RAINBOW TRIBE

Ed McGaa was born on the Oglala Sioux reservation and is a registered tribal member, OST 15287. Following the earning of an undergraduate degree, he joined the Marine Corps to become a fighter pilot. Captain McGaa returned from 110 combat missions and danced in six annual Sioux Sun Dances. The Sun Dance led him to the seven Mother Earth ceremonies under the tutelage of Chief Eagle Feather and Chief Fools Crow, two Sioux holy men. Eagle Man and the Rainbow Tribe people discovered each other during preparations for the Harmonic Convergence. Ed McGaa, Eagle Man holds a law degree from the University of South Dakota and is the author of *Red Cloud* (Dillon Press, 1971) and *Mother Earth Spirituality: Native American Paths to Healing Ourselves and Our World* (Harper & Row, 1990).

▼ ▼ ▼

Books on spirituality and philosophy tend to generate many letters. The author would very much appreciate the enclosure of a self-addressed stamped envelope by readers who write to him.

Rainbow Tribe

ORDINARY
PEOPLE
JOURNEYING
ON THE
RED ROAD

Ed McGaa, Eagle Man

HarperSanFrancisco
A Division of HarperCollins*Publishers*

Harper San Francisco and the author, in association with the Rainforest Action Network, will facilitate the planting of two trees for every one tree used in the manufacture of this book.

Illustrations by Barbara E. Coast   Text design by Katherine Tillotson

Library of Congress Cataloging-in-Publication Data

McGaa, Ed.
 Rainbow tribe : ordinary people journeying on the red road / Ed
McGaa, Eagle Man.
   p. cm.
 Includes bibliographical references.
 ISBN 0–06–250611–0 (alk. paper)
 1. Spirituality. 2. Nature—Religious aspects. 3. Dakota
Indians—Religion and mythology. 4. New Age movement. I. Title.
BL624.M397 1992
299'.785—dc20   91–55325
                      CIP

94 95 96 HAD 10 9 8 7 6 5 4 3

DEDICATION

To Frank Fools Crow, Oglala Sioux Holy Man. Spiritual Chief of the Traditional Lakota Sioux. 1890? 1891?–1989.

To Chief Eagle Feather, Sichangu Sioux Holy Man. Sun Dance Warrior Chief for the Return of the Sacred Tree. 1914–1979.

I deeply admire the rare warriors with that special courage to go out to the lonely edge—the chasm of change—where the detractors are many and the supporters are few. Bill Eagle Feather went to that edge and brought back the Sun Dance piercing. Publicly, boldly, defiantly, out in the open. And Frank Fools Crow pierced him.

▼   ▼   ▼

To all Rainbow contributors within these pages.

To Mark Salzwedel, editor, again, for his direction and perception.

To Rosana Francescato, production editor, and Anne Collins, copyeditor.

To Sun Bear, a brave warrior who sought spiritual unity.

To Morgaine Avalon.

CONTENTS

▼　▼　▼

FOREWORD

▼ ▼ ▼

It did not take long for the red nations to express their desire for the dominant society to change its way of thinking, its values, its ignorance of a living Earth. You can see this yearning in the speeches of Native American leaders from the colonial period onward. I thought this book was necessary because I have found a people who are making that essential change toward the Natural Way. What can most effectively curtail the past practices of human and environmental destruction? It is simple: the conveyance of knowledge about the best spiritual and cultural qualities of the Natural Way. Our destiny is linked to this change or we perish. I believe the change will have to come from those who are presently in control, not from those who stand on the sidelines detracting.

Too many of the red-way people are standing idly by complaining and not realizing that they can be of tremendous assistance to many across this planet. Maybe the luxury of doing nothing could be indulged in if we lived on separate planets. But that is not the case. We all perish together if we lose this earth to overheating, pollution, greed, and overpopulation. None of us chose to live in the aftermath of this Industrial Age destruction, but fortunately there are those who choose to learn what makes the Natural Way harmonize with all life forces and our relatives within. This book speaks of their knowledge quests, their grail that is made of bravery, courage, generosity, and wisdom. I hope that it will teach the new aspirants who seek this way of communion with nature and with the Mystery Source that manifests itself through the natural world.

The Rainbow Tribe is here. Each dawn, the numbers increase. No longer will the priceless wisdom of nature-based spirituality be ignored. We do not have any choice. Global warming, acid rain, overpopulation, and deforestation are real.

Old wisdom that has performed so well will now be allowed to work its environmental medicine where it is desperately needed.

Two-leggeds are coming together to bring forth a sacred hoop of harmony made up of many flaming hoops. An optimistic quest for peace will be an important benefit of this nonthreatening harmony. A spiritual fire now nurtures a communal commitment to a world-wide environmental undertaking. Rainbow energy will fuel that fire and give it great power.

Who are the Rainbows? Rainbow Tribe people work in cities and towns. Some are housewives still raising their young. Rainbows work, thrive, vote, pay taxes, abide by laws, are drug-free, abstain from or touch little alcohol, and do what almost everyone else does legally in this land. They also do ceremony and have found a closer connection to the created entity all around them. Rainbows have stepped back into nature, and this has become a glorious spiritual leap for them. Rainbow tribalism is bolstered by modern medical and scientific advancements. Rainbow spiritual perception is gained from natural participation in what many of the old tribal ways have preserved. Rainbows have found their path, their tribal unity, and a rich harmonic connection while they travel their earth-walk journey.

The harmony and deep peace of Mother Earth have brought many of the Rainbow Tribe people into a sacred perspective. Individual quests and group beseechments, blended with natural ceremonies held directly upon the soil and grasses of our planet, have deepened the spiritual quest of the *Wigmunke oyate,* the Rainbow Tribe people. In ceremony, Mother Earth has acknowledged Rainbow endeavors.

Out of ceremony, Mother Earth has issued some stern warnings that humankind's past practices of unchecked "dominion over nature" will no longer be tolerated. Nature is tallying devastating results of centuries-old suppression of natural spiritual enhancement. Despite human neglect, nature seems to be forgiving and is still offering its knowledge for those who have the integrity to observe and contemplate.

Startling world changes are occurring and, like Rainbow spirituality, they are fostered by communication and knowledge. It is becoming more difficult for those who think only of themselves to subjugate those who realize that we are all related. In this age of communication, the search for freedom and the search for a fulfilling nature-based truth have united. Man-designed religious fears employed by the old eclipsing regimes have no hold over the Rainbow Tribe. Rainbows will not follow the patriarchal hierarchies where fundamentalist-fomented fear, manipulation, and oppression have reigned. Rainbows use their minds to find their spirituality! Rainbows employ the natural intellect that God has given them and bolster it with courage, generosity, and acquired wisdom through observation and increasing knowledge.

Some Native Americans have come forth to offer knowledge and experiences. Over a half century ago, Black Elk met with a white man to tell of his deep and powerful vision. Later he sat with another non-Indian to expand upon the seven sacred ceremonies. These men, John Neihardt and Joseph Epes Brown, were writers. Black Elk intended that the knowledge of the Natural Way be preserved and passed on for the benefit of all two-leggeds, tribal and nontribal.

J. Epes Brown stated, "The old man [Black Elk] knew that he was soon to die, and he did not wish that this sacred lore, much of which he alone knew, should pass away with him."[1]

Fools Crow and Eagle Feather, two venerable Sioux holy men who rebirthed the Sun Dance, followed Black Elk's example. Their ceremonies did not exclude anyone because of gender, color, or bloodline. Indeed gifted, as evidenced by their spirit-calling powers, both holy men spoke out for unity and cooperation among the races of the four colors. These men traveled often, far from the reservation, to hold ceremony for the healing and acculturation of Indians and non-Indians who sought their counsel.

Frank Fools Crow said, "The power and ways are given to us to be passed on to others. To think or do anything else is pure selfishness. We only keep them and get more by giving them away, and if we do not give them away we lose them."[2]

Old books holding a treasure of shared knowledge from native men and women of world vision once sat dusty upon the shelves of time. But now in these enlightened days they have been reprinted and along with new writings are being voraciously consumed. Enlightened two-leggeds who have catalyzed world progress in the realms of freedom and scientific knowledge are now reaching beyond into environmentalism and spirituality and discovering that the two are related. They are finding the courage to cast off age-old fears and are beginning to walk forth within their own individuality. Vacant spaces of Mother Earth now dance with ceremony. Her stones, forests, and waters are becoming understood.

The *Wigmunke oyate,* the Rainbow Tribe people, have come forth to learn how Mother Earth can be revered and protected. I am thankful for the timely arrival of the Rainbow Tribe.

Note: The names *Lakota, Dakota, and Sioux* will be used interchangeably throughout this book. At this time, my tribe is still officially addressed as the Oglala Sioux, as is the adjoining tribe, the Rosebud Sioux. That is how the tribal councils have been referring to themselves for some time. The terms *Native American, American Indian, and Indian* will also be used interchangeably. Most older Native Americans have been called Indians all their lives and have become accustomed to that term; therefore, interchange is preferred here. Also, I am more concerned about spiritual content than about semantics, whose overplay too often distracts from harmonic values.

PART ONE

ƷƷƷ

ORIGIN OF THE
RAINBOW TRIBE

These Two-legged will be called the Rainbow Tribe, for they are the product of thousands of years of melding among the five original races. These Children of Earth have been called together to open their hearts and to move beyond the barriers of disconnection. The medicine they carry is the Whirling Rainbow of Peace, which will mark the union of the five races as one.

Jamie Sams, *Other Council Fires Were Here Before Ours*

$\frac{1}{6}$

RECONNECTING WITH THE NATURAL WAY

D own through time, tribal human beings (two-leggeds) lived in environmental tranquillity, but now, in only a few Industrial Age centuries, we have come to an ecological chasm of perilous pollution and exponential overpopulation. When rationally gifted beings became separated from the spiritual connection bonding them to the Natural Way, environmental destruction began.

While reaping a rich life-style, Native Americans preserved this portion of the planet for centuries upon centuries. I believe this high plane of living, which bore great gifts to the world, was a result of their deeply spiritual relationship with nature. In an age of unchecked industrial growth and the ecological disaster it has fostered, we had better start studying the first Americans' life-styles, values, and knowledge immediately. We could also well use a spiritual base that does not advocate "dominion over nature," but rather brings us to an intrinsic relationship with nature as dependent servants—not polluting, self-destructing masters. After we have observed and studied, we can approach some of the nature-based ceremonies to find values that will significantly advance us toward our goal of planetary preservation. Getting back to nature will be the key to saving the planet. Our day-to-day social and governmental endeavors will be ethically enhanced as well.

Most Native Americans do not attempt to describe the Great Spirit. We believe that it is rather foolish to attempt description of the Creator of space and time—things our two-legged minds cannot totally comprehend. How far out is space? Where does it end? Our minds cannot conceive of a total answer. When did time begin? What is time? How can we attempt description of the *Creator* of such mystery when we honestly realize that "It" is too vast to describe? We are truthful people. We cannot be liars to ourselves and to those around us! The term *Great Mystery* leaves adequate latitude to avoid an argument.

Many two-leggeds (human beings) share the belief that there is one beginning in this universe. It is called by many names: Great Spirit, God, Allah, and other titles. All animate and inanimate entities are usually accepted as created by this one essence. All occurrences are influenced by this one Creator.

Growth comes with an increasing awareness of and respect for Great Mystery in all people and things, with an awareness that this force of mystery is at work in all events. Growth comes through tolerance for the infinite variety of ways in which Great Spirit, the Infinite, may express itself in this universe.

Natural people throughout the planet are exploring revelation from created nature, exploring that extension made directly by the Creator, the Higher Power, the Prime Mover, the Ultimate Force, or the Great Mystery. They are learning from what is directly revealed and from what they can taste, touch, feel, observe, and study. Now, modern seekers (some of them call themselves the Rainbow Tribe) are beginning to recognize the visible powers of the universe. They are addressing, cultivating, and nourishing the heart of the spirituality that has been with their unbroken gene link, their beginning, down through the circles of time. Like the native tribal ones of old, they too are sensing that we, and all the life forces that surround us, are extensions of that Great Mystery force itself and have a great purpose for being here—especially at this time.

One tribe, in particular, is only a century removed from their natural life-style. The Sioux were the last major tribe to come in from their unencumbered freedom on the Great Plains. Maybe this explains why the Sioux have preserved much of their nature-respecting culture, more so than many of the other tribes who have had to endure a much longer diluting contact with the dominant society. Upon the plains, the Sioux heeded the visible six powers of the universe and related to these entities in balance, acknowledgment, and kinship. Their culture managed to survive despite the relentless assault perpetrated upon the Lakota/Dakota (Sioux) descendants, who were corralled into captivity by a biased and materialistic society.

The earliest Americans considered every day a spiritual association with nature. The culmination of this association was ceremony. Ceremony is beseechment, thanksgiving, or acknowledgment to a higher power, a higher force, or, if you are a traditional Sioux Indian, ceremony is directed toward the *Wakan Tanka,* the Great Spirit, the Great Mystery, the Great Unending Circle, through the six powers of the universe, the six powers that Black Elk's powerful vision speaks of.

Bill Moyers's interview of Joseph Campbell was shown on a national television series. One of Moyers's questions reflected on spiritual imagery.

Campbell replied: "The best example I know which might help to answer that is the experience of Black Elk" (referring to Black Elk of *Black Elk Speaks*).[1]

After Campbell explained a portion of Black Elk's vision to Moyers, Moyers interpreted. "This Indian boy [Black Elk as a youth] was saying there is a shining point where all lines intersect."

Campbell: "That's exactly what he was saying."

Moyers: "And he was saying God has no circumference?"

Campbell replied: "There is a definition of God which has been repeated by many philosophers. God is an intelligible sphere—a sphere known to the mind, not to the senses—whose center is everywhere and whose circumference is nowhere. And the center, Bill, is right where you're sitting. And the other one is right where I'm sitting. And each of us is a manifestation of that mystery. That's a nice mythological realization that sort of gives you a sense of who and what you are."[2]

In the chapter "Where People Lived Legends" in *Transformation of Myth Through Time,* the spiritual philosopher goes on to say, after speaking again of Black Elk, "The function of the ritual and the myth is to let you experience it here, not somewhere else long ago."[3]

The function of vision, ritual, and perceiving intellect is to allow us to experience our spirituality here and now. We are a manifestation of the six powers physically. Three of the powers make up our very life form, our visible being. These are earth (sixth power), water (west power), and energy (the fifth power—the energy from the sun). The other three powers make up our inner being and are more fully explained subsequently. These six powers are clearly visible, today and every day. They are a direct manifestation of the Great Mystery and are contained within the great circle wherein we reach our manifestation. The Sioux vision as told through *Black Elk Speaks* allows profound insight into the subject of spiritual imagery raised by Moyers. Over a million readers have purchased *Black Elk Speaks,* and there are millions more who have viewed Moyers's interview with Campbell.

Some believe that, centuries ago, the Sioux depended on their spirituality for their escape from the advance of the unsatisfied European. It seems quite probable that our foretelling ceremonies warned us of impending doom were we to remain in our peaceful and plentiful Carolina cornfields. There is some evidence that a Siouan-speaking people, the Kansa, migrated out of what is present-day New York, possibly to avoid the Iroquois.[4]

Before the Sioux saw the white man, the main body of Siouan-speaking people had migrated westward down the Ohio River valley, turning north at the Mississippi. The Kansa, Arkansa, and Biloxi went downstream at this point. Some Sioux bands, the Omaha and the Mandan, went up the Missouri. I am strongly inclined to believe that my tribe heeded the forewarning power of our ceremonies and was granted several more centuries of freedom, whereas the tribes that remained in the East were decimated and many disappeared. Eventually, we went out onto the Great Plains and left our mark on history. Now, a far more important mark will be upon the spiritual and environmental revolution that enlightened two-leggeds are beginning worldwide.

The Sioux, the Dakota/Lakota, ended their migration at the end of the last century on the federal reservations, located within the Dakotas and Minnesota. In leaving the eastern portion of this continent, we Sioux took with us a goodly portion of the democracy that the Iroquois League of Five Nations passed on to the early colonists. Freedom of speech, women's right to vote, the barring of the military from holding political office, freedom from unauthorized entry of homes, leadership by consensus, are some examples of the many Iroquois League gifts to humankind.

Europeans were unaware of these democratic social practices prior to their first association with Native Americans. Indian peoples never had "divine order" or "divine right of kings" in their elected governments. Indian nations put into practice a government that regarded leaders as servants of the people, not masters over

the people, and even made provision for the impeachment of leaders for errant behavior. Our successful environmental stewardship
and the absence of slavery were also great virtues that must be
mentioned. Seeking the Great Spirit through what the Creator has
created (the exemplary interplay of all natural forces—the animals,
the winged, the four-legged, the finned ones—and their example
of living as God has designed them) gave Native Americans insight
that led to a harmonic social structure and a highly civilized state
far ahead of what the Europeans brought to these shores.

Why did the Europeans come to this land? It certainly was not
because they had developed a utopia in Europe. European social
structure was not based on the equality that the Indian enjoyed.
The Europeans' spirituality wasn't working for them either. There
was too much religious persecution and social injustice during the
time of the great westward migration to state otherwise. The Europeans had allowed a class system to develop that had little regard
for the democracy and equality found among the North American
tribes. This system was led by a nobility class in league with a self-
serving priesthood that created fear-based rules, many upheld by
superstition, to control the ignorant masses.

The red people had no need to consider migration from their
nature-based system. Their land was kept pure and clean. It was
still very productive and was not overpopulated. Despite what the
snake-oiled Hollywood movie moguls have done to paint us as
cruel, bloodthirsty savages, the hard evidence clearly shows that
we were kind and generous people. We kept the Pilgrims alive and
took in the runaway black slaves. We taught the Pilgrims Thanksgiving and how to plant and fertilize the right way. The fact that a
people could show kindness and consideration to total strangers
from another continent tells of a "relationship" concept that is
unsurpassed in human history. (It is heartwarming to see a beautiful movie such as Kevin Costner's *Dances with Wolves,* however. I
hope that this is a new beginning for the film industry.)

North American tribes had no aristocracy that controlled the
land. There was no landed gentry to make them into indentured
servants. Besides rich spiritual experiences, a wide range of other
benefits can blossom when human beings take a close look at
nature and decide to incorporate its teachings. A harmonious sociology, unselfish leadership, warm family kinship, and honest justice system are other treasures that proliferated. Fortunately,
history books are finally being written that tell the truthful heritage

of this land. I strongly recommend Jack Weatherford's *Indian Givers* and *Native Roots* if you desire to explore the values, gifts, equality, and dignified life-styles of the Native Americans.

Such important gifts for humanity evolved through a close association with and resulting direction from the Creator's nature. For us, our nature bible couldn't be twisted and tailored to establish a man-made hierarchy of personal power. Our nature bible gave us straight, observable truth, unaltered; therefore, it gave us more. The impending environmental catastrophes warn emphatically that it is time for the new inhabitants of this land to start taking direction from nature. The proven stewards of this land did not color the truth that is a vital part of spirituality through nature. Before Mother Earth can be healed, modern man and woman must learn to recognize natural truth. It is how the Great Spirit designs and operates this universe. Nature does not work in untruth nor does she attempt to color it. The unexplainable intricacy and the continued functioning of all created entities prove this supposition. To do ceremony, natural ceremony that calls upon the Great Mystery, you must begin to understand the essence of truth; the essence of thinking and doing without ulterior motive and flowing in unison with the stream you are becoming. Without truth your endeavor will have no power. Conversely, when you comprehend and live your truth, it can be far more powerful than you would ever imagine. It is not a big mystery why some holy persons have discernible, "mystical" power, especially when in beseeching ceremony. They have lived their truth!

Many Rainbow Tribe people have learned that the truly powerful holy persons of the Sioux tribe deplored the use of any and all hallucinatory substances. Fools Crow and Eagle Feather, among others, warned against the use of peyote, alcohol, marijuana, mushrooms, and similar substances. The seven sacred ceremonies related by Black Elk to Joseph Epes Brown in *The Sacred Pipe* certainly do not recommend hallucinogens.[5]

Unfortunately, some who call themselves Rainbows do not heed the warnings of these naturally perceptive teachers and have gathered together openly to use hallucinatory substances and other drugs. Although these people are well meaning, are environmental, are unprejudiced, and respect the ways of nature, they are still hallucinogenic users and cannot be of the Rainbow Tribe. Rainbow Tribe people regret this undeserved association in much the same way that traditional Native Americans have to suffer their undeserved association with those Native Americans who use peyote in their ceremonies. Rainbow Tribe people do not believe they should have to change their identification, however, just as I would not be expected to change my identity as a traditional Native American simply because a minority of Native Americans use peyote in their ceremonies. But to be recognized and to differentiate, Rainbow Tribe people have chosen the Rainbow Tribe designation.

Rainbows realize that the ecology of the planet presents a much higher calling—and one that demands a clear head; otherwise, we can all suffer a tragic cataclysm. Nature will force the truth if the ecological disasters get much worse. We have no choice; we have to rediscover the Natural Way. Get close to nature and begin your truth. Stop the old practices of coloring and manipulating truth. With the gifts of communication and related technology, this rediscovery can progress even beyond the accomplishments of the League of the Iroquois.

Native Americans believed in an afterlife. They recognized that *Wakan Tanka* made everything in the form of the circle, and therefore the circle symbolized that life was unending. Certain Native American ceremonies, if conducted by people who are exceptionally truthful, do reach into "the beyond." This looking-into-the-beyond power was a convincing ingredient in their belief that their spirit would not end. After I experienced a *Yuwipi* Ceremony conducted by Chief Fools Crow, I was convinced that the afterlife does exist. A belief in an afterlife that based punishment and reward on one's truthful conduct went a long way toward fostering humanitarian ethics and morality for the old-time Native Americans. The preservation of pristine resources, for those of us who live here now and for the generations that will follow, was an added benefit.

The Indian repeatedly states to those who inquire about our spiritual concepts, "*We base our spiritual beliefs on what we see and experience while we are on our earth journey.*" Memory, we experience. Pride, conscience, regret, shame, achievement, honor—all of these are of memory; they are windows of deeds done or left undone while we travel this earth-path journey. This belief has an impressionable effect upon our conduct and no doubt was a strong factor in keeping the path of the old traditional Indian "straight." Traditional Native Americans were careful to nurture a respectful record, for they would be eternally reminded of what they did or did not do—good or bad—when they reached the beyond. Our memory and the memories of those we have associated with will be our "hell" or our "heaven" in the spirit world. I find this concept much more sound and realistic than what I was told by missionaries when I was little.

The white missionaries tell us of a hell they have created. There is no evidence of a hell (or a devil either) in nature; therefore, most traditionals do not swallow this belief of the white man. (No Indians have yet seen a devil, and they wonder if the white people truthfully have ever seen one.) Instead, we are very perceptive of memory. Even the *wamakaskan* and *zintkala oyate,* the animals and the flying ones who speak differently than we, have memory. Not only do Indians look to see what the Great Spirit has made, for their guidance and insight, they also well perceive and diagnose what the Mystery has allowed. Now, in this era of communication we have been allowed to discover that even a machine can be endowed with memory. A traditional Indian is not awed by a computer but rather can understand it in a philosophical perspective unrelated to a white man's evaluation.

A computer is another revelation, a discovery, and not a mere invention of humankind. A computer works through natural functions much like our Creator designed for our neural systems. Electronics, sun energy, ganglia, transmission, memory, decision, searching, weighing, storage—all of these facets are reflective of the computer to a considerable degree. We are all born with a basically blank disk, and some of us make the choice to put a lot on it, while others choose to input very little or to input only a narrow, knowledge-avoiding set pattern.

Some accept a perilous risk that knowledge will come *after* they die. How will this knowledge suddenly get there? Isn't the Great Spirit showing us that a blank disk remains empty until we put something on it? We repeatedly place knowledge upon a once blank disk and in time remove the loaded disk from the computer. The computer is destroyed, but we have saved and transferred the memory into a much more sophisticated computer. Are we not being shown that knowledge and methods to seek more knowledge (memory) are selectively placed upon our disk (our life) and that when the computer is destroyed (our death), the knowledge from the disk can be transferred to a colossal computer (the afterlife) and the memory live on? The memory will not be altered either. This forgiveness concept pertaining to the afterlife that the dominant society has spawned contributes considerably to the lack of conscience that so many practice and display. It is as if they have no fear of carrying the knowledge of their misdeeds into the after-life. Maybe that is why a "Blue Man" (an untruthful, greedy, and destructive being) who came into my life and destroyed my employment could lie so easily and the public metropolitan com-mission that existed to regulate him could so easily look the other way. To them, such lies are part of their customs.

If one is to fathom from the direct example of what the Ulti-mate has allowed us to discover, our memories, like information cast upon a computer, can and will be permanent. What is evi-denced here can be there. The computer is a wonderful tool to fur-ther appreciate and relate to memory. I may take exception to the temporary damage I perceive done to my people's culture, but I also recognize and dearly appreciate the inestimable good that non-Indian technology has provided worldwide, especially in com-munications, medicine, food production, and the advancement of knowledge. (Knowledge communication—through books, televi-sion, radio, newspapers, and courageous people—brought down the Berlin Wall and crumbled the Soviet empire!) It seems far more plausible that our hell in the spirit world will be the memory brought forth by those we have intentionally harmed along our earth journey.

Can you imagine the deserved suffering of those who have caused incest to happen to their own children? They will be reminded for eternity—the circle of life—by their very own lin-eage. The degree of hell experienced will be the degree to which we have caused innocent beings to suffer. I know a man who told some very elaborate lies about me so that he could get his unquali-fied children and sons-in-law employed. My immediate superior went along with him and was rewarded by having his own son take my position in a publicly managed bureaucracy. I fought this nepotism and racism all the way to the state supreme court and found nothing but cover-up by politicians and untruth all the way through the so-called justice system. This person is a white man, but he resembles the Blue Man in *Black Elk Speaks*. Although he has managed to get away with his schemes and untruths, in the spirit world truth won't be bought or sold and memory will be for an eternity. Natural justice will wreak its balance. I predict that he will face a considerable hell from others he has harmed, as well as for his excess greed and power quest. Those who supported his lies because they lacked courage will also have to face the Ultimate

Truth. I intend to remind them eternally and in time will include him within a book about the Blue Man.

"It is said that, in the very early days, lying was a capital offense among us. Believing that the deliberate liar is capable of committing any crime behind the scene of cowardly untruth and double-dealing, the destroyer of mutual confidence was put to death."[6] On the other hand, Lakota people allowed the possibility of forgiveness, even for killing in retaliation if the provocation was severe. This allowance went a long way toward keeping conduct honest among the people. You pushed persons only so far in Dakota society and they could retaliate.

> Murder within the tribe was a grave offense, to be atoned for as the council might decree, and it often happened that the slayer was called upon to pay the penalty with his own life. He made no attempt to escape or to avoid justice. . . . He was thoroughly convinced that all is known to the "Great Mystery," and hence did not hesitate to give himself up, to stand his trial by the old and wise men of the victim's clan. His own family and clan might by no means attempt to excuse or to defend him, but his judges took all the known circumstances into consideration, and if it appeared that he slew in self-defense, or that the provocation was severe, he might be set free after a thirty days' period of mourning in solitude. Otherwise the murdered man's next of kin were authorized to take his life; and if they refrained from doing so, as often happened, he remained an outcast from the clan. A willful murder was a rare occurrence before the days of whiskey and drunken rows, for we were not a quarrelsome people.[7]

An effective check upon the actions and words of the old-time Indians was their belief that they would be accountable to their peers in the spirit world for all that they had said and done. Historians who interviewed the old-time warriors consistently acknowledged their honest recall and desire only to speak the truth. With regard to particular battles, such as the battle with Custer's troops at the Little Big Horn, historians would question an Indian warrior about a hill or bluff that he had fought on. The Sioux interviewee would give an excellent account of what took place. But when questions would be asked about another portion of the battle in which the warrior did not take part, the interviewee would suddenly become mute. "Come now," the historian would coax, "you were there after the main battle. What did you see?" The warrior would refuse to answer, finally explaining to the historian that he should talk with Two Hawks, who was on the particular hill in question during the fighting. "Go see Two Hawks. He was there during the fight. What I might say would not be the total truth compared with what Two Hawks saw."

Traditional believing Indians did not have an idea that they would be sitting at the right hand of the Great Spirit and would somehow have all memory vanish of what truthfully took place in their lifetime. Knowing that they would indeed be accountable for all time, they endeavored to be serious about their words and conduct. Native Americans were far more honest than the biblically based Europeans who tried to brainwash us that all is forgiven after death. If you disagree, then let us start with the treaties that we signed in good faith. We did not break them. It is a historical fact that the other party broke these solemn agreements declared upon paper—every one of them. And this was after the Indian treaties were propagandized with a great deal of show as to the truthfulness and honesty of the Christian whites.

I believe that this sitting-at-the-right-hand-of-God idea and the fact that Christians believe they can be forgiven for all their misdeeds, no matter how harmful to others, are the major reasons that Christians have historically failed to measure up to the honesty and truthful performance of the old-time Indians. In turn, a great deal of harm has been done to the world, since this belief allows Christians to shade or outright corrupt the real meaning of truth and selfless conduct. If this statement angers Christians, then they are failing to look truthfully at themselves. I am not asking them to give up their religion, but since we Native Americans have been such unfortunate victims (and the Jewish people as well), I hope we are allowed to speak forth on this very important matter. *If this "truth factor" is not seriously weighed by the dominant society, then I believe that the environmental salvation of the planet is doomed.*

I also believe that there is much good in Christianity. The Christians did not wipe us out entirely. That is a fact that cannot be overlooked. Some spiritual force must have kept them from doing that. That is my opinion. I tell fellow Indians to think what it would have been like had a non-Christian force taken over this land. There were many humanistic and charitable Christians who spoke up for us and sincerely wanted to help us back in those ignorant times of limited communication. The Quakers are one example. So I hope that my statements do not disturb too many people.

In a discussion of truth, one cannot write credibly (or truthfully) by trying to appease the dominant society, as so many writers have historically done when they explored Native American culture. These writers have been too quick to degrade our truth, or they never even attempted to get at the heart of it. Take a look at the volumes of books whose authors thought they could tape-measure our spirituality. Up to this time, only a very few writers have had true, respecting integrity when it came to the heart of our history and culture. Catlin, Weatherford, Joseph Epes Brown, Dee Brown, Vinson Brown, Tom Brown, Manfred, Erdoes, Neihardt, and Powers are examples of those writers. The Native American authors such as DeLoria, Momaday, Ross, Ohiyesa, Barbara Means, Sams, Sun Bear, and Standing Bear have also reached in deeply. I hope that there are some more courageous Native American writers on the way. My advice to them is, Don't be looking over your shoulder all the time. If it is happening in front of you, go forward with it. If you are on the battlefront of worldly change and you are worried about what people will say about you, *compose lamenting poems!* But don't attempt to be a writer.

CREATIVITY

The Man who follows the crowd will usually get no further than the crowd. The man who walks alone is likely to find himself in places no one has been before.

Creativity in living is not without its attendant difficulties, for peculiarity breeds contempt. And the unfortunate thing about being ahead of your time is that when people finally realize you were right, they'll say it was obvious all along.

You have two choices in life: you can dissolve into the mainstream, or you can be distinct. To be distinct, you must be different. To be different, you must strive to be what no one else but you can be.

Alan Ashley-Pitt

I would like to add: You may eventually lose most of your old friends and maybe even the society to which you once belonged.

You might even lose your tribe, or rather your tribe might want to lose you if you have explored too far into other realms and they are not ready to recognize such change. You may also discover a whole new set of friends if you find that you need them. But in the end, your mind will certainly be rewarded, and it is your mind and nothing else that you will take with you to the spirit world when you leave here. I can now understand why many writers of courage choose the mobility of reclusion when they seek the necessary freedom to continue their exploration into the sheer canyons of that mystery-shrouded chasm of change. You learn to become like the mountain lion and discover how to divorce yourself from hindrances.

The Indian Way promoted a high-minded leadership incomparable to what we see in politicians today. Are our Congress, our presidency, and now, our slanted Supreme Court really all that truthful when compared with the leaders of the Iroquois League? Are they equivalent to a Chief Sitting Bull, Red Cloud, Chief Joseph, or the unselfish Chief Crazy Horse who were raised in the Natural Way? This adversarial legal system, this appointed judiciary that is accessible and bendable for the privileged, this lobby-controlled Congress and corporation-controlled presidency are not working for the good of the planet. They lack the truthful spirit exhibited by the leadership of the original stewards of this land. Someday, when this nation can get around to understanding and facilitating truth—that all-important virtue—we can bring down the wall of untruth that is holding back this country. A spiritual concept reflecting the truthful performance of those who followed the Natural Way can go a long way toward renewing leadership in this land. A new concept will have to come sooner or later, and I hope it will be a balanced one.

Conversely, our heaven will be established by those to whom we have been compassionate, considerate, and truthful. I intend to acknowledge the many good people I have been fortunate enough to know. In the sweat lodge I acknowledge out loud, during the fourth endurance, those who were good to me and who are now in the spirit world. It is realistic to believe that those who are in the beyond will want to be with those of like minds and similar knowledge. Those of you who have explored a spiritual path will not have much in common with those whose highest goal on this planet was to hate, lie, become addicted, be a perpetual jealous detractor, or support Ku Klux Klan meetings. I can't believe that people who were the victims of racial or religious hatred will want much association with the spirits of their oppressors other than to point out the suffering that resulted from such disharmony, ignorance, and hate.

"Heaven" will be the association and appreciation of those of like minds who strove to attain a harmony and equity while upon this planet in two-legged, free-rationalizing form. There are more and more people who are now soaring like the eagle, observing and learning from all that is put before them. "Hell" will be a blank passage without any trace of the higher knowledge and communication that were available but ignored while one played the role of the grasshopper. The grasshopper sees little and hops about haphazardly, unable to perceive a world of wisdom and adventure, and then is killed suddenly by a cold winter. Maybe the grasshopper just dies. It is clearly much more of a blank disk than an eagle. The Great Spirit shows us the extreme difference between an eagle and a grasshopper.

As we say, we can observe, see, and touch our religion. Think of the Archie Bunker blank disks that you know. Worse are the loudmouths who know everything and yet have had little or no actual experience with what they proclaim to know so well. I like to check myself and say that all human thought is mere supposition, when we consider the great mystery of this life. Yes, it will be interesting, quite interesting, when we go into that "Great Beyond."

Most of us have sought a teacher to learn more about the Natural Way. My answer is to let nature be the foremost teacher. But when you do come across a person who has knowledge that you believe will be beneficial to your path, then at first test the teacher. Does he or she exhibit jealousy or animosity? Does he put down others who are also respecters of the Way? Is she letting ego get in front of her? Do they want to control you or things in general? Are they loaded up on taboos, superstitions, or strange rules that restrict sincere beseechment? Are they purposely making it difficult for you to understand so that you will have to keep coming back over an extended time? Are they telling you to never go to anyone else's ceremonies or to avoid other knowledge? If their rules or procedures can be explained for practical and harmonic benefit, then by all means respect them. I know a teacher who is fairly strict, but underneath he emanates a deep harmony along with some very worthwhile wisdom. I consider him a good teacher.

Two traits that I seek first in a teacher are courage and the admission that he or she can be wrong or in error. Have your teachers had the courage to stand up for the need to recognize the spiritual yearnings of people of all colors and both genders? Have they coupled their courage with integrity to realize that this age of communication is a time of profound earth- and people-changes? Do they see that the population increases are bringing about a great deal of natural-earth destruction, besides increasing pollution? Do they recognize that woman must have ceremonial equality in order for her essential and needed power to come forth unrestricted? I guess that one of the most profound abilities to be found in fruitful teachers is their ability to admit that they do not know the answer to most of life's mysteries. Above all, allow your teachers to be human and grant them the freedom to make their share of human mistakes.

▼　▼　▼　▼　▼

Upon the plains the Sioux discovered the horse, *tashuunka wakan,* which means "big holy dog." When they first saw a human riding the animal, their impression was that it had to be a special gift from the All-Providing One because it allowed people to hunt the abundant buffalo. An endless supply of meat resulted. *Tashuunka wakan* allowed the Sioux to range in a territory from present-day Minnesota to the Bighorn Mountains.

One day in our spiritual history a very important event happened. Two scouts were out hunting on the plains when they discovered a beautiful maiden dressed in white buckskin and carrying a bundle. The woman sang a song as she approached:

> In a sacred manner I am walking.
> In a sacred manner I am walking.
> Behold me, for in a sacred manner,
> I am walking.

One scout had bad thoughts and approached to do the woman harm. A mist settled and when it lifted, he was nothing but bones covered with crawling worms. The spirit woman established that harmful acts would be severely punished. The woman was a powerful spirit woman and had been sent to the Sioux by the Great Spirit to give the people the object in the bundle—a red peace pipe. The woman, who was called Buffalo Calf Woman, taught the people the use of the pipe in seven sacred ceremonies. These ceremonies were:

1. The Sweat Lodge
2. The Vision Quest
3. The Sun Dance
4. The Making of Relatives
5. The Keeping of the Soul
6. The Womanhood Ceremony
7. The Throwing of the Ball.

Some of these ceremonies, including the Sun Dance and the Keeping of the Soul Ceremony, were actually banned by the federal government. Two ceremonies, the Peace Pipe Ceremony and the Spirit-calling Ceremony, evolved to replace or alter some of the original seven ceremonies. Some ceremonies changed very little and their essence or meaning remained the same. I call the new versions the seven Mother Earth ceremonies; they were developed after my ancestors were forced to give up their plains freedom and were herded to the desolate reservations in the Dakotas. I call them the Mother Earth ceremonies because, if practiced, they can convey a meaningful connection or spiritual relationship with Mother Earth and all the rest of the Great Spirit's creation.

Unlike the ceremonies of the dominant society, Sioux ceremonies are very balanced. Woman opens the ceremonies and sits in the place of honor holding the pipe in the Spirit-calling Ceremony. Woman is the first to circle the Sun Dance tree at the annual thanksgiving. When woman is present, it is she who will be the first to enter the lodge. Woman is not barred from conducting or leading ceremony. This would be an imbalance against nature, for it is she from whom we come. It was she (Buffalo Calf Woman) who brought us the red sacred pipe, and everyone knows that woman is half of the two-legged population. She is our Mother, *Ina Maka* (Mother Earth), upon whom we are conducting the ceremonies! A great deal of power and harmony never manifests when she is not allowed her equal place in ceremony. Probably more important, a great deal of wisdom is lost when she is not allowed her rightful voice in spiritual leadership. This statement will bear fruit in some of the later chapters, where wise, moving messages and soulful experiences of Rainbow women come forth. I do not expect the dominant society to rush to the pipe or the sweat lodge, but it should at least pay strong attention to these words about woman for the benefit and betterment of its imbalanced, male-dominated ceremonies and religious leadership.

Eugene V. Debs has written:

> Man has not yet reached his best. He never will reach his best until he walks the upward way side by side with woman. Plato was right in his fancy that man and woman are merely halves of humanity, each requiring the qualities of the other in order to attain the highest character. Shakespeare understood it when he made his noblest women strong as men, and his best men tender as women. The hands and breasts that nursed all man to life are scorned as the forgetful brute proclaims his superior strength and plumes himself so he can subjugate the one who made him what he is.[8]

▼　▼　▼　▼　▼

Just before the Sioux left the freedom of the Great Plains, one of our own had a powerful vision. Black Elk was a young boy when he was taken up into the rainbow-covered lodge of the six powers *(Shakopeh Ouye)* of the universe. These powers are the four directions, Mother Earth, and Father Sky. Above these powers, naturally, is *Wakan Tanka,* the Great Spirit or Great Mystery. The six powers are very visible and are with us every day of our lives.

The six powers brought Black Elk into their lodge. The west power, *Wiyopeyata,* gave him a bow and then spoke first. "I have the power to make live and the power to destroy." We acknowledge the life-giving rains as the power to make live. The thunder and lightning is the power to destroy, but we realize that far more life than death comes with each rain. Following the immeasurable life that springs from each rain is a rainbow of beautiful colors. Darkness comes from the setting of the sun in the west; therefore, black is the representative color of this direction. Black Elk was told that he could have the power to make live and destroy.

The second power was the spirit power of the north, *Waziya.* The north power gave Black Elk the healing sage herb and told him to use it for healing. We think of endurance, cleanliness, truth, and strength as associated with the north. The white blanket of snow puts our Mother to sleep on this portion of the planet so that the land can be revived fresh to bring forth the growing bounty of springtime. When the snow melts the earth is washed clean.

The east power, *Wiyoheyapa,* told Black Elk that out of the red dawn new knowledge comes forth with each new day. The power of light brings peace, which comes only from understanding. This is the beginning of the age of communication. New knowledge is reaching out to all parts of the globe. We have seen great progress from the power of communication, and this gives us hope that our planet can be saved from past practices of destruction. We have no choice. We must communicate and work together. We have also seen in Desert Storm what can happen when human beings refuse to communicate.

The fourth power to speak to Black Elk was the yellow south power, *Itokaga.* The sun's zenith rises and lengthens with each spring day. Growth, shelter from the standing ones (trees), and medicine from roots, stems, herbs, and fruits are associated with the south power. Abundance is another great gift from this direction.

The colors to be remembered as representing the four directions are: black (west) and, following clockwise, white (north), red (east), and yellow (south). Blue, for the life-giving rains, often represented the west also.

Father Sky spoke and said that the things of the air would be with Black Elk to help him in his struggle. Could these "things of the air" be the open space of communications that can now span the globe? Could they also be the satellites—things of the air—beaming back video and radio waves that allow us to see and talk directly across the skies so that truth is more difficult to distort?

Mother Earth, the sixth power, spoke and told Black Elk that she would be in danger and that his knowledge would be needed in times to come. Below, a Blue Man was seen. This Blue Man symbolized the corruption, insensitivity, greed, and ignorance that was upon the earth. The Blue Man would wreak great destruction using lies and untruths and would have to be addressed or else all creatures, including two-leggeds, would perish. Untruth is the Blue Man. The six powers attacked the Blue Man but were beaten back. They called on Black Elk for his help, which was the knowledge he was receiving and had the power to communicate. His bow changed to a spear and when he attacked, he killed the Blue Man. Could this mean that the six powers need two-leggeds to eradicate the corruption, lies, and greed of humankind that are destroying our environment (Mother Earth)? Could the natural knowledge from Black Elk's vision be the spear in this age of communication that can save the world environmentally and free it from war-fomenting greed and wasteful detraction? This is certainly a profound perspective.

We can visualize the six powers as extensions of the Great Spirit who reveal much of the mystery of what the Great Spirit is. In a way, we ourselves personify, to a degree, these powers. Our mostly fluid bodies flow and move because of the life-giving rains of the west power. The Earth, the sixth power, makes up our bodies; and the sun, which is the heart of the fifth power, Father Sky, is the source of our energy. Truth, endurance, strength, and courage are inner virtues that we can develop from perception of the north power. The east power, the bold red advancing dawn, can stimulate us each day to rise to more wisdom and communication wherein we can become peaceful, understanding knowledge. The south power is within us because we grow, replace, are healed, and can help heal.

Black Elk rode to the center of a village where the people gathered. A voice said: "Give them now the flowering stick that they may flourish, and the sacred pipe that they may know the power that is peace, and the wing of the white giant that they may have endurance and face all winds with courage." Black Elk thrust the stick into the earth and it leaped mightily to become a cottonwood tree with birds singing in its branches. A sacred peace pipe came flying on eagle wings and stopped beneath the tree—the Sun Dance tree—spreading deep peace.

The daybreak star rose and the voice said: "It shall be a relative to them; and who shall see it, shall see much more, for thence comes wisdom; and those who do not see it shall be dark." A red stick was cast down to the earth by the powers, and where it landed a sacred tree bloomed and flourished.

The reservation missionaries made a strong attempt to dislodge Black Elk's vision but were unsuccessful. Fortunately for this era of two-leggeds, Black Elk's story was preserved through Neihardt's book *Black Elk Speaks*. The old holy man gave Neihardt the name *Pta Wigmunke*, Flaming Rainbow. To Black Elk, Neihardt was a talk maker, a word sender. "This world is like a garden. Over this garden go his words like rain, and where they fall they leave it a little greener. And when his words have passed, the memory of them shall stand long in the West like a flaming rainbow."[9] The rainbow symbolizes fresh spirit life, and from the rainbow little flames of knowledge fall. Where they land, flowers grow.

Flaming Rainbow bridged across into the natural world through natural native people. His bridge touched back to his own people, although it took some time before his own people crossed over on his new bridge. John Neihardt was probably the first Rainbow person—at least the first to be named by a member of my tribe—and since that naming I have discovered an entire tribe, the Rainbow Tribe. The old prophet and *Pta Wigmunke* have entered the spirit world, but they live on forever in the pages of *Black Elk Speaks* and a host of related works that have been inspired by it. The powerful vision was meant to be preserved in accord with the six powers because it reached us despite a seemingly insurmountable adversity from the dominant world. The spirits of Black Elk and John Neihardt must be quite pleased with the Rainbow Tribe people who are taking a serious look at Native American spirituality. Some call it Mother Earth spirituality or simply the Natural Way. Whatever it's called, the Rainbows are not only looking and appreciating but are actually doing and participating within the values and beneficial aspects of the past tribal ways. They too have discovered the visible six powers of the universe and are now relating these daily entities in balance, acknowledgment, and kinship. They are searching to bring forth that ancient tribal gene link that cultivates an innate spiritual consciousness, a natural, harmonically flowing guidance that led native peoples to personal and collective earth-enjoyment for thousands of years. These enlightened ones are the Rainbow Tribe.

▼　▼　▼　▼　▼

A Rainbow Tribe person allows nature to touch into his or her own inner source of wisdom—one's own heart. Rainbow Tribe people definitely have their own vision, but they readily observe what has been placed upon their path. They are not afraid of new visions or to reach out to a higher plane, a plane that allows more growth and a close immersion within nature and its revelations. From this natural connection they convert knowledge to spiritual wisdom.

A beauty of the Rainbow Tribe people is that they never try to convert the nature-based people from whom they learn. I also find a lack of deviousness, almost a total absence of dishonesty among Rainbows. These characteristics, among many others, have won my admiration and respect. Consequently, a trusting energy is generated when I am among them.

▼   ▼   ▼   ▼   ▼

2

THUNDER OWL AND THE RAINBOWS

My friend Thunder Owl is a Mdewakanton Dakota. They are the easternmost band of the Sioux tribe and are presently located in Minnesota. Most of the Sioux moved out of Minnesota to travel westward onto the plains. Mdewakanton means "they camp by the holy water." Thunder Owl lives on a reservation close to the Twin Cities. His reservation is next to a town called Shakopee, which means "Six" in the Dakota/Lakota language.

Joe Thunder Owl is a descendant of Chief Little Crow. It is his belief that his ancestor's spirit has found its way to him through his lineage, and no doubt that is why he prefers the Natural Way when it comes to believing in the Great Spirit and the way he will follow as he travels his earth journey. We have been close friends for some time. We have done many sweat lodges together, and at first we only did them with our fellow Indians.

Before I met Joe, I had a close Ojibwa friend named Eddie Benton, who was the head of the Red School House for Native American youth. Eddie was raised in the old way and knew his language and ceremonies very well. Bill Eagle Feather, the Sichangu Sioux holy man, told us to build a lodge on some acreage I had purchased at the edge of the Twin Cities and to do ceremony. We held sweat lodges for urban Indians for quite a while until I moved away and eventually Eddie moved back to his reservation.

Once while Eddie was at my house I received a phone call from a local college. It was summertime and the college had been sponsoring a workshop for international journalists. People from all over the world were attending this workshop and the college wanted to give them a taste of Native American culture. A professor asked me on the phone if I would consider having the writers experience a sweat lodge. I didn't know how to answer because at that time I had even objected to a white woman being allowed to dance briefly for one day in the Sun Dance back on the reservation. This was in the days when the missionary priest still had a lot of power. He had even driven his pickup truck into the heart of our Sun Dance grounds to set up his altar, and our ceremony was limited to only three days. I objected because many of the traditional older people were fearful that the old ways would not be allowed to come back.

I explained to Eddie about the professor's request. Up to that time only Indians had attended our "sweats," although I had to admit that quite a few of the Ojibwa looked "white" since their tribe had been much longer with the white world than the Sioux had. Eddie Benton looks like a full-blood, however, and knows his Ojibwa culture deeply. I remember asking Eddie his opinion about what we should do. I asked the professor where the writers were from and explained back to Eddie that they were mostly foreign journalists and named off a bunch of countries that the professor had volunteered. Quite a few were European and Iron Curtain countries. Eddie Benton pondered for a while and then said, "Tell him to bring them out. Those aren't white people anyway."

Within a few days a long bus pulled into my driveway and disgorged enough journalists to fill several sweat lodges. I learned a good lesson in those sweat lodges that we conducted for the journalists. We had Muslims sitting next to Jews and Russians alongside Americans and Germans. When it came time for each person to pray in the third-endurance portion of the ceremony, they all prayed reverently and in a spirit of brotherhood and sisterhood. Those sweat lodges showed me that natural ceremony can truly bring people together in a bond of harmony and respect for the earth. It must be remembered that this was at a time when the Cold War mentality dominated and many of us were pretty well brainwashed with this ideology that our government fostered. A great deal of diversity was being promoted during this time to keep different cultures and nationalities separated and suspicious of one another. The age of communication was not nearly as strong as it is now. Few positive results had yet to happen and the Vietnam War was still raging. All the journalists in the *Inipi* (Sweat Lodge Ceremony) seemed to be awed by the ceremony. They especially liked the Lakota term *Mitakuye oyasin* with which we ended the ceremony. It means "We are all related" or "We are related to all things."

As time went on, I began to realize more deeply the philosophy of Black Elk, Fools Crow, and Bill Eagle Feather. They were not exclusionary holy men. These were my teachers and their openness has been a great influence on me. But I am a two-legged and their example took a while to sink in. It took a while for me to forget the priest who had always been around like a ferret trying to weasel in to dilute our own tribal reemergence with his way. Even after we beat him, I still remembered the haunting faces of the old who would come up to shake the hands of the sun dancers after the final ceremony day, the fourth day—the piercing day. They always seemed to convey the message, "Don't let them take our ways away." It must be remembered that this was when there were very few young men participating in the Sun Dance, just Buddy Red Bow, Sam Stands Holy DeCory, Sonny Larive, and myself. It was ironic that three of the four were off-reservation Indians, meaning we no longer lived on the reservation. Buddy Red Bow lived on the reservation but spent a considerable amount of his time traveling throughout the country singing in shows and writing some good songs reflective of our culture. Titus Eagle Feather was a young child then and would dance beside his grandfather, Bill, to give him strength. After a Sun Dance, Titus would be out cold. In those days, many reservation Indians were under the influence of the missionaries and the total-assimilation–minded Bureau of Indian Affairs. Bill Eagle Feather and Frank Fools Crow, along with other brave traditionalists, suffered much ridicule. Credit must be given to the many AIM (American Indian Movement) members who finally came to the reservation and were instrumental in breaking the power of the priest and others like him.

I was a speaker on "Cultural Return" in Minneapolis at a National Indian Education conference when I first encountered AIM. Some of its members came to hear what I had to say, and after my presentation Clyde Bellecourt, Dennis Banks, and Russell Means introduced themselves. We sat down in a bar and I told them what was happening at our Sun Dance. The following summer Russell Means, Clyde Bellecourt, and Lehman Brightman, among others, saw the priest boldly enter the Sun Dance circle just as we dancers were making our entry. In fact, Father Paul Steinmetz, S.J., stepped right in front of me in his black suit and waved a peace pipe. A confrontation took place during the recess period under the shade bower. I couldn't say anything while we were out in the Sun Dance arena as it wouldn't have been proper. Russ, Clyde, and Lehman came over to support me and warned the priest not to go back out into the dance arena. The priest then rushed to the microphone to stir up his followers, but he was sent packing and we went on with our ceremony without having to dilute it or cater to his beliefs. The next summer I danced alongside Russell Means, and, after this event, the priest and his supporters no longer interfered so openly. They still scheduled a rodeo and a carnival during the event, but it wasn't long before the traditionals regained their power. AIM has never received credit for this confrontation to preserve our way and this acknowledgment is long overdue. The tribal chairman, the late Enos Poor Bear, whom I am proud to claim as a blood relative, was also an ardent supporter, and without him we would have been set back.

Now it is a new time. There are literally hundreds of young, vibrant sun dancers, and traditionalism has swept the reservations. I am just an old has-been when it comes to sun dancing. I no longer have to fear that these nature-based ways will be relinquished. I still do not think that the dominant society is ready for ceremonies such as the Sun Dance, because it has taken centuries of supporting values to tribally hone that ceremony. The *Yuwipi* Ceremony speaks for itself. Only a few can conduct that beseechment, and I would find it hard to believe that an "outsider" would ever be able to conduct it. But then, who could have predicted the dissolution of the USSR and its military threat?

We are moving now into a new time—the age of communication. The far right is still a dangerous threat, and some of the Natural Way can be a formidable protection against their narrow zeal to make us all like them. They do not use truthful tactics, so the People of the New Dawn should not become naive or too conciliatory. For the beginning ceremonies, the Sweat Lodge, the Vision Quest, and the simple beseechment to the four directions (or what some refer to as the Medicine Wheel), I think it is better for this ailing world that non-Indians have the opportunity to experience these ways since it will make them a better people. That is how powerful these ceremonies are, and we do not have much environmental time to be arguing over it.

On the other hand, as I mentioned earlier, it is my belief that some ceremonies should remain on the reservation, for they are much more intricate. They require special songs and seem to need a tribal participation based on centuries of development. At present, a controversy has developed over whether non-Indians should be allowed to participate in the Sun Dance other than as spectators. There have been some rather large Sun Dances held on the major Sioux reservations where at least half of the sun dancers were non-Indian men and women. I counted at least 160 such dancers at one gathering and almost as many at an earlier Sun Dance on an adjoining reservation. The participants were all good, sincere people from what I observed. Some of the Sun Dance intercessors (leaders) have been quite adamant that this has been their vision, and of course they have followed their vision by allowing so-called outsiders to come and beseech around the spiritual tree of life as reflected in Black Elk's vision. I believe that these Sun Dance leaders are brave spiritual men and that a vision should be respected. On the other hand, a person with whom I sun danced years ago, Titus, the grandson of Chief Eagle Feather, is adamant that non-Indians should not be participating in the Sun Dance and has restrictions at the Sun Dance he conducts at his grandfather's old cultural grounds.

This whole situation has become something of a dilemma. Time will no doubt resolve these conflicts, but in the meantime I would like to request that Rainbow Tribe people turn their energies and attention toward the resurgence of Earth Day recognition at least every four years and toward other global healing events similar to the Harmonic Convergence. Never forget that the Berlin Wall cracked shortly thereafter. An explosion of positive world change has continued. Rainbow Tribe people should consider what is happening in their own geographical area and how they can help promote environmental and harmonic concern.

This is a free country and I hope it stays that way. No one, including myself, should be telling fellow citizens what they should believe or be limiting forms of beseechment as long as it is respectful. International Sun Dances will probably go on regardless of what I or anyone else has to say, but the focus on the worldwide situation should not be diluted. Earth Day and events like the great

Harmonic Convergence should not be lost sight of. Maybe traditional Indians doing their Sun Dances back on the reservation in restricted form is not such a bad idea if it will help the non-Indian spiritual seekers to concentrate more fully on events that they have held successfully and need to continue doing. In time, all colors will dance around the tree of life, but right now there is still some development to do. I am just a two-legged and can be as wrong in my observations as anyone else. But these are options to consider as we all head down our spiritual trails.

A friend wrote a letter of advice that addresses this dilemma of choices:

> Ah me. The purists vs. the eclectics: those who would preserve the old ways unchanged, and those who would seek to shape [them] to new uses or users. As I look historically at the evolution of spiritual and artistic traditions, it seems that those that have been able to adjust and mix are those that survive. On the other hand, pondering the tragic history of abuses that Native Americans have suffered at the hands of the whites, it is understandable that many are being cautious about embracing extraneous elements into what they have fought hard to preserve from annihilation. In a world where plastic cards and automated data handling is so rampant, slowing down enough to do things mindfully seems worthy to me.

Maybe we can slow down somewhat and not rush pell-mell into seeking out all the ceremonies to explore and take part in. A good firm basis of understanding within the visible extensions of creation would seem to be more fruitful for those who are just crossing over into the Natural Way.

One fact that I am adamant about is that no one owns the four directions or the six powers as revealed in Black Elk's vision. I cannot understand why anyone would not honor a respectful person's simple beseechment to these entities. Let us picture a Vietnam veteran in a wheelchair in his living room holding up his own personal *wotai* stone to the rising red dawn. This veteran served in a war for his country and came back without some important parts to his frame. He can't get up on a high mountain but he can go into a lodge and has discovered some newfound hope. This veteran turns to the south and beseeches the south power for warmth and growth that day. And then he turns his chair again to continue making his connection with all that is. Not far away, a woman gets spiritual comfort from her morning beseechment in a similar manner before she goes off to work. She has not been satisfied with organized religion and has sought a new path that will eventually lead her to a healthier understanding of creation. I hope no one finds fault with the simple yet powerful manner of praying that these two examples utilize to reach out to the powers that cannot be owned. Maybe the detractors of spiritual growth will find a chorus of castigation when they enter the spirit world from many such innocent people whom they would seek to limit.

At this point I want to make it clear that I do not regard myself as a medicine man just because Bill Eagle Feather told us to lead some ceremonies. He told us this mainly because the distance was too far for him to be traveling from South Dakota. I want to avoid living in a glass house and having people examine everything I do with a fine-toothed comb. I also wouldn't care to put up with the jealousy that is always dropped on a medicine man, especially the successful ones. I am just a two-legged who has made my share of mistakes in life, and I don't think that will change. I'll make a few more or a lot more, so I don't care to be placed in one of these infallible roles that society loves to assign people just because they might have done a ceremony or two. I don't believe you have to be a medicine man or a holy man to simply beseech or acknowledge God, the Great Spirit, or a Higher Force. I don't believe you have to be a medicine man to sit up on a mountain with some thoughts or go into a lodge to lead a beseechment. I respect highly the holy men and women it has been my privilege to know. I also respect practicing medicine people who have well demonstrated a truthful power to heal. But I am no medicine man and never will be. My conduct, at times, is not reflective of the extreme patience that I have seen demonstrated by many spiritual leaders. I just do not make the grade in that area. It's tough enough just being a writer, just having the courage to call a few spades, spades.

Those *Inipi* ceremonies conducted for the visiting journalists gave me an insight as to how the Natural Way can bring diverse peoples together. Now it is decades later and we are aware of ethnic groups fighting each other as a result of the tremendous world changes that are happening. These people should all get into some sweat lodges or go out into nature and beseech to one great common entity that is an admitted mystery—a Great Spirit if you will. Maybe they could find a harmonic understanding like the journalists did. Maybe these fighting ethnics or differing fundamentalists should sit down with their so-called enemies and say *"Mitakuye oyasin"* together in a natural lodge. I am sure that Joe Thunder Owl or Eddie or myself would donate our time to build them one and conduct a ceremony for diverse leaders beseeching together in a lodge.

During this time I was called on to give cultural talks at schools and in prisons, where I also held sweat lodges a few times. At those ceremonies, a non-Indian would occasionally want to participate. In a federal prison, even the warden and some of the guards took part after several of the Indian inmates eagerly encouraged me, saying that it was agreeable with them. Once we had the warden in there, one of the inmates said in Sioux, *"Lelah kahtah"* ("Make it real hot"). When I returned to the Twin Cities I met Joe and we did some lodges for an Indian alcoholic rehabilitation center. Once in a while a non-Indian would attend with some of his Indian friends. We didn't mind. The ceremony certainly had a positive effect for the goals of the AA (Alcoholics Anonymous) program and that was what mattered. After a while, more and more non-Indians would come to our sweat lodges. It seemed they were hungry to express themselves in the Natural Way.

Native American philosophy will never hurt a Twelve-Step program, because it demonstrates that people can lead a very harmonic life-style without alcohol, a substance that was absent from native culture before the white man. Maybe that is one reason why the earliest Americans developed democracy and reached a high plane of spiritual thought that blended so well with their life-style. Of course there were other reasons, but this certainly was a beneficial ingredient.

Once we were asked to speak at a church. It was a different kind of church, different from what either of us had been exposed to as children. The white people in this church seemed genuinely interested in our Indian culture and especially our native spirituality. So many of them came to our talk that they had to move us from a big room to the main part of the church—the place where they hold the Sunday services.

None of the people in this church tried to convert me as do most Christian religions that I have come across. Believe me, if you are an Indian, you will soon discover that Christians go out of their way to proselytize us Indians. They are even rude and insulting when we tell them that we have our own way of seeing and communicating with the Great Spirit. Well, none of these people tried to convert Joe or me the night we gave our talk and that impressed us.

I remembered back to the time Eddie and I had held the lodge for the journalists. We invited the church people for a sweat lodge. We didn't realize that so many of them would come the next Saturday night. We had well over fifty at the ceremony, and the lodge was small. Some of these people had already been in sweat lodges. Thunder Owl did the first sweat lodge; I did the second; Joe did the third; and I did the fourth. We were pretty tired by then and, luckily, Joe's son was there. Tony said he would do the fifth lodge, so I was fire-tender and handled the stones. Joe listened through the canvas cover of the lodge and was proud of how well Tony did the ceremony.

That was our first sweat lodge experience with the "Rainbow Tribe people." I do not want Joe and me to be accused of starting all this, however. In my travels I have met many, many non-Indians who experienced their first "sweat" long before Thunder Owl and I had our event. Across the nation, people had been—and still are—experiencing nature-based ceremonial beseechment primarily through the Sweat Lodge. In time, it was Joe who was responsible for the name *Rainbow people.* We noticed that many of them had a crystal or two that they brought to the sweat lodge. We had told them in our speaking engagement, in response to a question from the audience, that it was agreeable with us for them to bring what they regarded as holy or special articles. One woman even brought a peace pipe that she had purchased years before at the Pipestone quarries in southwestern Minnesota.

The sun was just going down when we built the fire for the lodge. Joe always starts the fire an hour or two before we intend to have the ceremony. You want to get the rocks hot, and with elm and oak for firewood you get a good hot fire, but it takes a little longer to get started. Elm and oak throw fewer sparks than pine. Actually, cottonwood is the best for not making sparks, but in this portion of the Midwest the other trees are more available for firewood.

Some of the "Rainbow Tribe people" were there early also. We always have our sweat lodges away from the hustle and bustle of the big city, and many of the city dwellers enjoy the peace and quiet of our locations so much that they come early just to sit around the fire or wander through the woods and pastures.

One person asked Joe to read the images in one of her stones. He studied it for a while and pointed out some animals that he saw within the grain. She then asked him if he could see images in crystals. He said it was still a stone and all made by the Great Spirit. If there were images to be seen, he probably could find some of them.

She took the crystal from her neck and handed it to Joe. He held the crystal up to the setting sun and saw immediately a golden rainbow within. It was quite pronounced. He said that since the crystal was clear colored, unlike the stones, it had a special power or characteristic. Having such a vivid rainbow inside gave it an added dimension or, to an Indian, power. The rainbow within was a direct sign from the Great Spirit, who after all designed this particular crystal to have such a bright rainbow inside. Later on, Joe came up with the name *Rainbow people,* and I think that little crystal with its rainbow was the beginning in finding that name. In time, the Rainbow people chose to be called Rainbow Tribe or Rainbow Tribe people.

Thunder Owl and I were hunting once when a beautiful rainbow came close in front of us. It was so strong that we forgot about the pheasants in the field. We just stared at that rainbow. It was so close that you could feel the fresh new life that was emerging from the light rain that had just crossed over. From that dramatic image I guess I got the idea that the other half goes down into the earth with its life-giving mystery that comes forth for all the plants to drink. *Wiyopeyata,* the west power, is a live, powerful entity to me. I like to form my ideas about the mysterious Creator from what the Creator shows me directly. When you get a powerful natural image put right before you, it does give you some lasting impressions.

Too many fundamentalist white men scared both Joe and me with their predisposed, proselytizing ideas about God when we were little. Fundamentalists are scary two-leggeds and not limited to one faith. A fundamentalist is the type who tells you to do religion his way or else. He always thinks he has some special connection into God and that hardly anyone else does unless they think like him. We even have some Native Americans and some claiming to be Native Americans who think this way. You use their colors or face your sweat lodge only in the direction they prescribe or else something really bad will happen. Meanwhile, tribes across the land and even different clans within tribes will have differing colors or face a lodge in different directions and the spirit world doesn't seem to be punishing them. (I don't believe the spirit world is into punishing or controlling us.) I guess the archetype of fundamentalism can still be found in the Middle East. Desert Storm made these fundamentalists more evident. The woman doesn't have much freedom there because of fundamentalism—and because of oil, our State Department isn't going to say much about it. Well, so much for one-way thinking. Joe and I are free now. We prefer nature revelation to show us our spiritual connection.

These new Rainbow Tribe people made us consider the meaning of the crystal just by being around them. Thunder Owl and I talked about it and eventually formed our opinion. We concluded that the crystal is related to the rainbow, that it is reflective of the Great Spirit itself—and, of course, reflective of the Great Spirit's powers since so much is exhibited by such a beautiful stone. We still regard it as a stone, because it was made and designed by the Great Spirit and is a piece of Mother Earth regardless of how pretty and enchanting it may be. But obviously it has been granted special characteristics that we Indians call powers. The crystal can even conduct a radio wave. An advisory to those who make fun of crystals: The stones were designed, made, and empowered by the Great Spirit.

Sioux people always appreciated new discoveries that enhanced their spirituality. When they saw a tribe or a band doing something in a certain way and it was fulfilling to the spirit, they were not afraid to add it to their own customs. They did not have a sacrosanct priestly hierarchy to hold them back either. Maybe that is why many Sioux have been at the forefront of spiritual adaptability. Some of these leaders were Black Elk, Fools Crow, and Bill Eagle Feather.

The Rainbow Tribe people wanted us to do another sweat lodge. When the time arrived, Thunder Owl and I drove to the sweat lodge site. We drove from his reservation and headed north toward the outskirts of a city where there are still plenty of woods and lakes. One of the "Rainbows" had some wooded land surrounded by horse pasture. To get there, we had to go north and west and not in a straight line. It had been raining but not enough to worry about, especially when we were going to do ceremony. (It has been our experience that when we do ceremony, the powers in control of the weather usually either hold off the rain or make it go around our sweat lodge. During drought times it seems to work the other way. It has happened many times that rain has come to the area where we have sweat lodge, but a short time after the ceremony. I heard former presidential candidate Pat Robertson on his national radio program exhorting a storm to go out to sea, so I guess we Indians should be allowed to believe that mysterious powers exist for us as well.)

We were driving and a rainbow was up ahead of us. This rainbow seemed to be settling over the place where we were going to have our sweat lodge. We were driving west when we first saw the rainbow, and when we turned north it seemed that the rainbow stayed right over the area that we were heading for. We turned west again and it was still over our destination. Despite the twists and turns of a winding road the rainbow remained. Joe said he was lucky to be an Indian and could recognize a natural sign when it was so obvious. He said, *"Wigmunke hey, Wigmunke oyate."* He meant to say that the rainbow was showing us where the Rainbow people were going to have their sweat lodge. I laughed and said, "Joe, you have given them their Indian name. They are the Rainbow people, the Rainbow Tribe." Since then, they themselves call themselves the Rainbows and the Rainbow Tribe. We called them Rainbows when we finally arrived at the lodge site and they laughed and liked it. A lot of them said, "Don't call us New Agers; call us Rainbows or the Rainbow Tribe." Joe concluded with a good statement: "I like these people so much and have met many good friends among them. I consider myself a Mdewakanton of the Sioux tribe. I also say I am from the Rainbow Tribe."

▼　▼　▼　▼　▼

The Rainbows invited Joe and me to a meeting about the Harmonic Convergence. At our first meeting, the Rainbows assumed we knew what it was all about and of course we didn't want to appear too dumb, so we just sat through the meeting figuring we were there mainly to do some sweat lodges and that would be our contribution. After the Harmonic Convergence was all over with, some of the news media never did fully comprehend it, if one is to judge by their inaccurate and distorted reporting, so we decided our initial denseness wasn't so bad after all.

After a while we figured it out. Rainbow-type people all around the world would be gathering at different places. Some would be beseeching their concept of the Higher Power for world peace and harmony. Others would be projecting a concept of world unity and peace to the rest of the two-leggeds. People have gathered for a lot less. Joe and I thought it was an outstanding idea—sort of a world-class Sun Dance. People would be coming together like a big earth-circling tribe to beseech and acknowledge. Some earthshaking changes have occurred since that day in August 1987. Freedom has leaped across the globe. With those kinds of momentous events, I hope the news media will be able to gain more depth before the next global spiritual event takes place.

As I said before, we were impressed with these Rainbows; they were totally different from the white people that we were used to. Not that we hadn't run across good white people who wanted to be nice to us before, but it had been our misfortune too many times to discover some ulterior motive, usually a commercial reason, for someone or some group going out of its way to be friendly to us. Naturally they were going to be awfully "nice" until they got control of the business operation. I could tell some horror stories about reservation bingo halls that were controlled and exploited by outside interests. I have met some good corporate people who sincerely wanted to help the tribes and were very patient besides bearing considerable expenditure with little in return for their effort, and they should not be linked with the exploiters. Many generous people and corporations have donated gymnasiums, food, and clothing to our Indian reservations, but some of the bingo hall deals have made the tribes jumpy. If you could know more about our history, you would understand why it is difficult for the modern Indian to trust outsiders.

Missionaries were historically the worst offenders. You almost have to go to a reservation to understand what I am talking about. When you've been exposed to reservation missionaries, you can tell that most of them couldn't fit in with their own kind and that's why they are out on the reservations. If you think I'm hard on missionaries, read Vine DeLoria's book, *Custer Died for Your Sins.* In his chapter on "Missionaries and the Religious Vacuum," he says:

> Missionaries looked at the feats of the medicine men and proclaimed them to be the works of the devil. They overlooked the fact that the medicine men were able to do marvelous things. Above all, they overlooked the fact that what the Indian medicine men did *worked.*[1]

On my reservation the Jesuits became the largest landholders. I suspect some real mental difficulties when it comes to a two-legged who wants to save souls and believes that he has direct, exclusive information about the Great Mystery. I'll admit that I want to do what is legal and moral to help save Mother Earth, but despite my consuming zeal for our planet, to save someone's soul is not my forte. I'll be as honest as I can: I don't know how I could do it and I can't find any representation or signs in the natural teachings to indicate that we two-leggeds must occupy our time in soul-saving. How would we start out? By pouring wild rice on people's heads? Enlightening the spirit to God's created nature seems more practical in this age.

If thousands of ocean mammals are being killed every day by drift nets, illegal shooting, and oil spills, then our energies should be spent to save them. If peoples of differing colors or differing religions are not allowed to vote within the borders of their own countries, then the natural call of freedom within us should speak out against such inequality. If heavy metals or chemicals infest a populated area to the extent that deformed children and abnormal animal offspring are being born, then my natural self tells me, Mother Earth is speaking out that she is being harmfully imbalanced. Nature is issuing a strong sign for all to read, but I cannot find any such sign supporting what the missionaries are attempting to do to our nature-based culture. The missionaries claim to have divine justification for their actions, but so far all that I have seen is an ordainment of their actions by mere two-leggeds—not by the real, visible higher powers that all of us experience daily.

It appears that my spirit is circular and doesn't need to be saved. Not that it doesn't have to follow ethical and moral precepts. A circular spirit life means that you will be in communication with those who have gone on in time, and that you will endeavor to earn the respect, not only of your open-minded peers upon this earth journey, but of the future generations as well. (You are never going to impress your jealous, narrow-minded peers.) A circular spirit life means that you will have an eternity to be proud of your path or an eternity to be ashamed of the wrongful actions you took against others and the living conditions of future generations. I don't believe your spirit memory will let you off the hook for not summoning the courage to take positive action to safeguard the lives of generations yet to come.

The environmental concerns of the Rainbow Tribe people impressed Joe and me and gave us a strong bond right from the beginning. We found them talking about humpback whales, tropical rain forests, international arms spending, impending disaster from overpopulation—the list went on and on. They talked of the world heating up, and since we were in the midst of a drought, what they said seemed quite plausible. One of the Rainbows was investigating the contamination of the water tables by heavy metals leaching down into the aquifers. He told us about his theory that this could be a possible cause of Alzheimer's disease. These heavy metals entering the body through the drinking water might be producing short-circuiting of the fine transmission "wires" of the brain as they became increasingly coated with the metals. Now that was an interesting hypothesis. It was certainly worth exploring and should be worth the cost of a military tank or two.

Joe and I concluded that the Rainbows had a lot more to add to our lives. In turn, since the environmental-catastrophe list kept getting longer and longer, we asked them to take a close look at what had worked in the past and to think about incorporating some of the successful philosophy, some of the psychology, some of the sociology, and, yes, a great deal of the spirituality from the old caretakers of this continent (the Native Americans). They agreed that we should all take a serious look at what had worked so well in the past.

The Rainbows were from all walks of life, and most of them were well read and fairly well traveled. One was a psychologist. Others were teachers, artists, counselors, chiropractors, salespeople, housewives, entrepreneurs, and regular working people. Another owned a significant amount of land close to the city and kept a stable of horses. They asked Joe and me if we would build a sweat lodge anywhere that we chose. We selected an area near the horse pasture that was protected by trees and went to work building a lodge. We received an unexpected reward while we were digging. We uncovered some old bottles and jars that had been placed in the ground long ago. We must have found about a hundred real old ones that were not broken, even some pretty perfume bottles with glass and cork stoppers. People like to collect things like that, and with all the ceremonies we were going to be doing, Joe and I knew we couldn't be spending our time lugging a bunch of old glass around, so we had a lot of fun giving them away. It's funny how excited people get over something that was thrown away and lay in the ground for a long time. The woman who owned the land said that she did not "own" it but was only a steward of the land. She had donated a large amount of her land to the Parks department with the agreement that it would remain in its natural state.

Joe and I explored this area and found an adequate supply of saplings and firewood. In a short while we had a sweat lodge frame, and a ceremony was planned.

At our opening sweat lodge, during Joe's ceremony, we were greeted by the spectacular entry of a spirit, which we later learned was Gray Eagle Woman. She drew startled gasps from the Rainbows who were inside the lodge when a flurry of lights and a rush of wind came into the midst of Thunder Owl's ceremony. She was a spirit who had camped at one time near the shores of Lake Minnetonka in that area. I was outside the lodge serving as fire-tender and did not experience this phenomenon, so I was temporarily spared being called crazy. The Rainbows inside the lodge all claimed to have experienced the startling apparition. My "non-crazy" status didn't last long—only about a week. Gray Eagle made indications when she entered the Sweat Lodge Ceremony I was conducting the following weekend, but her entry was not as dramatic as at Joe's ceremony. I guess, in the judgment of a detractor, I could be rated as "slightly less crazy." I do love Indian humor.

After a few more meetings, a decision was made to procure a tipi, a large Plains Indian tent. Joe and I located a tent maker and the Rainbows gave us some money. Our next job was to go back out into the woods and cut long lodge poles for the new tipi. We cut a few hardwood poles but soon realized that they were too heavy, as well as somewhat crooked. We needed spruce poles because they are straight and light. The lighter the pole the easier it is to move around, especially when it has to be a lengthy pole, which we needed to accommodate the extra-large tent we had purchased. Another important reason for using spruce poles or similar light poles is that a heavy hardwood pole can be dangerous for an occupant should a strong wind blow the tent down. Of all places, a racehorse track near Joe's reservation allowed us to take light pine poles from its property. It is difficult to describe the aesthetic beauty that the tipi added to the meadow. The tipi, the horses grazing freely, a tiny stream, summer flowers, and our sweat lodge tucked in beneath the shading trees returned us all at least a century into the past.

The Harmonic Convergence date was only a month away when the Rainbows decided that a portion of Black Elk's vision should be reenacted, using horses that were available at the stable to represent the horses of the four directions that Black Elk saw when he went up into the rainbow-covered lodge of the six powers of the universe.

We held several more sweat lodge ceremonies and met more and more Rainbow Tribe people. One day I was asked if I would be the fire-tender for an all-woman sweat lodge to be held during a full moon. Joe was at my home when I received the call, and we both were invited to serve up the hot stones to be placed in the lodge. That evening we went to the site. The fire was already heating the rocks when we arrived. One other male was there, and he was glad to see us. He was a very shy Sioux named Arvol from the family that keeps our Sioux Sacred Pipe Bundle back on the Hunkpapa reservation. That is where I danced my last Sun Dance under Chief Fools Crow and Bill Eagle Feather. One of the ceremony participants was a close friend of the quiet man and was known to occasionally go out to get him and bring him back to the cities so that he could give some inspirational talks and encouragement to the urban Indian population. Arvol Looking Horse conducted a beautiful pipe offering to begin the ceremony and also sang a moving song in Sioux. The Rainbows were quite impressed. Joe and I were impressed as well. Here we were at an all-Rainbow-woman sweat ceremony and the Keeper of the Sacred Pipe was there also. (He did not have the original pipe with him. That sacred item stays on the reservation under the care of this traditional family that has guarded it down through time.)

Since that night, I have discovered that this man is very courageous in his mild way. He has impressed me as one whose beliefs are quite similar to Black Elk's; that is, he has the foresight to see that the Natural Way can bring world harmony. He has a hard road, however, because some of the extreme traditionalists not as concerned with this worldview seem to make self-serving demands of him. I wish everyone would lighten up on Arvol and show him more respect and admiration. For a while, even Chief Eagle Feather and Fools Crow had a hard road because of Indian people who did not appreciate them. To this day, some Native Americans attempt to detract from Black Elk by calling him a *heyoka,* a contrary. That is one reason why I would never want to be a medicine man. So many people never appreciate them and instead seem to want to make their trails more difficult.

The day before the Harmonic Convergence began we gathered to cut down a tree, a "tree of life," in keeping with Black Elk's vision. We approached the tree in the same respectful manner I had seen take place at our annual Sun Dances. A woman was the first to speak to the tree, a cottonwood tree. She explained why we wished to utilize the tree. She said we sought peace and harmony and that the whole world was going to pray together on the following day. She said our particular gathering would pray in a manner that reflected on the vision of Black Elk. She explained to the tree that the people would gather around a sacred tree and this would represent all nations and all colors. Needed peace and harmony could come to the land.

The cottonwood tree was moved to the center of the meadow where the tipi was located. It was adorned with the colors of the four directions, as well as with green for Mother Earth and blue for Father Sky. A rawhide cutout of a woman was suspended in the upper branches, and a rawhide cutout of a dove was placed close by the woman figure.

We held a powerful ceremony the following day. Mother Nature was there in strong force to show us she blessed what we were doing. Just as we were about to begin our partaking in the Harmonic Convergence on our small part of the planet, upon the first stroke of the drum, a low cloud barreled over us. The cloud flew directly at our site as if it were being guided. As an added mystical ingredient—and a powerful sign in the eyes of a traditional Indian—a pair of white doves hovered above the crowd in the heavy wind as the roaring cloud came across. Only gray mourning doves are native to this area, not white doves.

Several hundred people gathered around the tipi and the tree of life. Four colored horses representing the four directions of Black Elk's vision and carrying children as riders charged into the meadow. The children represented the generations yet to come. Four women dressed in solid colors walked up to the horses and took their places to represent the east, south, west, and north. The woman of the east power wore a red dress and carried a red peace pipe. Her pipe was presented to the center of the gathering between the tipi and the tree. The yellow-dressed woman of the south power placed a yellow hoop around the pipe. The woman in black approached from the west and, while the black horse with painted lightning across its sides looked on, placed a cup of water into the yellow hoop and beside the pipe. The woman in white approached from the north to place healing sage within the hoop and fanned a white wing of peace and harmony across the objects within the hoop. Mother Earth came forth from the lodge wearing a multicolored dress and handed sage to the crowd. "Behold, I am the Mother of you all. I have fed you, clothed you, and housed you. Every particle of your body comes from me." She swept an arc with her arm from east to west. "This is the dawn of the new age that shall bring peace and harmony. The old order is eclipsing." Father Sky, a Native American wearing a feathered headdress, came forth from the lodge, loaded the peace pipe, and offered it to the four directions, to the earth and the sun, and to the Great Spirit looking on.

Joe Thunder Owl began a drumbeat on a barrel-sized drum and the crowd joined in a circle dance around the cottonwood tree. Flowers were everywhere around the tree. Black Elk's prophecy was fulfilled. The Rainbow Tribe people had gathered and the tree of life had bloomed!

3

RAINBOW AND CELTIC RELATIONSHIP

Most archaeologists declare that men and women first crossed the land bridge from Asia to America via the Bering Strait during the Pleistocene or Ice Age. This would have had to take place around twelve thousand years ago. This theory is nearly universally accepted by those archaeologists who remain inhibited by a high degree of Eurocentrism. Some archaeologists and historians challenge this assertion and argue that intelligent human beings were here long before the Bering Strait was dry enough to be crossed. The author of *American Genesis,* Dr. Jeffrey Goodman, states in his notes:

> The test of any new theory is how it stands up to the new data that comes in after it has been proposed. One of the key themes of this book is that modern man was in the Americas at dates much, much older than the traditional 12,000-year-old date associated with the Bering Bridge Entry model. *American Genesis* argues for man being here at least 100,000 years ago, . . . so it is comforting to note that on April 22, 1981, the Associated Press (Toronto) reported on a new 150,000-year-old dating for mammoth hunting man in the Americas. . . .
>
> Dr. William Irving, an archaeologist with the University of Toronto, told the press that stone tools and broken ani-

mal bones found along the Old Crow River in the Yukon were 150,000 years old. . . . The 150,000 year dating was confirmed by the bones of an extinct species of lemming common there.[1]

I have always maintained that "One Way Only" signs were never posted on the Bering land bridge. Maybe humans crossed from east to west. No doubt the strait was traveled in both directions during the centuries it was open. There is conclusive proof, however, that Homo sapiens were roaming North America over twelve thousand years ago, and some authorities like Dr. Goodman hold that they were here over 100,000 years ago. Goodman cites a report by Dr. James Bischoff of the U.S. Geological Survey in Menlo Park, California, who used the uranium-thorium dating technique to get an absolute date of 200,000 years for the site studied by the late Louis Leakey at Calico Hills, California.[2] Dr. John Bryde, author of *Modern Indian Psychology,* also contends that Native Americans can be traced back 200,000 years.

Some historians and archaeologists like to associate North American culture with Aztec, Maya, and Inca influence and even origination. This assumption is partly based on agricultural technology, seed cultivation, and some medicines. Numerous plants raised by Native American farmers have been traced to their beginnings in Central and South America, in particular, corn, potatoes, and beans. Before these plants were introduced to the Old World, Europe was sustained almost entirely by grain crops such as wheat, barley, rye, and oats and consequently was frequently ravaged by dreadful famines.

The Maya recognized the four cardinal directions and even chose the same colors as those revealed by Black Elk's vision. Red represented the east, yellow the south, black the west, and white the north.[3] Specific deities were associated with the four directions, and the Maya had a supreme god, *Hunab Ku* or *Itzamna,* who could be interpreted as akin to the undefinable and infinite *Wakan Tanka* of the Dakota/Lakota. But the Maya pantheon of lesser gods and deities was far more complex than the six powers of Black Elk.[4] The interpretation and placation of this wide-ranging Mesoamerican pantheon was manipulated to become beyond the grasp of the common people. As in too many organized religions across the planet, this role was taken by an elitist, sacrosanct priesthood made up of self-perpetuating, power-oriented men.

Some historians have sought to link Maya, Inca, and Aztec temple architecture to the man-made mounds of the Mississippi and Ohio valleys. The large temples of the major Central and South American tribes never found their way north, at least not in vast monuments of stone or brick. In the continental United States there are few sophisticated architectural relics of pre-Colombian times other than the ancient settlements of the Southwest such as the cliff dwellings of Mesa Verde and Chaco Canyon. Earthen mounds of dirt and wood were found everywhere west of the Alleghenies—over ten thousand in the Ohio River Valley alone. Most were associated with burials and were conical in shape, but none were made of stone. In the lower Mississippi area, conical mounds were scarce and flat-topped pyramids were the rule. These structures indeed resemble the stone pyramids of Mexico and indicate a link with Aztec culture. In the Ohio and the Mississippi valleys colossal mounds rose out of the earth. The Cahokia Mound in Illinois was one hundred feet high and covered sixteen acres.[5] Only the pyramids at Cholula and Teotihuacan in central Mexico surpass the Cahokia pyramid in size and total volume.[6]

When post-Colombian explorers came upon the land, there were no inhabitants of the great cities associated with the mounds. They, like many of the Maya, had simply vanished. Other than the hundreds of mounds that still dot the land, early mound-associated inhabitants left little trace on modern society—except through the strains of cultivated plants that they no doubt improved upon and passed on, which of course was a great gift. The *absence* of mounds in one particular part of the country, however, may be an important clue.

In the thirteen colonies, where the beginning of modern-day democracy was borrowed from the Iroquois confederacy, there were no land effigies, not even of earth and wood. "The Atlantic coast, from North Carolina up through New England, had no mounds, but beyond the Alleghenies they were everywhere."[7] The Atlantic coast, from North Carolina up through New England, is the area where the ancestors of the Sioux and the powerful Iroquois confederacy lived. Some elements of the Cherokee may also trace back to this region.

This interesting discovery is supportive of a theory that a nature-deity connection, a common spiritual bond, may have existed between the British Isles and the western shores of the Atlantic. It is a significant indication that the northeastern coastal and inland inhabitants of North America were a barrier, a formidable force who shut out a high degree of influence from the mound builders further west.

Probably the most glaring evidence against a spiritual link between the North American tribes and the Central and South American tribes lies in the priesthoods of the Inca, Aztec, and Maya societies. Theirs was an establishment of personal and political power allied with the other ruling class, the nobility. Heredity, education, and wealth separated this ruling hierarchy from the majority of the people. Nor was such an arrangement confined to New World organized religions. A powerful Old World priesthood existed long before the Spanish conquest, and that priesthood also had a hierarchy that intertwined with the ruling powers.

In the Aztec, Maya, and Inca religions, animal and human sacrifice, supposedly to please the gods, was a controlling aspect of ritualism spawned by the priesthood. Wars were created to obtain more human sacrifices to appease Maya and Aztec gods. Hearts were cut from living subjects by the priests. A favorite Inca ritual was to place a living victim on a freezing mountaintop to die of exposure.

The allegation of human sacrifice could be downplayed as the fabrication of zealous Christian propagandists, whose history has always revealed an eagerness to disparage native religions. But the finding of too many frozen sacrifices atop mountains and sacrificial scenes clearly depicted in sculpture, murals, and ceramics, along with parallel representations in Maya pictorial writings, strongly indicates a practice totally contrary to what nature teaches. Our four-legged and winged cousins do not sacrifice to appease *Wakan Tanka,* and the Creator has been taking care of them quite graciously down through time. Religious death sacrifice is too unnatural to link with a people who founded democracy, kept the Pilgrims alive, and were enjoying a high state of natural and victimless freedom within organized society when they were first set upon by the migrating Europeans.

The medicine people, the oracles of the northeastern tribes, were not self-serving, nor were they selected by hierarchy or through heredity. With regard to spirituality or religion, there is ample divergence of theology, organization, and ceremony between the northeastern tribes and the Central American tribes to indicate little similarity or relationship. Between these diverse entities were the agrarian mound builders. Distance and time must not be discounted as modifying factors, however. They may have allowed the North American mound builders themselves to filter out or dilute considerably any controlling or self-serving social and religious customs inherited from tribes farther south and west.

I hope that modern readers have grown enough to admit that the human sacrifice of the European Inquisition was equally horrendous and revulsive. The power base of the Inca, Aztec, and Maya priests and the deception they fostered in league with political leaders and warrior chiefs are far more closely related to organized Christianity than to the position of spiritual seers within the framework of native North American concepts and, indeed, even Celtic concepts. In the study of history, we should all search for the truth, not attempting to color history simply because of a cultural or ethnic mind-set or a particular religious persuasion. Truth cannot be forced. Those of the proselytizing persuasion should come to realize this; otherwise, they will continue to be embarrassed as masquerading hypocrites.

Mother Earth herself is being explored in a new perspective, a living comprehension called Gaia. Numerous geographical areas in this land are also becoming focal and gathering points for spiritual inclinations. Many within this new wave beseech the visible six powers of the universe and relate these daily entities in personal development, balance, healing, and kinship. Black Elk's great vision has reached deep into their being. Rainbows abhor a spiritual hierarchy, especially an all-male priesthood. They prefer a balanced female-male approach to ceremonial conduct, with a definite assertion that women will equally lead ceremony and share a leadership role in Rainbow cultural matters. In this area, Rainbows are opening a new freedom for females and are out ahead of many of their modern Native American counterparts, who I suspect have been unconsciously influenced by the patriarchy of the missionaries. Few tribes have managed to keep their age-old matriarchies after being exposed to the missionaries for several centuries. Could this Rainbow matriarchal respect be a reaching back to the best facets of the Druidic spirituality that obviously held a powerful connection to the Creator-endowed extensions of the natural entities?

I have suggested that if the evidence of history is dispassionately weighed and considered, parallels can be seen between Mesoamerican tribal customs and early European socioreligious leadership and practice. Yet another fascinating parallel exists—this one between the northeastern tribes of North America and another tribal people, the Celts, from across the Atlantic. Could early Celts have influenced the spiritual insight of the Native Americans or vice versa? An article in *Heritage Line Newsletter* suggests that the Celts were in North America a long time ago.

Who were the first Europeans in the New World? It is highly doubtful that they included Columbus, although North America should be ever thankful that he landed so far south. The Spanish Inquisition never reached the northern land and at least Christianity was tempered with Protestantism in the northern hemisphere. Was the Viking Leif Eriksson the first European in America, or was it Saint Brendan of the Emerald Isle? It was probably neither. Recent archaeological finds in New England indicate a European settlement as far back as 800 B.C.! The evidence is threefold: in an ancient complex of stone buildings; in scores of tablets inscribed with a writing matching that used in western Europe around 800 B.C.; and in American Indian words that parallel those used in western Europe at that time. The study of these data inescapably suggests that the adventurers who crossed the Atlantic over twenty-seven hundred years ago were Celtic! This was the conclusion drawn by *Heritage Line Newsletter*. The article goes on to provide some details about these remarkable discoveries:

> On Mystery Hill, New Hampshire, the ruins of a burial tomb and oracle chamber are studied. Surrounding the hill are great stones, geometrically aligned for viewing such celestial events as the summer and winter solstices and seasonal star and lunar patterns. The parallel to Stonehenge and Newgrange in Ireland is remarkable. Near Woodstock, Vermont, another oracle chamber has been identified.
>
> The Celtic identity of these structures has been established through the science of epigraphy—the study of ancient inscriptions on stone. Dr. Barry Fell, Harvard Professor and President of the Epigraphic Society, identified and translated the inscriptions as Ogham, a system of cypher used by Celtic people over 2500 years ago. Dr. Fell's research is conclusive in dating the Celtic presence in North America. Some of the inscriptions identify graves, others taken from the oracle chamber contain religious writings, and still others contain land boundaries. Together, they suggest a Celtic settlement in the New World, when Ogham was in use about 800 B.C. Further, a study of local Indian words and

place names reveals Celtic roots. Other methods, such as the defining and dating of pottery, tools and implements found at the site, have also revealed the settlement to be Celtic, matching items produced in the Celtic regions of western Europe during the Bronze Age.[8]

The archaeological conclusion is that a Celtic society existed in North America long before other Europeans came. Dr. Fell has released a book on his studies called *America B.C.* In it he writes:

> We find in New England some two hundred stone chambers, many of which are oriented and constructed in such a manner as to make them astronomical observatories for the regulation of the calendar of festivals. There are also systems of standing stones that indicate a calendar divided into eight half-seasons, all based on the annual cycle of the sun's motions in the sky. All these objects yield calendar observations to this very day for those astronomers who understand the use of ancient stone structures for this purpose, and the calendars so observed prove to match those which we know to have been Celtic. Since some of the stone structures are also labelled in Celtic script with indications of their function, we are obliged to conclude that they are the work of ancient Celts. Evidence by ancient European writers tells us that the Celtic astronomers were known as Druids. We therefore must draw the final conclusion that Druids were active in New England. They were still practicing their astronomical craft in the time of Julius Caesar, whose reformed calendar they adopted in part, and with it the use of Roman numbers, but they retained the Celtic habit of beginning the new year on the day of the spring equinox.[9]

In the British Museum in London, I viewed the circular character of ancient Celtic art and shield designs. I was amazed when I saw the four directions medicine wheel designs, which featured the circle of life enclosing the intersecting four directions. This is a major symbol for the Siouian (Dakota, Lakota) people.

It is likely that Native Americans influenced the Celts or Druids, since the Atlantic, like the Bering Strait, did not have a one-way flow. If Dr. Fell's research is borne out, then it is highly probable that early traders returned to pre-Christian Europe with many of the new continent's (later to be called North American) values. It certainly explains why northeastern tribes had traces of Nordic physical features. It may also explain why these tribes are different in appearance from the southwestern tribes such as the Navaho and Pueblo and from the west coast tribes as well. Maybe there was an inspirational trade-off of values and spirituality between the best of what both naturally inspired peoples had to offer. In my opinion, Dr. Fell is not some cowardly appeaser. He has made factual discoveries and reported them to the world.

Academia that blocks out startling discoveries reminds me of the Catholic church in 1493 when word went out that Columbus had landed in Lisbon with human beings from the New World. At that time, the biblical account of creation did not mention any new tribes or new continents. The "absolute truth" of Genesis was about to be challenged. The fifth Lateran Council was summoned by the pope, and American Indians were certified as human beings. We were considered to be descendants of Adam and Eve through the sinful Babylonians, who were postulated to have been destroyed by the Great Flood except for a few survivors who were banished to the wilderness. Yet, in retrospect, we were far more truthful and spiritual than those who tried to put their ownership and fictional history upon us. In archaeological discoveries, when the evidence of dwellings, inscriptions on animal bones, and tool markings are all ignored, such an attitude resembles the earlier church conduct aimed at manipulating our origins. I believe that some of these modern archaeologists and anthropologists harbor a religious zeal as intense as the ostrich-lock (head buried in the sand) of the church in times past—and in modern times as well. Some of these scientists have pointedly ignored carbon-dating proof also. Their lack of courage teaches me why the old-time Sioux declared this virtue (courage) one of the four cardinal virtues needed to be a truly beneficial two-legged on one's earth journey.

My lineage drew me back to the British Isles on a recent trip. I visited the Great Circle at Stonehenge and even had a fascinating dinner with the chief of the Order of Bards, Ovates, and Druids, Philip Carr-Gomm. His book *The Druid Tradition* explores a parallel spirituality to the Native American way. There are many startling similarities between Native American and Druid teachings and practice. The Spirit of the Circle, the Spirit of the Stones, and related stone circle (medicine wheel) ceremonies suggest a possible common past. The Bards, Ovates, and Druids use the term *Great Spirit*. The following day I beseeched at the tor in Glastonbury with

my peace pipe and four colored stones of Black Elk's colors. Everything went so well following that simple beseechment ceremony.
Maybe the Celtic spirits were pleased. That day, I met with the
noted Celtic author Geoffrey Ashe and with Robert Stewart, England's authority on Merlin, King Arthur's seer. It was as if I were
being told that there was a connection, a powerful connection,
between the two nature-respecting spiritual cultures on opposite
sides of the Atlantic.

Perhaps the Atlantic Ocean was not such a barrier after all. The
following are excerpts from an article by Mary Lou Skinner Ross,[10]
who provides a window through which we can view Celtic life
and through which women readers in particular may breathe in a
refreshing, invigorating spirit, a newfound vitality that can possibly inspire them with its balanced, equal-gendered "Manifest Destiny"—one that is long overdue today if this planet is to be saved!
Maybe early inhabitants of the Misty Isles foretold the sacrificial
Inquisition through Druidic ceremony. Most likely, they knew of
the continent across the Atlantic. Did they make a timely exodus
like the Sioux from the Carolinas? This hypothesis would have
them boating across the Atlantic long before the Pilgrims. The following should appeal to the ancient tribal traits that still inhabit the
DNA blueprints of every one of us who are red, yellow, black, or
white.

CELTIC WISDOM

When Rome spread its empire over the whole Medi-
terranean and into part of western Europe, it took care to
eliminate anything that might harm its socio-political organization. This was very evident in Celtic countries where
the Romans pursued the Druids (the Celtic priests) until
they disappeared. The Druids were an absolute threat to the
Roman State because their science and philosophy danger-
ously contradicted Roman orthodoxy.

The Romans were materialistic, the Druids spiritual. The
Roman State was a monolithic structure spread over territo-
ries deliberately organized into a hierarchy. The Druids followed a freely consented moral order with an entirely
mythical central idea. The Romans based their law on the
private ownership of land; property rights were vested in

the family. Celts considered ownership collective. Romans looked upon women as bearers of children and objects of pleasure. A woman entered into the husband's family upon marriage and became property. Celts, on the other hand, included women in their political and religious life. Such subversive assumptions seriously threatened Roman order.

In time the Romans defeated the Celts in Gaul and moved into Britain, although they never conquered the far flung edges of Celtic culture in Wales, Ireland and Scotland. People there retained their integrity. After the Romans left Britain, an upwelling of Celtic culture occurred in the years 400–600 A.D. and into the 8th century. Unfortunately, Celtic history was not written down by the Romans who never understood the culture and religion and who distrusted and were hostile to it. As a consequence, we have never been told the whole story. The most significant information, for me, pointed broadly to these facts: the Romans saw life from a very linear view, and Roman culture was structured this way through a hierarchical system; the Celts did not fit into this structure because they held a different understanding of their world.

Truly the Celts had a partnership culture; their organization was the family, consisting of relatives as far as the ninth removed. When the central family grew beyond a certain point, another family would form with compulsory sharing of communal goods. Several families became a tribe—a *tuath*—the basic political unit. Each king was elected by the community and became the administrator. Each *tuath* was self-sufficient, possessed of a well defined social structure, with goods owned in common, its own rules and regulations, and its own gods. Ultimately this decentralized approach had consequences and illustrates the difficulty (seen today) of political unification characteristic of Gauls, Britons, Welsh, Irish and Scots peoples.

The oldest money was cattle. Those who received cattle contracted obligations to the whole. Women could own herds and were not excluded. Contracts could only be agreed upon in the presence of the Druid, which frustrated Roman administrators. When we are told that Celts were an oral people, we can't fully understand the power of speech to them. They believed that to write anything down was to lose memory (a correct assumption). Their sense of the transmission of tradition and history was vastly different from that of the linear-minded Romans. Celts had a high culture that was not recognized by most Romans. There is poignancy and loss when memory is taken from a people.

Druids had a long, intense and arduous training; however, anyone would enter a Druid School because education was a central value. Druid colleges were centers of learning, and many centers existed. We know that at one time 3000 students were enrolled at Glastonbury. These colleges taught Latin, Greek, mathematics, art, literature, the healing arts; they had hospitals and surgery, law, morality, poetry and music. In those days, if anyone spoke Latin, it was a Druid or a person who had been taught by a Druid. For centuries, to be a scholar and an Irishman were identical. When a youth in Europe wanted the best education, he went to an Irish monastery. The monastic pattern was set by Druidic colleges. In fact, the Celtic educational centers, and those who went out from them, kept knowledge alive during the Dark Ages in Europe into the 15th and 16th centuries.

For thousands of years all history, story and celebration were oral. Bardship was an esteemed second discipline and a high art. A bard was required to make a long-time commitment to study. Bards often took twenty years preparing for final exams in which they had to compose poetry and song extemporaneously in a prescribed and difficult meter. Bards kept alive for people their identity and history, creating a communal imagination that wove together the past, present and future.

The Celts were inheritors of non-patriarchal societies that stood half-way between non-Indo-european influence and the patriarchal/dominator model. There is a well documented Celtic law in which women enjoyed privileges that Roman women could not have. Harmony reigned between the roles of men and women not dependent on the superiority of one sex over the other. It was an equality in which each felt comfortable.

Often the head of the *tuath* was a man, but there are known examples of women rulers. Women had equal power in early Briton, and they fought beside or led men. A woman could not be married without her own consent. She did not enter the husband's family as a possession. Celtic marriage was a contract and like all contracts could be revised. Women taught the healing arts, could own and manage their property.

Pre-Christian Celts were at home with the mystic and intuitive aspects of life. They understood that every human being is intrinsically free, and they appreciated metaphor because it revealed deeper levels in events. Synchronous events were accepted with awe as having meaning. There was a strong belief in a unity as the Source of Life. All came from that one creative Source, and Energy emanated from the Source in a triad. One of the three streams of energy was always deeply feminine. The sacred Source was not the sun, but was represented by the sun, and they believed the physical universe was not all there was. Spirit and mystery were interwoven through the universe and open to people. Because the soul was immortal, they experienced no fear of death. They expected to live other lives and might literally loan money which would be repayable in the next life. The interweaving characteristic of their art reflects their underlying philosophy; head and heart connected, no separation between spirit, the divine and matter—no one fixed dogma. For them the heart of such mystery could never be reached by one Soul path; it was always open to other people's understandings.

The Celts could not understand the Roman Christian position that the sacred Source was separate from life. They sensed the ineffable dignity of human life as holiness; humans did not live in a fallen state. The authority of individual experience was in the heart—no mediation was needed between an individual and God, although one might have or be expected to have a Soul friend.

In the end, the decentralization of the Celtic Church got in its way. Roman organization did have an advantage. English kings, seeing the advantage, sided with the Roman Church. Thus, Christianity inherited all the structures of the Roman State and continued to destroy Celtic values systematically.

▼　▼　▼　▼　▼

Had the Celtic tribes endured, even if confined to some kind of reservation system as were the native North Americans, then a vast reservoir of natural, connecting knowledge would have been available in our time. This supposition assumes that the Celts would have been allowed to retain their cultural identity and nature-based spirituality by their eventual conquerors.

This did not happen, however. Unfortunately for modern two-leggeds of European lineage, the Romans and the English kings, the "anti-Mothers," destroyed the truthful records of Celtic Earth-knowledge. We are fortunate that the Native Americans are available to reach into that "sacred Source" of which Mary Lou Skinner Ross speaks. Or possibly that sacred Source is reaching back out through North American native transplanting. It is not a remote possibility that the ancient Celtic and Druidic wisdom could have been transferred in part to the northeastern tribes and of course the Lakota/Dakota, who trace their origins to that area where the Celts explored and landed.

By attempting to understand Celtic wisdom we can draw a fulfilling parallel to the natural wisdom that is available on this continent and more fully appreciate that the connecting bridge *has not* been destroyed. There may be a great deal of credibility to Dr. Fell's hypotheses. It seems highly probable that the Celts, and the Norse too, were here centuries ago. From a geographic and navigational perspective, it was certainly possible. People were no doubt as keen on trade in the past as they are now. Maybe there was more trust and understanding in those days, since the people's nature-based religion admitted the existence of many mysteries in the vast, vast world.

This Celtic interest on my part must be a drawing from my bloodline. I am part Scotch-Irish, almost as much as I am Native American. It certainly is a nature-based combination. I am not a full-blood, nor do I claim a famous chief as an ancestor. There are many non-Indians with no traceable Native American lineage who declare all sorts of relationships with past tribes. Do not be untruthful to yourself. You are what you are. I am what I am. People are people, and almost everyone in this hemisphere is a mixture. I understand it makes for healthier genes. It is intriguing to search back into that past and imagine the old Celts and possibly the Vikings traveling and trading, setting the stage for a worldly influence much larger than any of us are yet able to imagine.

PART TWO

ᔕ ᔕ ᔕ

INTRINSIC POWERS
OF CEREMONY

Memorializes Hanged Sioux

For a few hours the monument to 38 Sioux hanged in Mankato in 1862 bore a mark of respect. Ed McGaa, who had come here to speak to the League of Women Voters, paid his respects in the Indian Way by attaching an eagle feather to the monument.

"You know, it really doesn't matter if this eagle feather is gone five minutes from now." McGaa commented as he unwound a ball of 35-cent string around the cement block. "What is important is that it was finally given to them."

The eagle feather traditionally is presented to individuals who have performed an outstanding service to their people.

To attach the eagle feather to the monument, McGaa wound the flimsy string around the headstone four times. "Four is an important number in the Indian Religion," he said.

In fewer than 36 hours both string and eagle feather were gone.

Mankato Free Press, September 1971
Joyce Levin, Staff Writer

▼   ▼   ▼   ▼   ▼

Note: Not long after the ceremony was conducted, the City of Mankato removed this monument, which bore the cold inscription:

HERE WERE HANGED
38 SIOUX INDIANS.
DEC. 26TH 1862

4

THE PATH OF THE RAINBOW

If I were asked what group of people best perceives the natural concept of spiritual imagery in this land, I would answer, "The traditional practicing American Indians."

If I were asked what group best perceives the spiritual imagery of Black Elk, I would answer, "The Rainbow Tribe people I have met across this country and in foreign countries as well."

Over a million copies of *Black Elk Speaks* have been sold. The vast majority have been purchased by non-Indians. The book has been printed in several languages, including Japanese. Not all of these readers are Rainbows, but I would venture to say that they have a strong leaning toward Rainbow philosophy. The Natural Way philosophy has a long way to go, however. I am under the impression that despite the progress of the Rainbow Tribe, the greater number of non-Native-oriented people in this country want to keep things too complicated. This is no doubt the main reason why the simplicity of the Natural Way has such a difficult time reaching people within the dominant society.

Although Black Elk's vision has influenced and inspired Rainbow people to an appreciable degree, ironically, his vision has not been as persuasive for the older members of most Native American tribes. Unfortunately, in my opinion, a high percentage of elder and middle-aged members of my own tribe have never read *Black Elk Speaks*. I do not blame the tribe, however. So thorough has been the abusive cultural denigration practiced by reservation missionaries in collusion with the federal government that the account of one of the world's most practical and understandable visions, coming directly out of the native people's own lineage, has been rejected or ignored. Many reservation people have yet to demonstrate the Black Elk message or his colors, aspects of the vision that are readily appreciated by the Rainbow Tribe people. In ceremony, most Lakota do not specifically use red, yellow, black, and white, beginning with red for the east and following clockwise in that order. Even the two colleges on the Rosebud and the Pine Ridge reservations do not depict these "Power of the Hoop" colors in the order named. The three Sun Dances that I viewed recently did not display them, and each had a differing arrangement.

In Black Elk's youth there was no alcohol and little disunity. The degree of unity was such that the Sioux nation was the last to come in of all the major tribes. And this was after the most famous battle of all, the Battle of the Little Big Horn, where the other side lost to the unified Sioux forces. This once magnanimous unity suffered through several generations of reservation boarding-school indoctrination by missionaries and federal government practices that suppressed leadership. Of course, in that time span Black Elk's great vision was never encouraged. Such a preposterous act of religious and Manifest Destiny superiority! Here was a vision that could have brought a great bond of unity to a suppressed people. It emanated right out of the tribe, and yet smug, know-it-all religious fanatics were allowed to come in and suppress Black Elk. Historically, Black Elk is on record as being attacked by overzealous priests for conducting innocent ceremony. The first priest stormed into the midst of a ceremony and threw out Black Elk's peace pipe, along with other sacred objects. This person was reputed to be Aloysius Bosch, S.J., who was killed by being thrown off his horse. Several years later, another priest, Father Lindebner, actually choked Black Elk to "chase out the devil" while he was beseeching to the spirit world to heal a young boy.[1]

After attending a conference of American Indian colleges I am more optimistic, however, because younger reservation tribal members seem much more aware of the old seer. I have even greater optimism when I see the hundreds of young sun dancers, regardless of what colors they are under, and the antidrug and antialcohol awareness that is so strong at these events. The young have risen up, and the old Earth-connected ceremonies now blossom across the land. The unity of Black Elk's vision could be invaluable in bringing a spiritual commonality to tribal people as it has to the Rainbow Tribe. Some Sioux tribes are already establishing leadership, and I am optimistic that more will be done because of this communicative age and the almost wholesale return of the young to traditional beliefs; these two incentives can move tribal people back to a renewed unity. Black Elk's vision speaks for itself, as do the million copies of the book that have come out across the land.

The Rainbow Tribe's timely recognition of Black Elk in this environmentally aware age is their own unique spiritual achievement and has certainly served as a stalwart basis for their emerging unity. To put it bluntly, Rainbows should not feel that they are robbing native culture when they follow Black Elk's vision and its representative colors. Rather, it is they who are recognizing a great vision in a more complete form by also using the associated colors.

This whole area is still new and largely unexplored territory for non-Indians, such was the thorough decimation by dominant organized religion in their own past as well. I base this conclusion, in part, on the hundreds of letters I have received from readers of *Mother Earth Spirituality*. Communications technology has changed everything, however. It is equivalent to Columbus coming to see a whole New World; such will be the change for many peoples. People are no longer afraid to use their own minds for spiritual perspective. Age-old fears exert less and less of a hold in this modern era. Discerning two-leggeds are starving to learn of an environmentally proven, culture-based advancement into this new realm. It is a teaching from the vision of Black Elk that the dawn of knowledge can bring each two-legged what she or he is capable of learning, and this can begin with each bright new day. We now need to learn how to find and how to perceive the Great Spirit in nature and humankind.

Mother Earth Spirituality attempts to teach that nature-based ceremonies intertwined with tribal cultural knowledge can weave human perception, four-legged and winged example, and a living Mother Earth into a spiritual relationship. It is a timely communication. Tribal wisdom from all parts of the globe is finally being recognized to help ward off the impending ecological and social disasters that all global citizens face.[2]

To achieve power to do ceremony you have to become familiar with the four directions and the six powers of the universe. Of course, balance and a sense of stability are also necessary ingredients for successful ceremony. For a respecting effort and a persistence to seek heightened and increased familiarity, the establishment of the spiritual veil comes into play, according to many experienced persons. From my own experience, after a period of time in conducting the basic Sweat Lodge Ceremony, intense, significant activity happened that did not occur before. This spiritual veil seems to lift and more acknowledging power from the spirit world seems to become evident.

I have heard testimony from Chief Eagle Feather and other respected traditionals that the spirit world that visits natural ceremony frowns upon the use of drugs and alcohol, and these ingredients are strictly forbidden at Rainbow Tribe ceremony. An age-old adage found in many cultures that are free from sacrosanct, man-based definitions and rules is that nature flows in harmony and will continue to do so with or without humankind. To find that flow, one can utilize ceremony and nature-based knowledge, but the use of hallucinogens or the practice of materialistic or disruptive acts based on disharmony simply won't work. If that kind of person indicates a piercing of the spiritual veil in ceremony, then he or she has found a means to false-image the participants.

Some very supernatural experiences can occur in ceremony. A *Yuwipi* Ceremony is an example. The conducting individual has to have a particular power, along with knowledge and special training to conduct the ceremony. In the more common forms of ceremony, so-called phenomenon power appears to be indicated through the one conducting the ceremony, but I believe it is really the participants within the ceremony who most influence the indications that take place when the spiritual veil becomes thin and the significant phenomenal activity begins. In later chapters, this power appearance is illustrated and spoken of by contributing writers.

Along with spiritual harmony, knowledge is a compelling ingredient as well. Some have wondered why early pioneers or non-native ancestors do not appear in Sioux *Yuwipi* ceremonies in which departed Sioux traditionalists make an appearance and impart wisdom. Early pioneers and their offspring did not believe in Native American ceremony nor did they have firsthand, respecting experience. They were, therefore, not in knowledgeable concert with the spiritual intricacy or intimacy of such dynamic ceremonial beseechment. They were little different from those today who are unfamiliar with the complex mathematical formulas that scientists and engineers use to build communications systems and other vast projects in this world. If you are not aware of and do not become familiar with certain realms, you cannot enter into them. Most of us have to admit that we cannot enter into the complex knowledge of a physicist, mathematician, or research engineer.

A simpler illustration might be a computer disk that one uses to place memory upon. The brand-new disk, which is totally devoid of implanted memory, must first be initialized by the computer before it can be worked with. The new disk is placed in a slot in the machine, and the computer prepares or formats the disk in order to accept it. Only after this initialization can the computer utilize the disk. After "becoming in concert" with the rest of its new but related environment, the disk can proceed within the system for beneficial results. From a native spiritual perspective, this process is not an invention of two-leggeds; rather, it is the discovery of a power that the Creator has endowed. How presumptuous and egotistical for mere human beings to think that they have "invented" some phenomenal discovery. This is the great failure of science: believing that scientists invent, when really, they discover. A so-called invention has already been made to function by the Great Mystery, *Wakan Tanka*. In time, as Rainbows depart for the spirit world, they will come back into ceremonies with which they were familiar, since they have been "initialized." Maybe this example can explain why early pioneers do not make an appearance in native ceremonies. They were not familiar with the ceremonies and certainly were not in harmony with Native American beliefs and values. The afterlife is all a mystery, but I believe that there are numerous clues as to its actuality if we are wise enough to perceive what is before us here in this life. After all, the Ultimate that has created this worldly medium has, no doubt, created the spiritual medium (so-called heaven) as well, and there is probably a degree of pattern in that medium that may be reflective.

Natural beseechment is not as difficult to fathom as mathematical formulas or computers, however. Three ceremonies can establish a good foundation in the Rainbow Way. These Mother Earth ceremonies are suggested because they are accessible and "do-able" by modern people who are seeking an understanding of and closer harmony with the revealed extensions of the Great Spirit. These ceremonies are: the Sacred Stone Ceremony or Pipe Ceremony; the Sweat Lodge; and the Vision Quest. It seems that the more familiar one becomes with these basic ceremonies, the more "power" or "spiritual intuition" one seems to acquire.

Native peoples should be reminded that early Christians and pre-Christian Jewish people went up on the mountain or out in the wilderness to beseech their concept of the Ultimate Power (Vision Quest). We Indians do not "own" this ceremony, or the Sweat Lodge either. All over the planet, people have huddled together as a group in a sapling-ribbed or thatched hut and beseeched their Higher Force. That is what we are doing in a sweat lodge if we are to really get down to it.

As for the other Native American ceremonies, I believe that the Sun Dance should remain on the reservation and should be conducted only by knowledgeable, respecting Native Americans. Other ceremonies that are deeply rooted in the tribe, and especially those that need the language and song, should also remain where they come from. But the three forms of beseechment mentioned above, in accord with some powerful holy men—these ceremonies can do the whole world a lot of good by coming out. To hold a Making of Relatives Ceremony or a Giveaway Ceremony honoring a departed spouse or other departed loved one should also be available to all.

BESEECHMENT WITH YOUR SACRED STONE OR WITH A PEACE PIPE

The peace pipe played a significant role in the survival of Sioux religion, Sioux spirituality. The Buffalo Woman enhanced the use of the pipe in ceremony. Black Elk's vision portrayed the pipe as an important instrument for bringing back the Sun Dance tree—around which the people would gather. The Sun Dance symbolized a return of the old Sioux spiritual customs; for many, its return is also believed to be a means for stimulating universal harmony among diverse peoples around the globe.

Black Elk went through a disparaging time. Soon after the Sioux were confined to the reservation system, our sweat lodges were no longer allowed. The annual Sun Dance thanksgiving was forbidden by government edict, while our peace pipes and medicine bundles were gathered up and destroyed. Lakota people had to stand and watch oil poured on gathered piles of their sacred articles, which were then set afire by the cavalry that had ruthlessly murdered women and children at Wounded Knee. Actually the Seventh Cavalry cared little whether or not we retained our spirituality; it was the fanatical missionaries who caused our ceremonial items to go up in smoke.

The peace pipe was concealable, however. The peace pipe was portable, and many of the people never lost their spiritual tenacity because this small, special item kept the ember of hope for cultural survival glowing. Some believe that the pipe was meant to be a sustaining gift by the Buffalo Calf Woman, who foresaw that Native American spirituality was to undergo a devastating test for survival.

The peace pipe is a highly respected personal object among Indian people. Native Americans abhor anyone misusing a pipe for any form of drug, and such a use is unthinkable among traditional native people. I believe strongly that no form of drugs should be used in association with ceremony and have found that Rainbow Tribe people are just as opposed to drugs or alcohol and avoid such things. Some who call themselves Rainbow people are not adverse to drugs, but there is little relationship between them and Rainbow Tribe people. Some Native Americans object to "outsiders" using the pipe. There are many Indians, however, who do not object and even carve the pipe from stone and make it available. Arvol Looking Horse, the present Keeper of the Pipe, was quoted in the *Lakota Times* (August 1991) as stating, in effect, that no one should be denied a peace pipe, but there is yet a considerable degree of dissension in this regard.

If my present pipe should accidentally be dropped and broken, I would need pipestone to carve a new one, or I would obtain a new one from a pipe maker to whom I would offer to give something in return, as did traditional warriors of long ago. It takes a lot of effort and time for pipe makers to reach the deeply overburdened layer of pipestone. Where would we who are not as artistically gifted get a truly aesthetic pipe that expresses our personal symbolism? I certainly am not one who wants the pipe makers or those who laboriously hand dig the stone to vanish.

I think most Indians would prefer to see the dominant society of today become acculturated and progress toward a healthy Mother Earth spirituality rather than have it return to the "Dark Ages." The learning of some of our spiritual concepts will have to be a portion of that acculturation. I would rather see this happen than experience a return to the old ways of religious persecution. I would hope that healthy-minded American Indian people will never advocate a return to power of the religious far-right that was so instrumental in having us placed in boarding schools and that would unleash a new round of cultural and religious destruction upon those of us who are not of their particular faith. Some ceremonies may have to remain on the reservation or in the hands of capable Native Americans, however, and these ceremonies will be discussed later. I like to avoid conflict, and yet I do not believe in sweeping important matters under the rug as most politicians have a tendency to do. And since I am probably too honest ever to be elected as a modern politician, I think this matter should be addressed.

I believe that if a person has a healthy respect for a religious item and sincerely utilizes it to connect to the Great Spirit, it is difficult to fault that person's use of the object for ceremonial purposes. I have observed repeatedly the respect exhibited by the Rainbow Tribe people. We Indian people have suffered severely from rule-making religious institutions that set themselves up as God, and I believe that we ourselves should never fall into that way of thinking. Now that we have so many new allies, we should make them feel welcome—as many Native Americans are doing. These allies will make our lives better as well, and they can exert a great deal of pressure on those who are still attempting to oppress us or would like to throw out our treaties and the other protections we have gained. Our new allies should reciprocate by not rushing in to "become Indian."

For those who wish to avoid conflict regarding the use of the peace pipe, I suggest that you seek a meaningful stone—your *wotai* stone—that has or will come into your life, and use this stone instead of a peace pipe to beseech the four directions, the six powers, or your concept of a higher connection. A crystal is a stone as far as I am concerned—in case you are particularly attached spiritually to a crystal. Crystals were also designed by the Great Spirit, the last I heard, although it seems that those who seek to detract from well-meaning New Age people do try to demean crystals. "If it is made by the Great Spirit, don't criticize it" might be a good rule. Actually, the use of your own personal *wotai* stone is a practical answer to the question of whether non-Indians should use or not use peace pipes or crystals as beseechment articles. This is a big, big world and, from a practical perspective, most people will not have access to a peace pipe any more than they will have easy access to a Sun Dance. More and more, I find myself using my *wotai* stone as a personal, portable beseechment object in which I can initially focus on the six powers when I do ceremony. Using a meaningful stone opens up the Natural Way to far more people as well. I like to avoid conflict, but I certainly am not going to go so far as to give up my beseechment and acknowledgment through the Natural Way or revert back to non–Native American beliefs just to please a detracting group of people. This is still a free country, and when innocent people are told that they cannot beseech through nature in a respectful manner and are repeatedly subjected to religious criticism, then this policy assumes some of the characteristics of right-wing fundamentalism, or worse, Nazism, which condemned and singled out the Jews.

The Pipe Ceremony is paramount and also fundamental for those who want to conduct ceremony in which the four directions are beseeched. For those who wish to use a stone instead of a peace pipe, simply substitute your stone for a peace pipe when you beseech.

The morning is a good time to begin your beseechment to the six powers. Look out upon the red dawn and hold forth your pipe or stone. Greet the rising of the sun at earth's edge and realize that a new day is to begin. Acknowledge the fact that new knowledge from a new day will come into your life. Realize that from knowledge can come wisdom. Wisdom leads toward understanding and ultimately peace for yourself and the whole world as well. If you happen to be participating before a group of supporters, then speak out firmly.

Turn to the south and think of growth, shelter, and healing. Speak out your appreciation for the long summer days that bring this planet food and for shelter that comes from the trees. Think of the medicines that the plants and herbs provide. For those into holistic healing, beseech the south power to impart its energy into your blessings.

Turn to the west and be thankful for the life-giving rains that come predominantly with the winds from the west. The power to make live and the power to destroy come from the west. Endeavor to help our earth live; seek to destroy the pollution and curtail the ignorance that harm all life.

Turn to the north and think of the cleansing snow that comes down from the cold lands and allows our Mother Earth to rest beneath a white blanket to rise refreshed when spring comes forth.

Touch your pipe or your stone down to Mother Earth and tell her you shall endeavor to protect her, that you acknowledge your relatedness to all things created from her.

Hold your spiritual item up toward the sun, or if it is evening hold it toward the moon that is reflecting the sun. Thank the sun as part of Father Sky for the energy that courses through your body. Tell Father Sky that you will use your energy to seek harmony and balance upon your travels, that you will use your blessed energy to promote true brotherhood and sisterhood by first respecting the many visions that are so abundantly allowed by the Great Planner.

Lastly, hold your pipe or stone straight up above and thank the Great Spirit, *Wakan Tanka,* or your concept of the Higher Power for all that is.

"Mitakuye oyasin" is a good expression to use to end your personal ceremony to the six powers that watch over us. *Mitakuye oyasin, mitakuye oyasin.* We are all related, we are related to all things.

After the basic beseechments have been studied and practiced, we should bear in mind that each of us comes from a unique background. Every day we all have different experiences, even contrasting from those of our brothers and sisters. Let us take a look at an exemplary Rainbow person who has blended the basic ceremonies with a healthy relationship attitude. Rainbows can pursue the same natural knowledge regardless of the many diverse paths they have walked in this modern world. The following is an account of an aware Rainbow representative who has reached out to that knowledge through ceremony and observation.

Let us learn from a Rainbow woman's initial familiarity with the red path. I first met Bright Earth Warrior in a Native American cultural seminar. She exhibited a notable degree of awareness with some of the material I was teaching. Bright Earth Warrior tells how Rainbow spirituality is essentially a personal path, a journey without guidebooks. She sees the ceremonies as a means to "thin the veil between ourselves and the spirit world, and at these times, the spirits can help us understand what we are meant to do and who we are meant to be." Bright Earth Warrior has her own pipe and even made her own pipe bag. As a pipe carrier she mirrors the Sioux image of a strong matriarchal woman; she is also very successful in the business world.

Bright Earth Warrior is serious about her spiritual obligations, as most Rainbows are. She is a generous person. Just a short while back in this modern day of technical advancement, I was still plodding along with note taking and a typewriter as my major writing tools when she introduced me to her computer. Later, due to her business acumen, she won a computer and insisted that I take her older model, which was essentially simpler for a computer beginner to understand and operate. The memory machine opened a whole new dimension of knowledge for me and proved the point that one is never too old to advance into new realms.

A SPIRITUAL JOURNEY WITHOUT GUIDEBOOKS
Bright Earth Warrior

From the time I was a child, I had to find things out for myself. When I was thirteen, my parents decided to send me to the local Congregational church for confirmation classes, arguing that since we live in a Christian culture, I needed to learn about Christian belief. I went, like any normal thirteen-year-old, and proceeded to make the minister's life miserable by asking unanswerable questions. Like, if God loves us so much, why is there so much suffering in the world? Or, if God sees every sparrow fall, how could he exclude them from heaven because they don't have souls? Needless to say, I was excused from further religious instruction.

My parents were equally appalled when at age twenty-six, after a severe spiritual struggle, I joined the Roman Catholic church. My father refused to speak to me for several months, convinced that I was the dupe of "some smooth-talking priest." I had no way to convince my father that, in spiritual matters at least, I took no one's teachings at face value. Unfortunately, I found that the church hierarchy took a somewhat different approach to spirituality than the contemplative nuns who had been my teachers.

So for me, Native American spirituality was an area full of questions. Isn't it presumptuous to participate in the spiritual tradition of a people who have been oppressed by the white culture? Isn't this whole set of beliefs something to be studied by anthropologists under the heading of comparative religion? Or is "shamanism" simply the latest fad of a spiritually hungry people who have sold every religious teaching to the highest bidder?

Would I have chosen Native American spirituality if I had been offered a menu? Probably not. Have you ever tried to respond to someone who asks what you did the night before, when what you did was go to a sweat lodge? And I am not yet done with my questions. How serious am I? How much am I willing to walk my talk? Is this just a game, or do I really use the spiritual tools that this path gives me to live a better life?

Although there are many ceremonies that are community events and are shared with others, this is essentially a personal path. As Eagle Man says, "We don't have any popes or bishops. Our holy men and women must each follow their own spiritual vision as they travel their earth path, their earth journey."

It is also a spiritual journey without guidebooks. Although you may go on vision quests or pray in sweat lodges or smoke your pipe, there are few set rules for what you experience. The role of the holy man or woman is to guide you, but my own experience is that their guidance is more likely to throw you back on your own resources. And while I, like everyone else on a spiritual path, want someone to tell me if I am "doing it right," I am refreshed and strengthened by being forced to do it on my own and to build my own relationships with the spirit world.

I had taken a class with Eagle Man. He had said that he would be building a sweat lodge in LaCrosse two weeks later, and that if anyone wanted to come, they could. That's it. That was the extent of the invitation. No printed circulars. No detailed directions on what would be expected and how to enroll. No itinerary for the trip. So I took a deep breath, considered how much I wanted to experience a sweat lodge, and called. He was wonderfully matter-of-fact, and we made arrangements to meet at his house on a Friday. Details after that were still fuzzy.

I am a planner. I like to have all my reservations made when I go on a holiday trip. In fact, I tend to fret if the details aren't ironed out. So I began on lesson one: You can only hold yourself in readiness. You cannot foresee everything that you will need to know.

When we finally left the Twin Cities, Ed, his wife, Mary, three of his children, his son's friend, and Rexie, the dog, were distributed between two cars. I was driving the three boys, two of them teenagers, and Rexie. I hesitate to admit how long it had been since I had made conversation with teenagers, but they were patient with me—and I was delighted to find myself enjoying the whole adventure.

We stayed in a motel that night, and in the morning Eagle Man and I went out to the property where the sweat lodge would be built. Before getting down to work, he spent some time educating the group of about twenty people on Native American spirituality. He talked about the six powers of the universe, about White Buffalo Calf Woman, and about the place of the *Inipi,* or Sweat Lodge Ceremony. He also shared his vision of women as spiritual leaders.

When we started on the actual work of building the lodge, I was surprised at how well the process came together. Although Eagle Man told us what to do, he did not supervise every aspect. The group worked simultaneously on each part of the process, some digging the fire pit, some gathering the saplings, some marking off the circle and digging the holes for the first ring. Others stayed in the house and made tobacco ties to be used in the ceremony.

It was a bitterly cold day for May, even in Wisconsin, and the work was hard. We ran out of saplings for the frame of the lodge, and new ones had to be located, cut down, and carried. Rocks of the right size and composition had to be gathered and carried to the fire pit. The saplings had to be carefully bent and tied, a job impossible to do in gloves and one that often required substantial strength.

At one point in the afternoon, I was tying part of the frame together and the sapling kept slipping out of my grasp. I was cold and frustrated. One of the men in the group came over and asked if I would like him to hold the branch down. He was a large, strong man and, from what I had seen of him earlier, very experienced in out-of-door tasks. Yet he hadn't come over to take my work away from me. There was no tone of disdain or of superiority. Just a simple question of whether I needed his help on that particular branch.

I began to watch the group more closely after that encounter. And I was surprised to see that that same communal attitude characterized almost all of the work being done. One group was in the kitchen preparing the meal for that night and being sure that those working outside had tea and coffee to warm them up. Stronger people were helping those who were less strong to bend branches and carry rocks. Taller people were reaching up to get things that no one else could reach. Smaller people were crawling under the lower spots to get those tricky knots. And Eagle Man was just one of the group—not a guru with disciples at his feet; just the work-crew foreman. Although every member of the group had been a stranger when I arrived, I felt the warmth and comfort of being with old friends.

The sweat lodge that night was wonderful, a trip back into the womb of Mother Earth. It is an odd experience to feel the closeness of your hoop around you, to hear their prayers, and yet to be totally enveloped in darkness. The rocks hissed and chattered with their own language. The darkness felt furry and full of spirits. At one point, I touched my eyes to be sure that they were open and I was not dreaming. I felt as if I had come home after a long journey.

There were other lessons on that trip. The next day, when I took the wrong fork in the road and turned a three-hour trip into a five-hour trip, Eagle Man behaved with perfect aplomb, making me feel much less stupid. I learned about patience and human frailty and acceptance in an immediate and simple way.

I have thought about that trip over and over. It became almost a symbol of the red road, a primer in spiritual journeying. We are excellent in Western society at segmenting our lives. Here's the physical exercise piece, here is the social piece, here is the career piece, here is the intimate-relationship piece, and over here, in its carefully defined corner, is the spiritual piece. I have learned this lesson well and I have a very successful career that depends on my ability to segment myself. For me, Native American spirituality has given me a way to once again become a part of the universe.

The Lakota use the phrase *mitak oyasin* often. It is used at the end of prayers and in many cases is the only portion of the prayer uttered aloud. It means "all my relatives," and it contains within it the key to the Lakota view of the world.

We are all related—human beings, four-leggeds, the winged, the insect people, the tree people—all of us are linked into a chain of being in which each has its place and in which none is more or less than another. We live whole lives by knowing our place in the chain and by standing strong in our place and being who we were born to be. That is why events such as the Vision Quest, the Sun Dance, and the Sweat Lodge are such important ceremonies. In these ceremonies, we thin the veil between ourselves and the spirit world, and at these times, the spirits can help us understand what we are meant to do and who we are meant to be. Our lives are the daily acting out of the visions that we receive from the spirit, and we may spend years studying and trying to understand the meaning of such a vision.

I received my name, Bright Earth Warrior, in a dream. I don't know what it means, but I know that it is part of the vision. It is up to me to take that vision seriously and to use the information that the spirit world gives me to understand who I am and what my place is in this universe. Every day I think about what it means to be a warrior and how that applies to me. I think about being named for the Earth and the obligations that go with that.

When one first encounters Native American spirituality, it is difficult to really take this worldview seriously. Western society is extremely homocentric. We believe and act as if we are the center of the earth and that everything has been put here for our use and pleasure. Just read the story of Adam and Eve and compare it to the beliefs of the Hopi, the Lakota, or the Cheyenne. Our self-centeredness has brought down on us ecological disasters that we cannot even comprehend. I don't claim exemption from this accusation. It is hard to break the habits of a lifetime, but I am working at it.

For me, that change began with taking my own spiritual obligations seriously. I became a pipe carrier and I pray regularly with my pipe. It goes with me on business trips and often has helped clear my head and reestablish my balance and contact with the natural world. In good Lakota tradition, I made my own pipe bag and have begun the decorations that may take years to complete, and will in themselves be an expression of my spiritual growth.

When I pray with the pipe, I link myself with the six powers of the universe, I invite in the Grandmothers and Grandfathers, I call on my power animals, and once I take my own unique place in the world, I can pray for those who need help, or comfort or understanding. The pipe is such a strong symbol of that link between the natural and the spiritual. Made of the most basic natural materials, it joins earth and sky. The smoke is my visible breath, the symbol of the sincerity of my prayers.

Several summers ago, I went with Eagle Man and about a dozen others to South Dakota for a vision quest. Along the way, he stopped at the Cheyenne River and had people search for a *wotai,* a talisman. Many people were uncertain about what to look for and how they would know that they had found their sacred stone, or at least a temporary one. As I listened to the conversations around me, I suddenly realized that we approach the whole problem from the wrong end. All rocks are sacred. The question is, how does the special one that we need find us?

And it is not only rocks. I have begun to learn down deep, not just intellectually, that everything around me is holy. I look at the people on the street and think there go I in a different face. I turn on a light and thank *Wiyo Ate,* Father Sun, for the energy that makes our lives easier. I am grateful to *Waziya,* the power of the north, for the snow, and I try to remember, as I shovel and struggle through the traffic during a storm, that I am not the center of the universe and that Mother Earth needs both the cold and the moisture of the snow to complete her cycles.

I love the practicality of this Natural Way. Unlike most religions, it is not confined by a specific building or ceremony. I remember driving home from the vision quest and running into the worst thunderstorm that I have ever experienced. We literally could not see more than twenty feet ahead of us. As the two in the front seats drove and managed the defrost and windshield wipers, the two in the back threw tobacco offerings out the windows and said prayers honoring *Wakinyan,* the thunder beings. All four of us laughed the whole time, yet we respected. We didn't fear the lightning and the torrents of rain that could have washed us off the highway had they increased. Maybe that is why we could laugh, and yet we let the west power know that we respected its torrential onslaught against a severe drought. We knew the land needed all that rain, but we were still going to send our signals to *Wakinyan* to be aware that we were inside all that fury. Looking back, I can see my progression toward becoming one with all the forces that affect us. I do love the practicality of Native American spirituality.

▼ ▼ ▼ ▼ ▼

We have observed how a Rainbow woman has found her natural path. Bright Earth Warrior represents a "normal," stable individual quite unlike the flighty, flitting stereotype that some cultureless facets of the New Age movement have projected. She also has a sense of humor. Her candid observations offer an admirable image with which to identify. In the building of a sweat lodge she exhibits the balance between male and female roles. She has gone forth into Sioux language classes, as well as drumming, and she regularly meets with a group of Rainbows to practice their ceremonial singing in Lakota from a Lakota language instructor. She travels occasionally to Spirit Mountain to vision quest, usually with other Rainbows.

A comment on matriarchy: Among the various concepts of matriarchy is that of a dominant woman devoid of feeling for the opposite sex who perhaps exhibits an animosity—backed by strong suspicion—toward all that the male undertakes in his role. Matriarchy need not come across in this form, however. Rather, the female role can be one of balance, with respect for male perspectives and a recognition of the areas in which both sexes need to cooperate so that a higher harmony can flow. Nature-based matriarchy need not relinquish those areas in which woman, with her perception and intuitive gifts, has been especially blessed. Old World strongholds of sheer, unbalanced patriarchy need to be challenged, however, since centuries of imbalance have set a disastrous example.

The Persian Gulf War exposed the severe limitations placed on Arab women by a fundamentalist, man-dominated religion. We witnessed extreme brutality from both sides. Were those countries to allow women military, political, and religious leadership, I am sure we would see much less brutality and more humanistic concern. Doesn't it make sense that a female commander would not look lightly on the rape of captive and refugee women? Look at what the all-male authorities allowed to happen to foreign women in Kuwait after Desert Storm was over.

Churches in this land should get their own houses in order as a beginning and should no longer restrict female leadership. The occupation of Kuwait by Iraq and the resettlement by the Kuwaitis was an example of how an extreme disregard for humanity can develop under religious fundamentalism that is totally male-dominated. Long ago, Native Americans showed the Europeans that women are a vital balancing force. Iroquois women voted and even had the power to recall and remove politicians from office; such was the wisdom of a people who followed the Natural Way.[3]

There are many Rainbow men within the Rainbow Tribe. In later chapters they will appear in vision quests, personal stone quests, and name searching as well as other adventures. They are balanced individuals and do not feel threatened by the new advance in power of the Rainbow Tribe woman. Rather, these men appreciate this new balance. Actually, it is an old balance that is seeking to be restored, if we realize what the Celtic Druids once had and recall the matriarchies of some of the northeastern North American tribes.

At present there is a new realization called the men's movement. Books by Robert Bly and Sam Keen are being read by modern men who are seeking their own identity. The spirit world seemed to manipulate my airplane ticket once. I found myself sitting next to Robert Bly on a flight, and we had a pretty good conversation. Later, I bought his interesting and insightful book *Iron John*. It was interesting how that little boy let the Wild Man out of the cage, wasn't it? And then how he and the little boy got along after the little boy got away from his mom and the busy king? And then all their adventures? I'm sure glad Fools Crow, Black Elk, and Bill Eagle Feather let me out of my cage.

I attended a men's movement conference in Colorado and conducted a session for Vietnam veterans besides speaking on the Natural Way. I spoke of Black Elk's vision and the six powers of the universe. It is amazing how this powerful philosophy can reach in a helpful manner into so many facets and problem areas that we two-leggeds come up with.

Years later, we war veterans are still honored. I recently was awarded the Red Feather Eagle Feather honor at the Yankton Sioux tribal powwow. After the award, we veterans all danced in a circle formed by twenty-two drum singer groups, and many people came forward to shake our hands. It is a sad commentary that the non-Indian Vietnam veteran has had to undergo such a hard time from an unappreciative country—because you are just as dead from a bullet in the jungle as in the desert. At the end of my short lecture we all went out into Mother Nature to a spot where the cut saplings had been placed. The veterans all pitched in and we built a sweat lodge.

It was good to be back again with just fellow warriors who had been in the same foreign land. It was almost like reaching back into the past and being with a group of Oglala Dog Soldiers or a Kit Fox Society. I have a Yankton Sioux friend named Leonard "Sonny" Hare. We are both members of the all-Indian Yankton Sioux Veterans of Foreign Wars Post 1353. Sonny is a true warrior, having been a Navy Seal and wounded twice. Vietnam Seals had a casualty rate of 80 percent either killed or wounded. He volunteered from his hospital bed for another combat tour. We have a camaraderie that I imagine the old-time Sioux warriors had. When I am with him it is a throwback to what seems to be many warrior pasts. That evening in Colorado we warriors held our cleansing sweat ceremony and, here again, it was the Natural Way that could fit in so well with a gathering and help out, especially for combat veterans.

An equal number of women attended this men's conference. Their presence added to the event's success. Toward sundown, two long lines of the different genders wound their way in opposite directions. These participants were led by a considerable number who had drums. They chanted and drummed and then both lines filed into a large campus building. I missed out on this part because of preliminary sweat lodge preparations. A Navaho friend, a Korean War veteran, was waiting for me to begin the sweat lodge fire and to help with the firewood and stones. After the gathering had concluded its drumming ceremony, many of the women came over with the Vietnam vets to take part in the lodge.

I want to point out that men's gatherings across the land have been utilizing the Sweat Lodge Ceremony. They recognized its therapeutic powers long before I attended one of their gatherings. Maybe it will help them if they can learn to approach the ceremony from a more culturally aware base, which will also give their ceremonies a semblance of commonality. I am sure that the spirit of Black Elk will rejoice if his colors are used along with the recognition of the six powers. His vision was about the races coming together in harmony, and it appears that we just might be headed in that direction.

When I am at a Natural Way–related conference or a Rainbow gathering I notice that the women usually outnumber the men. Is this because women are more spiritual? Are they more perceptive in the field of relationship and identification with the created entities? Even in the Christian churches on Sunday mornings, the women outnumber the men. Strangely, they even outnumber the men in those churches where women are forbidden to be leaders in the clergy or speakers from the pulpit. My observations are certainly not startling revelations to anyone, but sometimes what is patently obvious needs to be stated at least as food for thought. The women's movement is older than the men's movement in these modern times. But even the women's perspective seems to have changed from what it was several decades ago. Eventually, I believe, both movements will join together in a recognition of balance and respect. That combined movement will take a more spiritual avenue toward the life forces of the Earth, not unlike what the Rainbow Tribe has already done. Many will become Rainbows because the Rainbow Tribe movement, the Path of the Rainbow, is already within this recognition.

5

RAINBOWS IN SWEAT LODGE

The *Inipi,* or Sweat Lodge, is becoming a sought-after ceremony across the nation. Many non-Indians as well as off-reservation Indians living in cities have found vacant spaces to build sweat lodges. The holding of sweat lodge ceremonies off the reservation is certainly nothing that the Rainbow Tribe can lay claim to. Throughout North America, this ceremony has been conducted by numerous Native Americans and non–Native Americans. The lodge can be built in only a few hours out of saplings, and it provides a spiritual experience that no cathedral can match.[1]

In my experience, most sweat lodge conductors, water pourers, or lodge leaders have their own particular way of conducting a lodge. I have never seen two leaders conduct their ceremony exactly alike. But many lodge leaders seem to have some things in common. One method or practice is to beseech each direction separately and uniquely during the course of the ceremony.

Inipi means "to live again." No one should claim a patent on religion or spirituality. The people I have been associated with in natural ceremony simply want to pray in such a way that they can draw from the power of created nature. No one tribe or group of people can lay claim to the forces of nature. Across the planet, down through the ages, tribes of all colors have prayed to a natural, Great Mystery form of power. Just because organized Christianity put a stop to natural beseechment in most parts of the western hemisphere does not mean that European descendants should be held back from natural beseeching in a simple lodge that they choose to construct. I hope that no one nationality or ethnic group owns the willows or the saplings or the fallen firewood of the forest. If white people were praying and working together in their newly constructed lodges to put all Native Americans back into boarding schools and were planning to have us all forced into one religion through government manipulation, then by all means I would not want them in any ceremony. But this is not the case. I do not believe that sweat lodges and related forms of beseechment structures existed in the Americas alone. People are now going back to spiritual yearnings linked mysteriously to their genes, yearnings that reach back to Celtic, Germanic, Nordic, Lap, Mongolian, and a host of other tribal pasts. Natural Way beseechment people will be strong allies of Native Americans and the Earth as time moves on.

We should never take it for granted that the old ways of prejudice, religious persecution, and far-right oppression are gone for good. Review the Supreme Court decision of June 4, 1990, in *Board of Education of the Westside Community Schools v. Mergens*. Missionary groups are now allowed to invade public schools. A president of Christian educators stated, "Our jobs are to evangelize [and] our schools are the battlegrounds." Another missionary group intends to "raise up Holy Ghost swat teams on every campus who will lead every campus to God."[2]

Look at the expected progress after the civil rights movement. A lot of rhetoric was spoken and some laws were passed, but jobs and fair-hiring practices have been loopholed away and throughout the country, the old restrictions and inequalities are creeping back. Black brothers and sisters are still suffering despite the great sacrifice of Martin Luther King. Look at the way the far right is stacking the courts across the land. It would be very foolish for Native Americans not to realize what true friends we are cultivating through the movement of the Natural Way. It is an opportunity to follow in the footsteps of Dr. King; we can all advance together in a highly spiritual progression.

In the Sweat Lodge Ceremony the participants are smudged with sage or cedar, and the four elements—fire, air, water, and earth—are utilized. The four directions are beseeched within the warm womb of Mother Earth. Fire (*wiyo,* the sun) heats the stones, and water (*wichoni mini,* the life-giving rain) is poured onto the heated stones. The water is mixed with the sweat, the waters of the participants, and with air. *Tate Topa,* the four winds, carry forth the mixture of steam to the four quarters of our planet. This carrying forth of a part of ourselves out to the four directions tells us we are partaking in a universal ceremony.

Black Elk said:

> We regard all created beings as sacred and important, for everything has a *wochangi,* or influence, which can be given to us through which we may gain a little more understanding if we are attentive. We should understand well that all things are the works of the Great Spirit. We should know that He is within all things; the trees, the grasses, the rivers, the mountains and all the four-legged animals, and the winged peoples; and even more important, we should understand that He is also above all these things and peoples.[3]

Wochangi can also mean a spiritual power, such as may be manifested in the Sweat Lodge. I take exception to Black Elk's genderizing of the Great Spirit (and the six powers), but I believe that the depth of Black Elk's vision and his related wisdom are far more important than trivialities such as gender terminology.

Sit quietly and project yourself in a steaming lodge, sitting on spring grass within the moist womb of Mother Earth. Others are with you, others who have had the drive and ambition to discover the depth of ceremony. You are clad in a T-shirt and a pair of swimming shorts. The ground is cool even though the steam is spreading out from the first dippers splashed onto the glowing rocks in the dishpan-sized pit at the center of the lodge.

In the darkened interior, the lodge leader calls out to the west power. This is the first endurance, the first of four endurances that will beseech the four directions, the first four powers of Black Elk's vision. Mother Earth is present. You are sitting upon her. Father Sky is present. The sun's heat is within the glowing stones and brings forth your lifeblood, your sweat, to mix with the lifeblood of the world, the water within the bucket beside the lodge leader. All within the lodge are introduced to the onlooking spirit world through the west power. Each person calls out his or her name and a respectful greeting. A simple beginner's song is sung.

> *Wiyopeyata hehhhhhh* (west power). *Hehhhhh.*
> *Wee yohhh-peee-yahhh tahh hehhhhhh.*
> *Wee yohhh-peee-yahhh tahh hehhhhhh.*
> *Wee yoh-pee-yah tah hehhhhhh.*

If the lodge participants are experienced, a more elaborate song might be sung. The following is an example of a Sioux song.

> *Wiyopeyata kiya etunwin na cekiya yo hey.*
> *Cekiya yo yo hena nitakuye yo hey.*
> Look to the west and pray to them.
> Pray to them because those people are your relatives.

It is obvious that a goodly amount of practice would have to be devoted to learning just one phrase, but many people are making that commitment. Some Indian tribes will be unhappy to hear me say this, no doubt, but it appears that the Lakota language is fast becoming the spiritual language of the nation. *Wakan Tanka* and *Ina Maka* are now common terms in many non-Indian households. People are seeking out Sioux language dictionaries and are listening to the tapes of Sioux singers that are available.

The second endurance will beseech the north power, and a time of contemplation will take place. Possibly, more heated stones will be called for. A song will be sung or the participants may take up a chant to encourage the endurance.

> *Waziyah hehhhhh* (north power).
> *Waziyah hehhhhh.*
> *Waziyah hehhhhh.*
> *Waziyah hehhhhh.*

A more elaborate song may be sung instead:

> *Waziyata kiya etunwin na cekiya yo hey.*
> *Cekiya yo yo hena nitakuye yo hey.*
> Look to the north and pray to them.
> Pray to them because those people are your relatives.

The third endurance to the red east will be made in recognition of the power of knowledge. During the third endurance, those within the ceremony will have the opportunity to express their personal beseechments or prayers. All present gain strength and knowledge from these very moving prayers. At times, some of the participants receive their natural names during the third endurance.

At the beginning of the third endurance, the song in Lakota to the east power can be sung.

> *Wiyo heyapa hehhhhh* (east power).
> *Wiyo heyapa hehhhhh.*
> *Wiyo heyapa hehhhhh.*
> *Wiyo heyapa hehhhhh.*

The more elaborate east power or direction song would use the word *Wiyohinyanpata*. For the more formal south power song, *Itok-agata* would be inserted for the first word.

The last endurance will be directed toward the south power—the power of healing, growth, abundance, and holistic strength. Healing and acknowledgment of ourselves for being in the lodge, healing for a loved one, recognition of one who has been good to us and has gone on—these things may be part of the fourth endurance. Lastly, as a form of recognition and beseechment, the participants will place their hands forward toward the center of the lodge to touch the tree of life. You will ask for world peace and promise Mother Earth to watch out for her, protect her, and do what is in your power to end the pollution that is harming all that grows upon her. I tell her that I am a warrior against the Blue Man.

Beginning the fourth endurance, all can chant this song:

> *Itokaga hehhhhh* (south power).
> *Itokaga hehhhhh.*
> *Itokaga hehhhhh.*
> *Itokaga hehhhhh.*

"*Ina Maka awan yan ke*" is a simple beginner's wording of "Mother Earth, I seek to protect you."

The lodge can end on the statement, "*Mitakuye oyasin*" ("We are all related"). Some interpret this phrase as "We are related to all things."

The following took place in the southwest near Sedona. Like the *Paha Sapa* (Black Hills) of Dakota, this area is considered a special place by many people. I was fortunate to meet a group of people who are spiritual leaders in their own right. Their attitude, knowledge-seeking, and—probably—the location caused a startling event to happen within a sweat lodge.

THE NIGHT THE BOTTOM FELL OUT

Eileen Nauman, Tashuunka Winan Wichasta, Wolf Woman Warrior

About a year and a half ago I asked the Grandparents to send me a teacher if I was ready to learn Sweat Lodge Ceremony. Soon afterwards, I happened to be at a bookstore in Sedona and was guided to *Mother Earth Spirituality.* When I picked it up, the first thing I saw was the photograph on the rear jacket. My heart slammed into my ribs. I knew this man, and I knew him well. Old past-life memories were stirring strongly. I didn't care at that point *what* this man had written, because whatever was contained inside the pages was Truth as I knew it. So I bought the book without even opening it up to peruse the contents.

When I got home and read it, so much was double-checked for me. Finally, here was a Native American, like myself, who followed the old ways—a man who revered women as being equal, who didn't place taboo upon taboo in ceremony, whose eaglelike sight was laser-focused on several primary objectives: women taking back their power, and using it for all our relatives, and the healing of Mother Earth, our caretaker. After I finished reading the book, I sat down and wrote the author a two-page letter telling him who I was, what I was doing, and inviting him down for a sweat cere-mony. I enclosed a small eagle feather along with my request.

On Christmas Eve day, I received a phone call from Ed, who had just gotten my letter from his publisher. He said he'd come down for a sweat lodge, and we set a date in March for it to take place. As a medical astrologer, I wanted a full moon, and in March it would be in Libra, the sign of balance between the male and female energies. Like all Native Americans and those of the Rainbow Tribe, we are working toward one common goal: harmony and balance within ourselves that will automatically translate outward to encompass the other worlds in which we live simultaneously. Libra is the act of balance, and is ruled by Venus, which has a direct bear-ing on our heart *chakra.* With a full moon in force, it was a perfect time to set up the Sweat Lodge Ceremony from an astrological as well as a Native American perspective.

When Ed called I felt like I was talking to a mirror image of myself. He shot straight from the hip, didn't mince words, kept things simple, and, ultimately, utilized common sense and practicality. We found we had many things in common—among them, religious persecution. I feel this experience made our commitment to keep the old ways, and to bring them back, even more tenacious.

I am Cherokee Metis through my great-grandmother, who was of the Wolf Clan of the eastern Cherokee tribe. I have walked the old ways and the medicine path all my life. I call myself a healer because I work in many realms, using many tools to help people help themselves, and to help heal Mother Earth. When I refer to followers of the old ways, I mean people who used and followed the teachings of such great ones as Black Elk, Red Cloud, Crazy Horse, Sitting Bull, Chief Joseph, Fools Crow, and Bill Eagle Feather. The medicine women have always remained behind the scenes, but I want to acknowledge them also, for without the Grandmothers' guardianship none of us would have many of our Native American traditions and ceremonies left to us today.

Traditionalists, as I define them, are modern-day Native Americans who take missionary/church teachings that hold a burden-basket of taboos and contrive to combine them with ancient Native American teachings. The Great Spirit did not intend any of us to become so bound up with rules and regulations that we forget the real reason for performing ceremony or ritual: And that is with our heart. Love needs no rules or regulations, in my opinion. Follow your heart, that inner sense of *knowing,* and you'll never go wrong. Follow your head (left brain), which can get tangled up with third-dimensional complexities, and you'll find yourself in a box canyon.

I was taught that as long as your *intent* is pure, and your heart is combined with that intention, whether you know any ceremony or ritual, whether you are of Native American blood or not, and no matter what color or nationality you are, you will be heard, your prayer answered, or some change brought about—because you walk in a humble way, with your heart in the right place, on the good red road.

There is also a difference between ceremony and ritual. Ceremony is a tradition that has been passed down through generations by word of mouth (until very recently) and is followed precisely, without embellishment, without adding or subtracting anything from the song, the dance, the prayer, or whatever it is. For example, the Sweat Lodge, Medicine Wheel, and Pipe are all considered ceremony. Ritual, on the other hand, is being in the moment, flowing with the energies of that time and place, working with the spirits of that area and listening in an unconscious sense, and becoming a partner with it.

Many songs spring forth during or after a ritual, because you've opened yourself up to the possibility of becoming one with all. You may or may not remember a ritual once it's ended. Sometimes you do. If you remember that ritual, make it your own, and begin to pass it on to others (if you choose), then it may eventually become a ceremony—something that's passed on generation to generation. Ritual is just as powerful as ceremony. It utilizes the creative energies of the moment with you, the conduit through which the Great Spirit flows.

When Ed accepted my invitation, I was elated because I'd always been drawn to the Lakota language, people, and customs. I wanted my students, mostly of the Rainbow Tribe, to share the experience and learn from Ed's teaching. A good leader is a catalyst who creates situations not only for her/himself but for others. I sent out invitations all over the United States and to Brazil. Of the eighteen people invited, fifteen were going to be able to make it on fairly short notice. Some of these men and women had been students for many years; others, only quite recently. Because of their commitment to the red road for themselves and all our relatives, they were, in my opinion, ready to learn the techniques, take the knowledge back home, build a sweat, and begin creating ceremony not only for themselves, but for others who sought the sweat as a way of purifying one's self, as well as utilizing it as a major healing tool.

My husband, David, and I live in a canyon far away from everything and everyone. My profession is that of a full-time writer with over thirty fiction books and two nonfiction books published. I need a quiet, out-of-the-way place in order to create. My ninety-four-year-old grandmother, Inez, lives in a small house on the same property, and my seventy-four-year-old mother, Ruth, has her home here as well. We live the "Indian way," in that the entire family lives close to one another, shares everything, and each takes care of the other.

I call the land that we make our home on *La Casa de Tierra Madre,* "The House of Mother Earth." It is two and one-half acres next to a creek filled with trout, panfish, and bass. There are forty fruit trees on the land we steward, and two huge gardens. We have over a hundred bantam chickens and babies, plus we raise ring-necked pheasants. We're about 75 percent self-sufficient. We grow our own fruits and vegetables, and slaughter our chickens and pheasants as a meat source.

Oak Creek flows through the canyon, and there is a five-hundred-foot cliff composed of red sandstone and black basalt lava columns rising up from the other side of the bank. Our home sits directly across the creek from this canyon wall. This is sacred Yavapai land, where spirit guardians still exist to this day. There are also Apache and Navaho spirit guardians in this canyon. When Dave and I bought the land, we promised to be stewards to the area and to renew and awaken the ties to the spirit guardians who are caretakers to this potent, wonderfully female-energy area that is home to a large, powerful vortex.

Dave built me a hogan, an eight-sided Navaho structure, which I use as my medicine room and healing place, as well as for meditation. I lived on the Navaho reservation at Fort Wingate, New Mexico, when I was twelve years old. What I absorbed from the Diné culture, their morals and values, their way of walking, is with me to this day—and the reason for the creation of the hogan.

The hogan was placed beneath the bower of nine tall, old mesquite trees. A year earlier, before we moved here, my mother was the caretaker of the land for us. On one hot, muggy July afternoon the thunder beings built mighty thunderstorms around us. They came over the canyon and sent their lightning not only into our water well but also through the entire series of mesquite trees (twelve in total), blackening each trunk with a scorching fire. Each mesquite bears a black vertical mark four to six feet long on its trunk. The bolt walked from south (for the Cherokee, south is the home of the coyote and the element fire, so it was appropriate . . .) to north, and the south side of each tree is scored black.

I have always been one with the west, the home of the thunder beings. Even as a nine-year-old child, when I saw a storm approaching I would run up to the highest point (in this case, a huge hill of dried cow manure) and fling my arms skyward. The whirling of sudden, gusty wind would embrace me, and I could feel the thunder beings' electric energy tingle wildly down my fingers, through my arms, and course through my body to the Mother Earth in response to my supplication. To this day, wherever I travel around the world, thunderstorms crop up just before or right after I've arrived at the place where I'm to give lectures or seminars. So, for the thunder beings to place their lightning bolts across the land was indeed the highest kind of blessing that we could receive. A stamp of approval, so to speak. Their approval is evident to this day on each mesquite tree. And that was why I wanted the hogan placed on such sacred, blessed ground.

When Ed arrived, I took him to this place made sacred by the lightning and thunder beings. He quickly agreed that the sweat lodge should be placed right where the lightning had walked across the land, and it was to be situated about fifty feet away from the hogan, in a cleared area.

My students came from Arizona, New Jersey, Ohio, Oklahoma, New York, and Brazil. In the early afternoon on a spring day, we were like children playing and laughing as Ed showed us how to create a sweat lodge out of saplings gathered and utilized from the banks of Oak Creek. About halfway through the construction, Ed muttered, "Well, I've seen worse built," and then he grinned. Native Americans who walk the old ways (not to be confused with the traditionalists of the modern day) *always* possess a tremendous sense of humor. We understand that laughter is one of the greatest healers of all.

I looked over at him and grinned back. Suddenly, Diana, my pipe student from New Jersey, cried, "Look! A golden eagle!" We all looked up. There, high, very high, probably about seven thousand feet, was a golden eagle moving in a straight line from east to west right over the sweat lodge we'd been building with our laughter, love, and care. I glanced at Ed.

"Well," I said, "how's *that* for an approval rating on the lodge we're building?"

"Not bad, not bad," he said, obviously a little awed and pleased himself.

I pondered the eagle flying toward the west, the point of transformation, death, and dying. I knew it was going to be a tremendously catalytic sweat for everyone who sat in the lodge that night. Someone else spotted two red-tailed hawks flying in a circle in the northeast. They came through the "saddle," a dip in the canyon wall, hovered, and circled right over the creek, near our house. For me, the northeast has always been the magical position on the medicine wheel, that is, the place where seemingly impossible things are witnessed or experienced. Those hawks then disappeared. About an hour later they came back, lighted in the trees in the canyon, and simply watched us complete the sweat lodge. As far as I was concerned, we'd gotten the blessings of the Great Spirit that our heart, our intent, was good and true. I knew it was going to be an exceptional sweat.

I turned to Ed and said, "You know, this isn't any ordinary group of people coming together for a sweat. These women and men are strong, unique, confident individuals who are leaders in their own right."

Ed agreed.

I smiled a sly wolf smile and added, "So you'd better be prepared for what happens in that sweat, my friend." I knew that Ed was also going to experience things that had never happened in any sweat he'd ever conducted.

He laughed, and it was a good, hearty laugh. Ed sensed, as I did, as did all those gathered, that this was going to be a unique Sweat Lodge Ceremony.

I must point out that with the exception of two people, none of us had ever been in a sweat lodge before. I had had many opportunities over the years to partake of the experience, but I remembered what my teacher had taught me years before: You do not enter a sweat if you have an uncomfortable or uneasy feeling about it, or if you don't know the person conducting the sweat, or if there is someone among the participants who holds jealousy, envy, or some other negative emotion against you. I was taught to enter a sweat only with the highest of purposes with those who held the same intent. I felt completely comfortable with the people with whom I was going to enter the sweat that night. I sensed that their commitment was as strong as my own to go into the dark womb of our Mother, the Earth, with only our highest thoughts, feelings, and spiritual focus as our offering to her.

Father Sun slid behind Deer Mountain. This mountain spirit is a place where the deer people sleep during the daylight hours beneath the junipers, and it sits opposite the canyon cliff. As dusk fell, Ed quietly told everyone to get ready. The anticipation soared in the silence as each of us went to change into something loose and comfortable, and to collect our pipes, fetishes, *wotai* stones, or any other articles we wanted in the sweat with us.

It was a sweet, strong anticipation that hummed through me. I felt solid, confident, and good. I was excited, but in a subtle way. Getting to return to our Mother's body, her womb, was something I had ached to do all my life. Now, it was becoming a reality. And yet, there was this soft, gentle sensation within me, something so sacred that just being able to sense it was overwhelming. I knew the sweat was going to be completely unlike any other I would ever encounter in the future.

As I felt my way through what things might make it so, I knew that the caliber of my students, who really are my cosmic family, was a great part of that reason. Each is a Rainbow warrior from the Rainbow Tribe. Each has been tested through the fires of transformation, and they've come out tempered and stronger, like fine steel. I was so proud of them, because no matter what life handed them, they met each challenge, each fear, with an undeniable grace, a belief and trust in the Great Spirit, that is truly inspirational.

Ed and I, by the end of two days of his visit with us, openly admitted that we were like "twins." We were so much alike, except that he was in a male body and I in a female one. We were both warriors for Mother Earth, and both of us wanted to slay the Blue Man with equal intent and commitment. He had been doing this all his life, in many ways, and so had I. Further, Ed was a former Marine, and I had been in the Navy for three years. We'd both gone through the Vietnam War, he as a fighter pilot, I as a meteorologist giving weather data to pilots. I was also a student pilot, having gotten my license when I was seventeen. I went on to become a firefighter for three years, the only woman in our department. So I'd seen many forms of combat over the years. Our warrior spirit is our bond, and we realized that by being together in one place, it was going to create a focus of energies that would be akin to blending two powerful rivers into one.

As we walked toward the sweat lodge after the preparatory ceremony, I looked up to the west, and there, above Deer Mountain, was Mother Venus. She is called the Morning Star and Evening Star by different tribal nations. Mother Venus hung like a bluish white teardrop pendant in the cobalt velvet sky, and I thought to myself: She's in the west, the point of death and dying, the point of transformation. Venus, from an astrological perspective, rules the heart *chakra,* our love (on all levels of our being, not just the physical, sexual type), our friendships and affections. As I ducked into the lodge, I felt very good about having her radiance shining down upon us as we began.

Fifteen people sat in the lodge. I was on Ed's right, and Dr. Celso Alaeida, a medical doctor from Belo Horizonte, Brazil, sat on his left. We were to assist the lodge leader in various ways throughout the ceremony. David, who volunteered to be the fire-tender, brought in the hot lava rocks, glowing a reddish orange. We greeted each stone with *"Hau Kola!"* and it was placed in the pit. Ed said he wanted seven stones. David had brought eight. I watched and waited while they decided what to do. Ed told Dave to take the eighth stone back to the fire.

Seven, for the Cherokee, and most other tribes, is a sacred number. For the Cherokee, it reminds us of our real home, the Pleiades, which consist of seven stars. I felt that, unconsciously, Ed was honoring the fact that all who sat in the sweat this night were, indeed, star people. They might not have Indian blood in them this time, but they had the genetic memory of knowing that their home was also in the Pleiades. I smiled in the darkness, inhaling the dry, burned odor rapidly filling the silent, darkened sweat lodge. Seven was the right number for this group.

Dave came in and the flap was drawn down into place a final time. The first endurance began. As soon as Ed began to ladle water onto the glowing, living stone people, steam hissed and shot toward the roof of our lodge and rolled into billowing clouds. Ed began his prayer for all of us in Lakota, the words musical, vibrating, circling within the lodge in a clockwise direction. He poured three more dippers of water onto the rocks.

Another prayer was invoked. Ed began to beat the drum, the vibration shattering through the steam, permeating us physically, mentally, emotionally, and touching our spiritual being. He blew the eagle whistle, the sound shrill, not hurtful to the ears but certainly as piercing as if the Eagle had reached out with her claws and pierced through all our fears and defenses to get our attention, our focus. I saw the eagle enter from the east and rapidly wing her way in a clockwise direction around and around in the lodge. The energy heightened as she flew. I saw Grandmother Medicine Bear come in from the west, for she was the ultimate healer and brought death and dying, a form of transformation, into our presence. A herd of buffalo entered from the north. I felt a distinct shifting of energy within the lodge after that. I felt everyone opening up, receiving, absorbing, and digesting. Within moments, we were all dripping wet with the beginning of the perspiration from the stones, as well as from our own bodies.

Abruptly, Ed stopped drumming and whistling, and he added another Lakota prayer. Afterward, he asked each person, in a clockwise direction, to introduce themselves. This we did. Another prayer was said. Because David wanted to be a part of the sweat, we did not bring in stones for the second round or open the flap. We moved right into the second endurance.

More prayers, more water, were thrown upon those seven stones. As I looked down into the glowing stones, I saw the distinct face of Black Elk in them. I blinked. Understand that I wear glasses, and without them, I'm as blind as a bat. So, when I saw his face so clearly, it startled me momentarily. I watched his face dance in the fire pit, and I felt humbled. I wondered if anyone else had seen him: Ed did. This was the first time he'd ever seen Black Elk come into a sweat that he'd conducted. Fools Crow was there, too, and this was also the first time he'd appeared to Ed. I did not see him. Of course, neither of us knew this at the time, only afterward, when we shared our experiences with each other.

More prayers were said; steam was rolling, hot, but not burning. Ed threw some sacred white sage on the rocks and quickly doused them with water. The pungent scent rolled upward, curving across the bowed saplings and enveloping us as we inhaled deeply. Sweat had gathered at the top of the lodge and was dripping gently down upon us, making us one with all. Outside the sweat, I saw the Seven Grandmothers from the Bear Cave, which sits in Boynton Canyon, one of the major vortexes. These spirit Grandmothers stood around outside our lodge, stretched their hands across the top. When their fingers touched, I watched in awe as the rainbow colors flowed from their collective hands down into the lodge where they began to circle and flow in a clockwise direction, bathing all of us in those beautiful, uplifting colors. I thanked them for coming.

As Ed beat the drum, I saw colorful sparks coming off the drumstick as he struck the hide. It was like the Fourth of July in there for me. Then he stopped, passed the sage around, gave me the drum, and told me to play and sing a song. I chose my personal song, a song given to me by the Maidu Indian spirits who still guard and maintain the sacred fire circle deep in the northern California Sierra. Many of my students, who know the song, joined in, and it was beautiful, for we all felt the wonderful feminine power, the gentleness and yet the strength of it, flow through and around everyone. Afterward, I handed the drum back to Ed.

The third endurance began. Ed was beating the drum hard and blowing the eagle whistle when I looked up to see this luminous white light covering the top of the lodge. I didn't know what it was, but it was almost as if the top of the lodge was beginning to disappear. Ed stopped playing and asked each of us to pray. I sat there *feeling* each word of each prayer spoken by my friends and loved ones, and was humbled by their undying commitment to help heal our Mother, the Earth. Nearly everyone who wanted one received a name. The energy leaped, jumped, throbbed, and heightened with each prayer whispered from the lips of each person. I was the next to last to pray, and I felt a locking in of power within myself, so overwhelming that I could only sit there feeling the vibration of it. After my prayer ended, Ed told me that the spirit beings wanted to add onto my original name of *Tashuunka Manitou Mani,* "Walks with Wolves." He said instead they wanted me to receive the name of Wolf Woman Warrior. I couldn't cry, so deep was the humility I felt as the spirits spoke through Ed to me. I accepted the responsibility and mission of the name.

After Ed said his prayer, we lifted the flap and Dave went out to retrieve more rocks, and Celso, another gallon of water for Ed to use. At this time, as I sat there, I felt this incredible feminine energy, gentle yet strong, throbbing in the background. This was our Mother I was feeling, and I sat there like a sponge receiving all that she wanted to give me.

Rock after glowing rock came in, and we struck each one with the stick and greeting it with *"Hau Kola."* Ed asked how many new stones had been placed in the fire pit. I told him seven. Dave had an eighth. Hesitating, Ed said, "Bring it in."

Good! I thought, for the number eight, when placed on its side, becomes the symbol of infinity. Eight is the number of balance: two circles joined in the middle. It is the male and female in us all. Numerologically, the eight also meant you were going to get exactly what you deserved: no more, no less. I was inwardly thrilled that Ed had allowed eight stones into the fire pit. Now, I thought, things are really going to happen! We were going to be rewarded for our heartfelt intent.

The flap closed for the fourth round. Water was ladled into the pit, and steam hissed, rolled, and thundered throughout the lodge, touching and embracing each of us. Within a minute, we were immersed in the steam. Ed picked up the drum and began to play. This time, the tone of the drum had changed; her voice was deeper, more resonate, more shattering. Ed beat on the drum hard, the sound like a small earthquake shivering constantly through the lodge, making it shake like a young aspen in a summer storm. The piercing shrill of his eagle-bone whistle sounded, and I surrendered over to the powers that were there, waiting for us.

I looked up and saw the top of our sweat dissolve and disappear, the white light fading away. What I saw next was stars! A galaxy of stars all around us. I was entranced, held in a thrall of sound, whistle, power, and infinite love that now embraced us. I never wanted that music to stop, and, just by chance, I looked down. I saw stars under us! My mouth dropped open. And then, Ed stopped playing.

"Look above you," he said in a deep voice, "for you will see the galaxy of stars surrounding us. Look below, and you will also see the stars. We are out in space, we are surrounded by the stars."

Ed double-checked what I was seeing, and I was stunned by the beauty. We had all, literally, astral-traveled. No longer were we in a sweat lodge, no longer was Mother Earth beneath us, but we were surrounded by stars. I saw all of us sitting cross-legged, our knees touching one another, floating out in space in this beautiful circle of human beings, of star people. I saw the white light like an aura surrounding each of us, making the circle look like a glowing, fluorescent orb. As I looked down below where we were floating in the field of stars, I saw our Mother the Earth very far away. She was clothed in a mantle of the most beautiful blue I'd ever seen. Right at that moment of discovery, Ed said, "Look at the blue color beneath us."

I looked around us, and I knew that this was special even though I'd never participated in a Sweat Lodge before. None of us had been told what to expect, because Ed was very careful not to set us up psychologically beforehand. I saw millions of stars, swirling pintail-shaped galaxies, blazing suns, and felt my oneness with all. I understood as never before what "all my relations" really meant in the deepest spiritual sense. We looked like a space station built of people in a glowing white circle simply floating out in the arms of the Great Mystery, for what we were experiencing was the true mystery of Life. I sensed the importance of this for each of us, including Ed.

Ed began to beat the drum and blow the eagle whistle once again. I closed my eyes and simply felt the grace, love, and infinite contain me. A little later, he told all of us to place our *wotai* stones over one eye. He told us we'd see something. I had brought in the first pipe ever bestowed upon me, a four winds and spider pipe. I wanted her with me, even though I had a *wotai* stone with me, too.

She was my oldest teacher, and my bond with her is like the bond with a dear old friend. I held the small stone pipe up to my closed left eye. Instantly, I saw rainbow colors flowing from some unknown source, through the pipe, and into me. I was literally bathed in the rainbow colors. When Ed told us to put our *wotai* stone on our other eye, the color purple flowed through me.

The color purple holds special significance to me. For the Hopi, there is the Eighth Universe, the ultimate one, and from there flows the color purple. According to Cherokee tradition, the southwest direction of the medicine wheel is the color purple. The Apache have said that the red ray is now descending and that the purple ray, the ray of peace, is ascending. Since the Harmonic Convergence, this purple ray, according to Apache beliefs, has begun to be released. From now until about 2020, we will be in the chaos of the warlike red ray leaving and the peace-loving purple ray trying to gain a foothold. There will be such imbalance, that every day will become a juggling act, a challenge to remain in harmony and not be thrown off by the chaos of these two powerful energies: war and peace. The Apaches also worry that if nuclear war is to take place, it will be during this time of chaos.

As a result, in every ceremony or ritual I perform, whether for myself or for others, I always envision the purple ray, because it must be brought in, anchored, and encouraged in every way, by everyone. Just visualizing Mother Earth swathed in purple will help, and anyone can do that in meditation or just before going to sleep at night. I was taught that we're all conduits, empty vessels through which the power of the Great Spirit can flow providing we step out of the way, remain humble, and always walk with our hearts. Each time one of us does ceremony or ritual, we become that empty tube for the Great Spirit to send energy through to help all our relatives, including Mother Earth, as well as ourselves. So, I was pleased to see the purple color come through the pipe to me as I held it up to my right eye.

Shortly thereafter, the sweat was over. Over in one sense, but just beginning in another. We crawled out into the chilled late March air. As I stood up and turned to the east, directly behind the lodge, I saw that Mother Moon had just risen above the canyon wall. She was full; her luminous, iridescent white light touching us. I stepped aside and looked over at Deer Mountain. There, hanging like a lovely bluish white gem, was Mother Venus. I stood there assimilating the alignment of Mother Venus and Mother Moon, for they were exactly on opposite sides of us, with the sweat lodge in the middle of their alignment of energies.

Astrologically, the moon represents the feminine, the female in all of us. It is our emotions, our feelings, our mother in every sense (whether your biological mother, or our greater Mother, the Earth). Equally important, the moon symbolizes our subconscious, that treasure house of old, past, stored knowledge that we've accrued from hundreds, if not thousands, of lifetimes. I felt at that moment, with these two celestial beings watching over us, blessing our birthing, for the moon symbolizes birth, that we were indeed going to go forward from this sweat lodge as very changed people in the most positive sense.

I felt that, with Mother Venus there, we received her love and kinship and the recognition of the star people, for we were indeed out in space as a group. Mother Moon will gift each of us, in our own way, with unconscious memories, skills, talents, and new tools that will now come forth to the conscious realm so that we may use them, once again, in this lifetime—not only for ourselves but for all our relatives. The infinite love, gentleness, and mothering that I felt in the sweat lodge during the ceremony was explained, at least for me, by the astrological happening of Venus opposite the full moon. At no time during the sweat did I feel harsh or assertive male energy, even though four men were present among the assembled fifteen. But I must add that these four men were already in balance, with their femaleness well integrated into their maleness, so there could not have been any harsh, hard male energy present anyway.

Ed and I talked the next morning as I was driving him down to Phoenix to catch another plane to another destination. He, too, had seen Black Elk, and that was a first for him. Secondly, he said that he'd had the top come off the sweat before, but never the bottom! Another first. He said that he'd heard of that happening but had never personally experienced the phenomenon. Further, we were close to having a *Yuwipi* Ceremony occur, and Ed decided to back off from it, because he was concerned that some of the things that might take place would upset or scare some of the people. He said none of us, including himelf as facilitator, was ready for that.

What a way to start off learning sweat ceremony! The night the top came off and the bottom fell out of the sweat lodge and we were all one with the Great Mystery! *Mitakuye oyasin. Hetch etu aloh!*

▼　▼　▼　▼　▼

Wolf Woman Warrior indeed lives in a special area, as evidenced by the powerful Sweat Lodge that took place. The participants had all applied their hearts deeply to their earth journeys, and I believe that this was also a strong factor in explaining why such a dramatic event happened spatially for all of us. These two-leggeds had gone out into the Natural Way and acquired that higher plane through looking, learning, listening, and observing. They brought important ingredients that helped make this lodge so memorable. Wolf Woman Warrior is a very capable teacher as well.

I know little about astrology and astronomy but cannot downplay it since the constellations are also designed by the Ultimate. All things have a purpose. I did listen to that mysterious inner force during the lodge making and adjusted the doorway to move one frame to the left as I stood facing the initial doorway. It was the first time I had ever adjusted the direction of an established doorway, since I usually try to align them with a cardinal direction and mostly facing west. The first doorway simply gave me an unbalanced feeling, so I altered it. At the end of the ceremony, I discovered that the new doorway was in perfect alignment with the east moon and the western Venus. I have a newfound respect for astrology.

My first experience where the stars came across the top of the lodge was in Michigan. My friend Tarwater, who was fire-tending, saw a shaft of light come out of the top of the lodge heading skyward and then go back down into the fire. Black Elk's colors were present for this lodge. For the Sedona area lodge, we suspended Black Elk's colors from overhanging tree branches above it. I feel the most comfortable with these colors for myself but certainly do not object when I conduct a ceremony in a lodge that displays other colors.

This was the ninth time in a row that the top of the lodge came off. Wolf Woman Warrior is correct in stating that it was the most powerful Sweat Lodge that I have ever been in, except for some lodges where the Sioux holy man Bill Eagle Feather brought in *Yuwipi* power. In *Warriors of the Rainbow*, Vinson Brown tells of a dynamic spiritual phenomenon that he experienced for some time, and then it ended suddenly. I believe that this phenomenon with which I am being associated will end just as easily as it started, so I hope people's expectations do not rise too high if we happen to be in a lodge together someday. It is not the lodge leader, but rather the mind-set and sincerity of the participants, that brings forth spiritual phenomena. This concept reflects Chief Eagle Feather's influence upon me.

Actually, I intend for this event to end for me, because I prefer to remain free like a soaring eagle and have no desire to become some sort of mystic guru. Society puts you in a glass house when things like this happen, and you are never allowed to make a mistake and be human. I'll be damned if I will let anyone put me in a glass house and tell me what I can do or not do. Since I can't fly a Phantom jet nowadays, I might buy a Harley and head for a Sturgis rally someday. You never know. I will do fewer sweat lodge ceremonies in the future, but those who have been with me can't say that we did not experience some good acknowledgment. Life is not a race to see how much power you can accumulate in ceremony. It is more important that people gather together and quietly and respectfully beseech. I will always respect this happening, however, because it instills a high degree of confidence that the Natural Way is a good way and well worth following. It also tells me that Black Elk's colors and our *wotai* stones are being acknowledged.

As the Rainbow Tribe people progress down their own spiritual paths, I am sure that they will be experiencing some dramatic acknowledgments much more pronounced than what I have experienced. I hope that all Rainbows will be their own spiritual leaders, dependent only on the bond of commonality that is within the Great Spirit's created nature. If all keep that which is so truthfully revealed in nature as their principal guide, I am sure the natural phenomenon of reassurance will keep flowing and the Rainbows can keep on their journey well fortified to work for the salvation of the planet and human harmony.

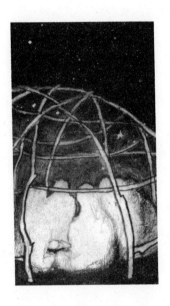

▼   ▼   ▼   ▼   ▼

6

RAINBOWS IN VISION QUEST

Hanblecheyapi (Vision Quest) or *Hanblecheya* (crying for a vision) is one of the most challenging and intensely individual ceremonies of the Lakota. After preparation and then purification in the sweat lodge, the vision seeker goes alone onto the mountain, butte, or high hill without food or water to meet with the Grandparents. The results of that experience are intended to increase nature awareness and spiritual discourse. The time may vary from one to four days, with the twelve-hour period from sunrise to sunset counting, by some, as one day and the sunset to sunrise period counting as a second day. When the seeker comes down from the mountain, he or she is again purified in the sweat lodge, at which time the seeker recounts the experience and begin to interpret its meaning. After this, there is a feast for those who have helped and supported.

As you think about *Hanblecheyapi,* keep in mind that you need to have a clear purpose to gain insight into a personal or world problem or to understand a previous vision or dream. In the old way, to obtain a sponsor you took your filled pipe to a spiritual leader and made your request. At that time, you discuss your purpose and present your pipe with a request for help to conduct your quest in a good way. If the leader agrees to help you with the ceremony, he or she will accept the pipe and smoke it. At that time, the leader gives you instructions on how to prepare for the *Hanblecheya,* on the making of tobacco ties and prayer flags, on how to prepare your personal songs, and on what to take with you. Nowadays and as a Rainbow Tribe person, I recommend that you take your special *wotai* stone and present this item before your helper. Conflicts relating to non-Indian use of the pipe have come forth in modern times and this is a means to avoid such conflict. Most who seek the Natural Path do not have pipes, and there is a growing trend toward sacred personal stones that are representative of the earth.

Following a Sweat Lodge on Spirit Mountain (Bear Butte Mountain), I helped a holy man carry several bundles up the side of the mountain to where a young Oglala would be placed for a vision quest. Four colored cloths were tied on to four separate sticks, and since the ground was so hard, these sticks were each held upright by a pile of stones. Each stick with its cloth banner flying in the night wind marked a corner of the four-cornered square within which the vision quester was placed. The holy man then unrolled 405 tobacco pouches to form the square boundaries around the vision quester standing barefooted inside the periphery. A prayer to each of the four directions was called out and a song was sung.

Although you are encouraged to fast during your *Hanblecheya,* there are fewer restrictions on water. This vision seeker had some water for a long four days because he was also required to swallow some medicine at times with the aid of the water. I read in an Indian newspaper of the death of a vision quester. No doubt the fasting and going without water added to the cause. Therefore, I urge caution in this regard, and if you are not sufficiently healthy, I advise that you should not try it. The holy man gave a parting word of encouragement to the vision seeker and I was asked to do the same. We left him on the mountain, the wind roared, and we found our way back down the trail in the dark hours of early morning.

As a vision quester, you are responsible for your own safety and for making reasonable decisions about your own limitations. Although a place like Spirit Mountain, a popular vision quest point and holy mountain of both the Lakota and the Cheyenne, is not wilderness, it is quite possible to get hurt if you are not attentive.

Whereas the *Inipi* is usually a group ceremony, Vision Quest is a solitary experience. I define a vision quest as one's individual attempt to meet with God or whatever word you use for your Higher Force, your Higher Power—or to use Sioux concept, the Great Spirit, the Great Mystery.

The quester seeks isolation on a lonely hill, a mountaintop, or a badlands butte. Woodland Indians, who did not have a high peak accessible, built vision quest platforms in tall trees. Traditional Native Americans have their peace pipes and medicine bundles with them when they vision quest and usually set out an area marked by four colored cloths or flags. Being a rock clan member, I now occasionally use four colored stones—red, yellow, black, and white—to mark the boundaries where I will spend most of my vision quest. I do the ceremony in this manner because I did my first vision quest under the direction of two Sioux holy men, Fools Crow and Eagle Feather, and was told to take four colored cloths and sit with my peace pipe within the square area formed by the red, yellow, black, and white flags. I do this because it establishes a relationship with the four directions, the first four powers of the six powers of Black Elk's vision. I believe the six powers were placed here by the Great Spirit and are looking on while I vision quest.

How long should a person stay in isolation? That is an oft asked and disputed question. Traditional Indians who have a strong background in their culture will go for as long as four twenty-four-hour days. Others say that a day and a night and another day and a night make up the four parts during which a vision quester should fast and take little or no water. I respect either way and admire the person who will endure for the sake of seeking higher enlightenment. I also believe that beginners are not causing any harm if they go up on the mountain for just one day and an evening, especially if they have to travel a long way to get to a mountain or other isolated place. After they have had more spiritual experiences and understanding, they can always set up a quest for a longer duration upon the mountain.

I do not respect those who set themselves up as judges regarding the length of a person's stay on a mountain. Many of these "experts" have never vision quested. Some say that the spirits will be displeased if a longer time is not endured. I say that the spirits don't carry a calculator and are probably quite aware that the world is in great environmental danger. They are probably pleased to see the great change in our non-native brothers and sisters, who are seeing the good within the Natural Way even though it was the parents or the grandparents of these new people who set the policies that placed us on the reservations and took our lands. The spirits are probably hoping that these new people can go forth and help change the values of that materialistic, polluting world that brought on the present environmental dilemma. They are probably hoping that even one night out under the stars will help these new people shape their resolve to continue caring and being considerate.

You know, I bet the four-leggeds and the winged ones are just plain happy to see all these non-Indians up on a mountain contemplating or going into a sweat lodge. I bet they are breathing a lot easier now than when some of them were in a critical extinction phase. It is too bad that the *wamakaskan* (the animals) cannot voice their viewpoint or sit down and write a letter to the detractors who do not want all people to go back to the Natural Way. I bet many of the animals would lend positive support for the continuation of this new direction that many people of all colors are taking.

Maybe some of you feel comfortable with Native American spiritual concepts, yet you have had your own discoveries, your own visions. As I have stated, with regard to the Great Mystery, none of us has *the* ultimate answer. But since we are attempting to be aware of such mystery, maybe we can consider that all human thought about spiritual mystery is mere supposition? We certainly do not have to go to war, or harm each other, over our spiritual suppositions. A Sweat Lodge or Vision Quest can still be very meaningful, regardless of your spiritual persuasion. I believe that even an atheist could benefit from sitting on a mountaintop out under the Great Vastness. It will make that person wonder about how this could all come to be. Actually, I feel more comfortable with a law-abiding, highly moral, truth-speaking, respecting atheist than I do with a religious zealot who wants to destroy our culture. Or with a zealot who would do me harm, who speaks lies about those not in concert with his or her beliefs, who would put little children in boarding schools to convert them or millions of people into death camps because they did not follow the zealots' religious concepts. I also have much more respect for an atheist who realizes that we all need to protect Mother Earth than I do for an ardent religious fanatic who believes that Man has dominion over Nature and that this dominion gives him license to pollute and not be concerned with world population growth.

There are some who have childhood fears of the night. I went outside the other night and beseeched on a lonely bluff right beside some ancient mounds that no doubt contain the remains of two-leggeds from a long-gone era. It was a moonlit night and the setting could have been termed "spooky" by those of that bent. While I was beseeching to a certain spirit guide, a noise came from within the dense sumac and sapling-covered woods behind me. I listened carefully and when I was satisfied it was some animal and not a clumsy two-legged, I continued on with my request. (Do safeguard yourself from other two-leggeds, however, when you quest; it is probably best to scatter out in a group or have a friend or several friends "down below" your area.) I laughed to myself to think how fearful I would have been in the old days when I believed the missionaries' devil tales and the horror movies. Their damage to my young, impressionable mind took quite a few years to shed; they made me afraid of Mother Earth's darkness and most surely of being beside a graveyard. I finished my attempt at conversing with the spirit world and went back inside. Within a few days, what I asked for happened. When I went back to the path next to the burial mounds, there was a piece of broken sumac on the trail left by a deer that had been scraping the velvet off its antlers. That was what was making the noise.

Maybe while you are out on a mountaintop you can contemplate deeply that the Creator has made all this vastness to intermesh with all the inner complexity of the innumerable operative forces, down to the tiniest regulated ant crawling in a sacred manner, at least for his colony. The sky hasn't fallen in yet and the living things keep on doing their magic—a "magic" force that we all have been conditioned to take for granted. How can all these observable things created and existing because of the Great Spirit have some form of eerie "evil" attached? Why would such a Creator, which demonstrates daily and nightly to us *its* perfection, allow a so-called devil to exist in its operative, demonstrated perfection? No honest person that I know of has seen this thing that the preachers scream at us over the public radio waves. Disharmony is thrown viciously at those who are finding the Great Spirit through what the Great Spirit has made and not through a bunch of scary imaginings that no one has truthfully experienced.

If the Creator is the Ultimate Artist, then it seems highly unlikely that it would be inclined toward blemishing its ultimate work, creation. Human artists do not desecrate or cast mud upon the best of their finished works. Only a much lesser force such as humanity can create this "evil" or allow itself to be so ignorant of the Natural Way that it becomes "evil." This so-called power of the devil can only be as strong as men and women allow it to become, and then strictly through human conduct and human actions. Anyway, this is the sort of reasoning you might utilize to dissipate any self-induced fear that is keeping you from some powerful insight while out in Mother Nature.

You might ask, "Then, how do you explain evil?"

Let us take an example of a rancher who lives close to an Indian reservation and has hated Indians all his life. Let us suppose that the rancher's favorite son happens to fall in love with an Indian woman and they get married. The rancher has a fit and disowns his son. In time, however, the rancher misses his son and even his new grandchildren. He discovers that his daughter-in-law is a good person and a devoted mother and wife. Eventually, the rancher relents and is seen driving his grandchildren around in his pickup truck. As time passes, he even begins to champion some of the Indian causes and some of their ways.

This example has happened in real life. What happened to the "evil" prejudice of the rancher? The answer is that he was not evil. He was *ignorant*. He did not have the knowledge that he later acquired. To me, evil is really lack of knowledge. Even Hussein and Hitler were not evil when they were born. They were as innocent as any other baby lying in its crib. They fell into ignorant, untruthful ways, however, and were joined by supporting two-leggeds who kept themselves in ignorance and consequently devastated millions.

Many people who have read *Black Elk Speaks* or *Mother Earth Spirituality* feel quite in concert with the six powers. It is comforting to be able to recognize what the Creator has put all around us and to identify with it in a relationship manner. I can see the red dawn of the morning; I live and grow because of the sun's long summers coming up from the yellow south. I can see the advancing wall of thunder and lightning bringing the life-giving rains out of the black west. I feel the cleansing, thought-provoking cold of the white northern snow. Mother Earth is beneath me and Father Sky is above me every day of my life. I am part of the six powers. Waters, minerals, energy, I am. My spirit surrounds and directs my composition of waters, minerals, and energy. Sitting up on a mountain on a starlit summer night brings forth this concept that we are extensions of all that has been created.

The following section describes the vision quest of a Rainbow man. His narrative provides a detailed account of what can take place. His preparation is also valuable knowledge for those who are considering such a venture.

WHERE SKY MEETS EARTH MEETS WATER

Red Dawn Wolf

Where Sky Meets Earth Meets Water—this is the name that my friends called the area where they live on the east side of Lake Pepin. This is the place to which I have been drawn for many years to do a vision quest, a time alone to think, pray, and listen. Finally the dream was realized.

With the rocks sitting on top of a blazing fire, soaking in the power of the flames, and a gentle setting sun shining into the open door of the sweat lodge, the five of us sat at the edge of the fire and drummed. Our minds were tuned into that which is beyond the powers of sight and sound. We were "thinning the veil," as Eagle Man calls it. We were preparing for our entry into the spiritual realm and waited until eleven o'clock when Suki and Jon joined us to begin the *Inipi* preparation ceremony.

The *Inipi* lodge, in symbol and reality, is the womb of Mother Earth. In the darkness underneath the canopy of bent saplings with tarps placed over them, sitting on the ground, smelling her musty smell, you are close to her. We put a sprinkle of sage and sweet-grass on the hot rocks as each was placed in the round pit in the middle of the lodge. The sweet smoke rose up to erase the negative thoughts that so easily linger in our minds and to help set our hearts into the receptive condition needed for this sacred ceremony. The rocks are greeted as old friends who have come to help. These rocks held a specialness in that they had been so dearly sought and seemed to have been specially placed for our use. The flap was closed and the first of the four "endurances" began. Each phase centers on a direction, usually starting in either the east or the west (depending on the purpose of the ceremony). We started this ceremony in the west. We called on the spirit guides to help us, and I heard loving prayers from my friends asking those helpers to aid me on my quest. More drumming and the flap was opened. The process was repeated for each direction; water was thrown on the rocks and they sizzled their reply. A sweat must be experienced again and again to be fully appreciated and understood. It is clear that if approached in humble openness, the ceremony is far more than just a "sauna" with sweat running off one's body.

After the *Inipi* Ceremony we sat by the fire until three in the morning talking the kind of talk that a good centering sweat can inspire. Then off to our tents we went to sleep.

A week later, on Friday morning again, we were back at the site. Marcy and Mike were the only ones who could get away on a Friday to help "put me out," but I knew that many others were thinking of me and were putting out their beseechments for encouraging strength. In my opinion, when a person is undertaking the Vision Quest in this way, with a whole "tribe" behind him or her, it is clear that what is sought is beyond just personal realizations. The vision-seeking is for the strength and growth of the whole group. This feeling was very strong in me, and it helped carry me through difficult moments.

We did a Pipe and *Inipi* Ceremony (we did it so hot that the fourth door had to be done outside!), and after the ceremony was finished and I had dried myself off, the three of us walked out over the cornfield to my spot on the bluff. My company sat with me a little while, making a few jokes, but all of us understood the realness and seriousness of this undertaking. Then they left and I was alone.

If you ever saw the movie *Never Cry Wolf,* where this guy is left out in the middle of a frozen lake by himself and the plane takes off, and there he is . . . well, you get the picture. There were a couple of things I had to do. First, I strung a string around the area I would stay in for the next two nights. My area was a diamond shape just over the top of a bluff, with a grand old birch tree and some scrub cedar below me and some little weathered sumac just starting to leaf out. Behind me at the top of the diamond clearing was the edge of a wood with deer trails running through it. I had made 405 tobacco pouches (one hundred of each direction color and my friends made the last five as they saw fit), and starting in the west I tied them onto the string. The different colors went up in random order. Each direction took me awhile (I didn't bring a watch). When I started it was sunny and a little windy, but by the time I had finished, clouds had obscured the sun and it was blowing hard and cold. It was starting to get dark and smelled like rain. I had brought a plastic tarp and found some branches to make a lean-to. It looked a little like a big blue clam with an overbite. There was no flat ground so it nestled underneath some of the branches of the birch tree for added protection. I knew that now I had done all the activity that I had to do for the rest of my stay. I had begun my fast the night before, so there would be no food to make, no coffee to heat, no one to talk to, no fire to stare into. Just me, the wind, the birds, and whatever else was to come to me.

Somehow I felt it was time to pray. First I called to my spirit helpers, Standing Bear and Yellow Man. That now-familiar warm presence ran up my back and I was glad to know they were with me. Then, slowly, to each of the directions I beseeched their guidance and asked for their teachings. I asked Father Sky to watch over me and not to be too harsh, for on this red road, I reminded him, I was but a baby and not so strong. Mother Earth I approached and thanked for all that she has given me: my body, my life, this place to give this small sacrifice of time. I thought of all her creatures— may I know them as dear to me as relatives. Then my thoughts turned to *Wakan Tanka,* the Great Mystery. As we cannot hold the whole ocean in a cup, our small mental capacities can never embrace all that is this power that is in everything. But we can feel it work and guide our lives. We can experience this Hand. It can play with us. These are the things I thought about.

As I sat in the spot I had chosen with the sacred pipe in my hands feeling small against the wind and the enveloping darkness, I felt the presence of others, the old ones, hearing my thoughts and prayers that I sometimes spoke out loud. I addressed them and asked for their help and guidance and for help for all those of the Rainbow Tribe, and all those on every path trying to learn to walk in balance. This went out to those who need help, but I felt as if I didn't know how to ask formally or in a precise manner for those who are in pain, and for those who cause pain. To all my friends and to all my relatives.

It was dark, I was cold, I was getting sleepy and, frankly, a little frightened. I didn't feel ready to confront what might be ready to confront me. I crawled into "the clam" and looked out for a while, thinking. Slowly, sleep took me. I slept in short spurts, woke for a while and continued my thoughts and prayers, and drifted back to sleep. This is how the first night went.

It drizzled rain most of the night and into the morning. There was hardly a daybreak, just increasing light that made it easier to watch the rain. As it became day the rain stopped intermittently, which allowed me to get out and stretch. I thought a lot about people I loved and my different relationships of the past. I went over my life and the many different stages of spiritual practices and yearnings. I sat in meditation with no thought on my mind, trying to be like an antenna pulling in a signal that wasn't always that faint. There's nothing like sitting alone for hours on end to give yourself time to put it all into perspective. I strongly recommend this way of spending time to anyone who can. Make time. It is that important and fulfilling.

A very interesting aspect of the experience was not knowing what time it was. No watch to look at and no sun to give me clues. So much of our lives runs on the clock, to be taken totally out of time is a challenge. Eventually it started to clear up. The wind died down and the sun broke free. It had traveled a good portion of its path across the sky. I suspected it was at least "dinnertime." Did I mention that I wasn't eating? There is an asking in the Vision Quest and for what you seek or "ask" there is a giving. Your fasting—going without eating, feeling the initial hunger pangs—is a giving up of something that you can offer in return. It is balance. An asking. A giving. And maybe the balance that is so evident in *Wakan Tanka*'s created nature answers the big "why"—why the spiritual power of the vision-seeking works.

Activity increased around me. The birds came out to sing and play. A blue jay who had introduced himself to me while I was putting out the tobacco bags came back and checked on me. There were a few boats out on the river below. Sound traveled up to me from the river very clearly and with a sense of harmony and melody. Among those sounds were the freight trains on both sides of the river that seemed to go by every twenty minutes or so during the evening hours. It all blended together and I was feeling very happy.

As the sun began to set I realized that I was as prepared as I ever would be, and that tonight was the night. I settled into my spot with the pipe in my hands and once again addressed the directions. I gave special thanks to Father Sky for the beauty that I was experiencing. At one point I had the pipe and was praying with my eyes closed, wanting some affirmation of my quest. There it was. I opened my eyes and saw an eagle (I later found that it was an immature bald eagle) coming straight for me and then passing about ten feet over my head. Wow!

In the setting sun my eagle friend had gathered around the next bluff with some more of his "tribe" and they were riding the thermals with such grace and beauty. At one point there were nine of them dancing in the air together, rising up until several were out of sight. Lovely, beautiful, magnificent. Powerful symbols, sculptured, shaped, and engineered for dramatic, breathtaking flight—all displaying their intricacy and inconceivable splendor that has emanated from this vast Power that can design so wondrously. Nine great winged ones whirled before me. I was a happy man.

The darkness slowly closed in, and my thoughts and prayers became more focused. I called again to my helpers in spirit and received their friendly chill. I could feel some of the old ones joining me as my "cry" went out. I thought I saw a green flash of light pass before me, and a distortion in my perception of the bushes around me as if something had passed in front of them. You can believe that my prayers weren't lazy and mundane. I had their attention and they certainly had mine.

It seemed to take a very long time before the first stars came out to greet me. Eventually the whole star nation was gazing down and I could see the Milky Way, the road that spirit walks, above me. There was no moon, and the lights from Lake City across the river were bright. I soaked it all in, feeling small in the vastness of space but at the same time significant enough to be given such an experience. This went on for quite a while, but eventually I was getting sleepy. Because sleep only seemed to happen in short doses, I crawled into my clam for a nap.

I awoke with a start and felt almost thrown out of my shelter back to my spot, and the world was a very different place. The moon was out, just a little past full and very bright. Her light overwhelmed the city lights and flooded my place. I cast a clear shadow (it was reassuring to know that I hadn't become spirit yet), and the reflected power coming from this older sister of ours went straight into me. I thought about this female "yang" energy and felt that it was showing me to be more receptive to it in myself. I sat staring at her, meditating on this for a long time as she slowly progressed on her path across the sky. Eventually the "nods" were catching up to me again and I went in for another nap.

If you guessed that I woke suddenly, was pushed out of my sleeping bag to the spot, and the world was a very different place, you win! This time I was standing on top of a cloud of fog looking across the top, and the only land that was visible was where I was standing. The entire valley below was filled with this white mist whose rolling top was lit by the moon. The moon had a double circle around it with wisps of fog that made it look just like a zodiac.

The fog formed animal shapes circling the moon, and I clearly made out the horns, legs, and body of a ram in one of the shapes. Coincidentally, my sign is that of Aries, the Ram.

The wonder of this scene is very hard to describe. It totally felt like another universe. I sat and watched this event, and slowly the zodiac drifted away, but the fog and moon stayed on. At one point the rolling of the top of the fog looked like the head and front of the wing of an eagle, which eventually lifted out and then dove back into the cloud. Most amazing.

A bank of regular clouds drifted in and then I was standing between two worlds, the fog below, clouds above, and a clear space illuminated by the moon in between. The scene just kept getting more incredible. This experience went on for some time, and eventually the upper clouds covered the moon. I had absolutely no idea how long it would be until daybreak, but I wasn't going anywhere. I sat on my spot and let the feelings and prayers consume me.

I thought that when day came, I'd probably be witness to a glorious sunrise that would burn off the fog and a new day would begin. What happened went a little differently.

It seemed to take forever for the first faint sign of the approaching light to show itself. The upper clouds were still around and the fog had become thicker and cold. I was really rooting for the sun to come and win the battle of night and day, but he seemed like a reluctant warrior. When a faint glimmer of light started rising in the east, the fog began to move. It very slowly poured out of the valley between my spot and the next bluff, emptying into the river. I thought "Oh boy, he's doing it!" But to my amazement, just as slowly, the fog poured back in, filling up the valley once more. This process happened two more times, and each time when the "tide" came back in, it filled up higher until I was totally surrounded by the mist, darker and colder than ever. Then it seemed to stay.

Trying not to hold a grudge against the sun, I resumed my post with my sleeping bag wrapped around me. Sitting there for a while I thought of the night's wonders, how it had been "the night of three worlds." Even through my shivers I felt the blessing of *Wakan Tanka* on me. I thought of the Rainbow Tribe and how, even though we are not all of Indian blood, and even if we don't practice ceremony exactly in the forms of the original Americans, our hearts are being taught and guided, our needs are being fulfilled. I was cold but happy. But I still was ready for a little warmth from the sun.

For some reason I got up and crossed my string boundary and went to the front of the birch tree to a lookout on the edge of the bluff. I was surprised to find that the fog had cleared off the river below. Evidently it had been rolling up the bluff as it lifted. The end of the long and eventful night was near. I could hardly wait, but of course I had no choice. It did finally clear off and became that glorious morning I had hoped for. The birds came singing, my friend the blue jay came and gave me a piece of his mind, and the eagles came out again to dance another dance for me.

I had taken down my tobacco offerings and folded up the clam; I was ready to leave. The way we had planned this part was that Mike, who had stayed at a campground on the river throughout the weekend, would go and start the rocks heating for a sweat, and Cindy, Marcy, and Jon would drive down from the Twin Cities. When they got to Suki's, Suki was going to bring her bay horse and they would all come and get me. I would know they were coming by Marcy's wonderful drumming. What a plan! I'm sure I heard that drum at least twenty times, only to have no one come over the crest of my hill. Finally I could wait no more, and I picked up my clumsy red bag and headed off on the twenty-minute hike back to the house.

At least maybe I'd run into them on the way. No such luck. When I reached the house Suki was brushing the horse, Mike had the fire going, but no cars were there with the others. I guess I was a little early. How was I to know—I didn't have a watch. . . .

The others did arrive, with Joyce also. We had a fine *Inipi* Ceremony led by Marcy—her first. At the end I tried to tell this story that I have just told you, and we smoked the pipe. It was *lelah wakan,* very holy. After Black Elk had his vision, he had to dance it for the people for it to take effect. I have danced my fingers on this keyboard and have told my story. As I felt in the beginning, things like this are for the strength and growth of us all. I hope that by hearing these exploits, others are inspired to take the challenge of the hill, to spend the alone time crying for a vision.

> To All My Friends
> To All My Relatives
> *Hetch etu aloh*

▼   ▼   ▼   ▼   ▼

There is strong symbolism associated with the participation of the eagles in this quest. An eagle is a very observant entity created by the Great Spirit. You can feel the magnificent power of the eagle if you are ever fortunate enough to observe it. It is like a visible prayer when you watch it in flight. This flying one scans the earth as it cruises effortlessly wherever it wants to go. The eagle tells us to go out and look at this world as much as we possibly can, to inspect every nook and cranny and appreciate the means that we have in this modern era to travel. Travel affords us the freedom to see and communicate.

An eagle is an extremely cautious creature that normally avoids coming close to most human beings, but in ceremony, eagles and other creatures seem to make their appearance in an unusual manner. The eagle flying low overhead is a highly unusual demonstration by such a cautious creature. Traditional Indians believe that it is acting out a blessing sent by the Creator, or by the extensions of the Creator—the six powers. The gathered eagles symbolize people of alert and intelligent minds who are gathering worldwide and have the ability to appreciate and learn from the millions of facets of nature, each of which has its own pearls of wisdom to tell and reveal. A tiny dragonfly can teach us of the four directions, and a gigantic elephant can teach us of a shared *tiyospaye,* an extended family living together in the herd. Red Dawn Wolf is at the beginning of a significant movement that highly respects nature. The gathered eagles at his vision quest are a strong sign that this natural return will surely grow in increasing circles. The eagles are the Rainbows that he associates with and have become so much a part of his new life. The new life is represented by the fog filling up the valley, covering all of the old way that used to be. There are different values, different insights within this new perspective, enough so to tell you that you need much less of the old creature comforts that you once thought you could not live without. Actually, many were false comforts and brought little happiness anyway. The sun was held back by the fog rising and lifting, telling the vision seeker that the Natural Way does, at times, save such powerful sights only for the seekers of new vision, a vision that is really a return to the ancient roots within all of us.

His natural name, Red Dawn Wolf, may have been a part of the power that let him observe something special when the red dawn came. Like the wolf, he is a scout, a teacher who goes out and brings back good experiences to his pack. They are nourished and refreshed from his spiritual quests and the lodge that he helped build. Rainbows who do not have access to willing Indian teachers must be prepared to go forth on their own when they have received the basics. Red Dawn Wolf is a strong follower of the Natural Way. He sets a good example and is a good role model to follow.

Everyone should take time out in his or her life to sit upon a mountain or in another isolated area and commune with nature. Take time out to observe even if your initial observation is but a tiny anthill that happens to be close by the spot you have chosen. Elisabet Sahtouris states in *Gaia: The Human Journey from Chaos to Cosmos,* "No place, or environment, on earth—from the barest mountaintop to the deepest part of the sea—has fewer than a thousand different life species, mostly microbial, forming it and doing different things to keep it alive and evolving."[1] Eventually you will progress to the greater dimensions of outer space. The vision quester looks up at the stars and realizes the immensity of space. You look up and see the Big Dipper above. It has been placed there by the Creator. The seven stars tell me that there are six powers to watch over us. The four stars that form the cup of the dipper are the four directions, and of course the fifth and sixth stars are the Father Sky and Mother Earth powers. The seventh star completes the Big Dipper and symbolizes the Creator, *Wakan Tanka.* This is the most visible star image in the western hemisphere. No other formation is as clearly visible as the Big Dipper (Ursa Major). It is always free from other stars as well. It seems quite evident that the Creator arranged these formations for our visualization. Such a telling portrayal of these six powers beckons every night of our lives if we simply have the high-mindedness to look for it.

Another powerful thought you might formulate as you look up at the skies from a mountaintop or other isolated spot is based on the stars. They are other suns really. Many of these great balls of energy are far more powerful than our own sun. Did the Great Spirit place all that energy there merely for us two-leggeds to view from our place here on earth? I hardly think so. Such energy must exist for a much higher purpose. Nature always seems to replicate itself, doesn't it? Dr. Sahtouris states:

> Our living earth is likely no more a freak accident than is the seedling that grows or the frog egg that matures. All are

the inevitable result of right compositions and conditions. Some scientists believe the conditions were so special that Earth is a rare phenomenon, perhaps the only such planet in the universe. But there is no better reason to believe this than there is to believe that living planets are as common in the universe as are the successful seedlings and hatchlings of Earth. And if this is so, there are billions of other live planets in the billions of galaxies, each with billions of star systems.[2]

A book the size of the one you are holding contains over 100,000 words and thousands of punctuation marks. A book takes time to create. For many writers it can take years or a lifetime. Yet in a few seconds a copy of one's complete work can be made on a computer. This is done simply by placing all the chapters in a disk folder on the computer's hard disk and then pressing the "Duplicate" button. Indentions, paragraphs, sentence structure, and chapter arrangement are also a part of what is exactly copied. Most people would probably explain this as a technological marvel, but in my opinion these events are allowances of the Great Spirit or whatever you desire to call your concept of the Higher Force. It is another of the endless revelations of the Creator's mysteries.

As I have mentioned earlier, the efficiency of a computer offers insight into the vast data-consuming and calculating ability of our Great Spirit Creator. Of course, you have to be of the mind-set that nothing exists or is endowed with its capacities or functions unless it is put there in the first place by this all-powerful Force. One can wonder further as one looks up at the stars: after the Great Force made its first sun and its first grouping of planets, it could have sat back and marveled at its creation. You never know. Maybe "it" was quite pleased and proud. Who is to say that it didn't reach over and punch that "Duplicate" button several billion or trillion times in ecstasy! I would! I think that these great balls of energy up above and completely surrounding our mere globe are made for other life. Doesn't our sun impart life? Are those other stars/suns made and created to not sustain life? I find the self-centered supposition that our lone planet is the only one to have life difficult to believe. If there were only one sun, then that supposition could hold some merit, but such is not the case. From a mathematical perspective alone, the magnitude of the numbers argues that there would have to be some planets in life-sustaining condition. Philip Carr-Gomm states in *The Druid Tradition:* "Science currently estimates that the

Cosmos contains three trillion galaxies, enough for each one of us to be responsible for a galaxy of our own."[3]

Some planets are, no doubt, in their trilobite stage, some in a dinosaur stage, maybe some in a stage equivalent to ours. Some may be highly advanced because they have found their balance and harmony much earlier than we who have yet to achieve that stage. These were some of my thoughts while I sat under the vast galaxies up on the peak of Spirit Mountain in the Black Hills. Maybe your suppositions will be more profound than mine.

7/6

RAINBOWS FINDING THEIR NATURAL
NAMES AND WOTAI STONES

I have had two natural names bestowed upon me. One name was my child's name. I was playing outside when a visitor came to our home. It was Ben Black Elk. His wife and her sister were close friends of my parents. They visited my parents often.

Ben called out, *"Wanblee Hokeshila,"* as he watched me play. It was quite an unceremonious naming and at the time I did not pay much attention. My mother called me over and said in a chastising voice, "Youuuuu! Ben Black Elk gave you your Indian name and you just kept on playing." I remember Ben laughing and not seeming to mind. "He called you Eagle Boy. So what do you say?" my matriarchal mother demanded. "Gee, thanks," I remarked and went back to playing.

I was again unceremoniously named, although my naming did take place in the sweat lodge just before I was to take part in the Sun Dance. I had returned from the Vietnam War and had been a fighter pilot. I was participating to honor my pledge taken in Fools Crow's *Yuwipi* Ceremony held for me before I had gone off to war.

Fools Crow (the Sun Dance chief), Bill Eagle Feather, and Ben Black Elk were huddled in a conversation while I was toweling myself dry from the morning sweat lodge before dressing for the Sun Dance. In those days there were few Sun Dance pledgers, and there was ample room in the large tipi for us to dress after a sweat. My name was called out by the three men. "You are going to receive a new name," one of them said as I approached.

"Your new name will be *Wanblee Wichasha,* Eagle Man, because you have been a warrior in battle and you followed our instructions. You have vision quested and are keeping your pledge by dancing here in the Sun Dance." I thanked them and went back to put on my sage wreaths for the Sun Dance. I guess if a point can be made, it is that your natural name does not have to come to you in some elaborate ceremonial form. This may disappoint some sacrosanct mullahs who are attempting to become rule makers, but this has been my experience and it speaks for itself. I advise them to forsake their narrow rigidity and read Black Elk's message in order to turn their energies toward Mother Earth.

Ben Black Elk interpreted every word of his father's and John Neihardt's book, *Black Elk Speaks.* Fools Crow and Eagle Feather were two extremely powerful holy men as evidenced by their *Yuwipi* calling power, and they were also courageous in their stand for the return of the Sun Dance. Yet, there was no elaborate ritual when I was given my name. I guess that is why I seem to follow their example and just let certain ceremonies happen. In the Sun Dance or in *Yuwipi* ceremonies, they did follow some established procedures, but, overall, to them ceremony was a means to pray and beseech; this was more important than having a set of rules for each and every happening. They did not get cemented in protocol, dogma, or excess ritualization. They provided an atmosphere that was open and nonstifling. You did not feel hindered or fearful when you beseeched in their ceremonial forums.

Let us take a look at a commendable person who has pursued a natural path from childhood. The following is an account of a young Rainbow man who has had some unique spiritual experiences and did not hold back in his active search for his natural road. He found many spirit guides at a historic battlefield. The birds of the air, two totems out of the sky, led him to his natural name. I first met Tim Ryan, Thunder Hawk, in a Native American cultural seminar. He exhibited a high degree of familiarity with Lakota culture and was well read in Black Elk's vision. He is a very genuine person with a heart of hawklike courage who definitely "walks his talk." His animal totem, the hawk, led him toward his natural name, and the winged one still enters his life occasionally as a reminder that he is pursuing a good path. Thunder Hawk tells how Rainbow spirituality can be a path to a world full of adventure. He understands the spirits of the ghosts of the past as beneficial helpers leading us toward what we are meant to do and who we are meant to be.

RED GHOSTS OF THE LITTLE BIG HORN
Thunder Hawk

This is the story of how one white man became red from within. I believe that the Great Spirit, *Wakan Tanka,* has led me here to tell these adventures, for they show the awesome power of acknowledgment, the literal truth of the power that is peace. *Hetch etu aloh.*

August 1976

A party of four left Minnesota, the land of much water and the origin of the seven council fires of the Dakota Sioux, to travel westward toward the cries of the *Wakinyan* (thunder beings) and the endless sky country of Montana. On the second day they crossed the Rosebud and looked south toward history. The vast plains ghostly echoed the war cries of June 17, 1876, and the meeting of Gray Fox Crook and *Tashuunka Witko,* Crazy Horse, at the Battle of the Rosebud.

I was one of these four riders and it seemed only right that I rode alongside my uncle. The western Sioux, the Lakota, gave the honorary name of Uncle to the buffalo. And *Tatanka Yotanka,* Sitting Bull, was the uncle of two very important fighting men at the Little Big Horn.

The wind howled and the four wheels buzzed beneath us. In 1976 we rode in a car; the white man's civilization has developed a few useful ideas. All we could see was wave upon wave of hilly green-brown Mother Earth under a pure blue Father Sky. In the distance there were puffs of white-smoky clouds rising above the Bighorn Mountains like the visible breath of *Chanupa Lutah Wakan,* the holy red pipe.

The journey to the Little Big Horn lasted only a few short, dream-filled hours. A rare August rain quickly brought coolness to the Great American Desert, although I didn't even notice it until later. Excitement grew inside me like a bud in springtime. As long as I could remember, my dream was to be at this great battlefield. I was growing into a man. At fifteen I would have been a man for several years had this earth walk been in 1876. The growth of energy made my mind drift—soaring into the past—to see the flowing warbonnets, honors from the spotted eagle. As we neared the battlefield the intensity pushed me against the car door. If I had been in the saddle I surely would have fallen off, for I almost jumped through the car ceiling when we rounded the corner and the monument came into view. There it was, the monument, the twentieth-century mark of remembrance. But the monument had little significance to this warrior's mind.

I was there because of the people of times past, the people with whom I was related and now am once again related; my journey was for the Lakota. *Wakan Tanka* had a powerful sign there to greet me: something unmistakably brought about by the Creator. *Acknowledgment.* For there, stretched over the glorious battlefield, were huge arches of flaming colors. An unexpected sign, a gift for my eyes, heart, mind, and memory; a bold vision into my future. An invisible prism somewhere in the valley of ghost lodges was displaying its truth, bending Father Sun's light for all the world to see. *Lelah nupa wigmunke!* Brilliance—a magnificent double rainbow!

As we wheeled slowly up to the monument, we passed the permanent marking of the white man. This sacred place that commemorates the courage and battle prowess of a natural people who turned and fought for survival is known to the white world as the Custer Battlefield National Monument and Cemetery. Now there is a brick museum building and an acre or so of World War I and World War II veterans' graves. So we who honor Mother Earth, as did the natural people, must look past this spot to the plains of old.

The museum does have some value in that it holds many artifacts from the battle and a wealth of books full of history about this event. And outside the building is a sign that carries the greatest message. There is a quote from the sixth Grandfather, the holy man Black Elk: "Know the power that is Peace."

We parked by the monument and rolled out of our modern stagecoach. The view of the valley below was captivating. The buffalo grasses were alive in the winds and the rainbow covering made the scene unforgettable. We took some pictures, grabbed a canteen, and made our way down the headstone-dotted trails to the river. The day was regaining its normal heat and it was time for a swim. We moved slowly down the trail, for the history of June 25 was heavily marked in white-marble graves. Several hundred yards down the trail, a fence blocked our path. Horse droppings were visible on the opposite side. We were quickly over the barbed wire and down to the water. The green weeds on the river's bank told the history of the Sioux name, "Greasy Grass" (the Little Big Horn).

I peered across the river into the cottonwoods where the Lakota encampment once brimmed with hundreds of lodges, snorting ponies, laughing children, cooking mothers, aunts, grandmothers, storytelling uncles and grandfathers, and warrior sons, fathers, and brothers ready and waiting to expel a foe from this planet that had little sense of what relationship was all about. A chill ran down my back as I imagined the fate of the intruding white men of Custer's cavalry. The chill vanished when my spirit helper told me that Custer deserved his fate.

We decided this was a good place and found the water cool and inviting. We played for an hour and then made our way up the slopes to the modern reality of the museum. After a quick tour we set out for Reno Hill and more pictures. By then the sun was sending long shadows to tell us it was time to journey on. So we said farewell and made a night ride eastward to the Black Hills.

June 1979

I had graduated from high school and eight years of studying the Lakota; it was time for my vision quest. I now carried the pipe, and my uncle and I had planned another Montana vacation. Little did I know that the spirits of the Greasy Grass were going to show me more acknowledgment.

The day before we began our journey from Minneapolis, my uncle asked me if he could bring along a friend. This trip was supposed to be for just the two of us, but the Great Spirit had plans too. I should be more precise and say that the six powers (Grandfathers), or whatever the force is that the Great Spirit lets act upon us, had plans for me. That power was now influencing my life, for I had read *Black Elk Speaks* several times and was able to identify spiritually with my natural surroundings through the vision of the old seer Black Elk. My uncle wanted to bring along his girlfriend, and I reluctantly agreed. She was an attractive lady and she played a vital part for me on this trip. Sometimes our purpose is disguised in the affairs of others. So, I had Lakota history, Black Elk's vision, and Mother Earth, and my uncle had his interests too. The woman's purpose in my journey was to be a distraction—a distraction to my uncle—so that I could be alone with the spirits of the Greasy Grass.

We made our way across the open plains to the Little Big Horn monument and had our usual adventure there. After the museum tour, we were informed that a movie would be shown at 7:00 P.M. This gave us enough time to take a drive to Reno Hill. On the way we noticed a herd of horses grazing on the slopes of Medicine Tail Coulee. And as the spirits would have it, my uncle prophesied my future. "Wouldn't it be great to ride those broncs?" Eight years later I'd be able to say that it was indeed a grand thing to do.

We got back to the museum in time to see *Red Sunday*. When the show finished it was dark, and the movie set the stage. The plan was in motion and my vision quest lay ahead on the slopes of the Greasy Grass. My uncle had his distraction and thought it a good idea to be left alone for the evening. We had traveled and camped together for several days and the "couple" hadn't had any time alone. It was my privilege to help out. Mother Nature had plans for all.

I slipped off into the dark Montana night and walked up the asphalt road past the monument. The electric lights on the museum and by the monument made white holes in the black vale of sleeping Father Sky. The night was cool and I wrapped my ancient wool blanket around me. The plan was to sleep right out there on the battle ridge. As I walked away from the monument I suddenly stopped. Before me was pure blackness, a wall of darkness, a door into "the other world." I had chosen the journey and my destiny; with God I walked on.

The darkness represented ignorance and the unknown. When I walked through the blanket of blackness, the door of knowledge opened and I saw the beauty of God's night. The electric light of the white man's world faded, becoming small and limited. I realized that I was on the ridge where Sitting Bull had made his night prayer 103 years before for "the rubbing out of Long Hair (Custer)."

The Milky Way was in grand form that night. It seemed that all the beings of earth were reflected there, smiling acknowledgment. At that time I had had no formal teachings on the Indian Way, except for books and the one special book, *Black Elk Speaks*. So I followed my heart and walked away from the white man's road, forever. The spirits of the Greasy Grass would guide me from now on. I need only listen. The *wanagi* (spirits) were all around that night. The whole place was alive with power, mystical power that would bind me to the past and the Greasy Grass.

I picked a spot on the west side of battle ridge. After my blanket and medicine objects were laid out, it was time to smoke the pipe. I offered my life to the four directions, Mother Earth, Father Sky, and *Wakan Tanka*. I gave thanks for all the abundance that is here for all, and prayed for all my relatives *(Mitakuye oyasin)*. I prayed for wisdom, teachings, and the red way. I prayed for peace, love, and *waableza*—clarity of understanding. Soon afterwards, the gift of sleep rested my mind and body.

Sleeping under Grandfather's dome was wonderful and I awoke to the early rays of *An Petuwi,* Father Sun. I watched the morning star bring its knowledge to the new day, gathered my relics, and headed east to learn. "We are all here to learn," the Grandfathers and Grandmothers told me, and I watched the fire in the sun float over Custer's ridge.

On the east side of the ridge I found myself among fifty-plus markers of Custer's I and L troops. The war cries and .45 caliber firing echoed all around me. I wondered how the red man could have ever been considered hostile after the history of violence and cruelty displayed by the white race. The Indian people were in their own lands, guaranteed to them by the white government. Perspectives and individual positions on the circle are sometimes hard to understand. But now is the time for peace and love, so we must learn to live in harmony with all beings.

My mind became filled with a hologramlike reenactment of the "last stand," and I was lost in the sounds of long ago. The shrill cry of a real winged one pierced my soul and brought me back to the present day. Down in the valley to the west my brothers were calling. I walked slowly back to the top of the ridge and westward down a ravine toward Deep Coulee.

A pair of small hawks began to circle me in an irregular manner. They seemed to be interested in this two-legged one. I could feel the physical energy of Father Sun mixed with the cool morning breeze. The smell of the sage-covered hills surrounded me, as did my feathered brother and sister. These wingeds were there to teach me. First I was to learn about fear.

The memory of this event brings to me the greatest teaching. Many times, because we human beings don't learn very fast, remembering brings to us the greatest treasures. I remember my apprehension and my lack of faith in the Great Mystery. Faith is something to always ponder. It is a lifelong challenge in discovery—discovering what is really important in life and discovering how and why we react to certain situations the way we do. These are individual lessons from which we can continually learn. Fear is usually based on the unknown. My fear that day was brought by the winged ones to be remembered by me in the future so that I could learn many times—about faith and about *awachin* (belief).

The war cry of a spotted eagle echoed out from the trees on the Greasy Grass. It was wishing me happy adventures and a life of learning. I smiled and thanked the winged ones for their beauty, for their wisdom, for their gifts. Another teaching from the great Sioux camp would be carried with me—onward—for the people.

A rainbow haze filled my mind with thoughts of *Tankashilah,* the Grandfathers. It was time to meet my uncle and continue our journey. But I would return to this place. *Lelah wah ste wakan.* This is truly a holy place. My teachings here were far from over.

July 1987

The third time out and another hot summer day. There were four beings again: a new woman, my uncle, a dog, and me. This time it was a real adventure—on a steel horse I'd ride, a loaded six-string on my back. It was the way it should be: I was the scout, on my motorcycle—a free bird with my guitar, shield, and pipe. I led the way to the open plains and to my spirit home at the Greasy Grass.

Montana is a broad, open, endless-sky country. Not much fun for a lot of folks. That's okay, I needed an excuse to be alone anyway. So, after a two-day journey and a half-day tour, the lady of our party had had enough. "I'll catch up to you all later," I said. They were off, and I was on my way to the biggest adventure of my life.

The land around the battlefield is on the Crow Indian Reservation, and the Crow raise horses and farm the valley by the river. I intended to set up my tent at the local campground, but first I was determined to see some of the old Lakota camp. The air was warm and the blue sky widely stretched above me. As I rode down the highway paralleling the river, I saw a few dark clouds on the horizon. And as *Wakan Tanka* would have it, the *Wakinyan* (thunder beings) would be paying a visit. They would have a lasting stay in my life. Father Sun was descending into a mass of purple-blue-black western sky as I made my way up a dirt farm road toward Medicine Tail Coulee ford. Ahead of me was my future, and my past.

I wheeled up to the river and noticed that the Great Spirit had permitted these people to build a gate in their fence, right there by the Medicine Tail ford, just for me! Of course the gate was open and there were no signs. So I just parked my bike inside the gate and scouted the area. The spirits must have brought me there, for less than forty yards to my left was a domed-shaped lodge. I'd never seen a sweat lodge before, but I knew what this was the moment I saw it—*lelah wakan* (very holy).

There were no signs of life and this wasn't my lodge, so I respectfully left it alone. Instead I headed to the river. Now I stood on the victor's side of the river, and the Indian in me smiled at the *minne wakan* (holy water) with a newfound pride. I love my parents and family, but I couldn't help that they're white; my blood and heart are red.

I waded into the Greasy Grass and stood in the middle, spellbound. This is where it happened; less than seventy yards upstream to my right, Custer was shot. The controversy is enormous but the truth is all the same: Custer was warned and he chose his fate. Maybe he didn't die in the river, but his end started there. *Hetch etu.*

When my spell allowed me to move, I took a hike on the "white man" side of the river. This land is huge and I soon discovered the limitations of a horseless man. As that thought entered my mind, the earth started to rumble; I felt thunder and when I looked back to the river I saw an inspiring sight—*shuunka wakan!*

The horses were racing down an age-old trail to the ford and hit the water with a splash of energy. Right on their tails came three modern-looking Crow warriors bent low over their saddle horns. I wondered how they kept their cowboy hats on at full throttle. The four-leggeds thundered through the river and filed through the gate with habitual precision. As the last rider reached the gate, a sky-blue pickup rolled out of the dust and squeaked to a stop. A man climbed out and started to close the gate. But something caught his eye, or maybe it was the wind whispering in his ear. He glanced over at my bike and then followed a straight line across the river directly to me. There we were: white man on one side, red man on the other. This time it was different, though. I had come in peace, and we would become friends.

"Whatcha doing over there?" he yelled in an unanxious voice.

"Just looking around this beautiful country. The gate was open. Is that all right?" I wanted to be respectful; it was his land and my race had intruded enough. I decided that it was best to talk at less of a distance, so I walked across the river and introduced myself.

"My name's Tim Ryan. Are these your horses?"

"Yeah, you wanna ride?" he asked as if I were already a good friend.

"I'd love to ride. When?"

"Well, you can ride this afternoon or all day tomorrow. I'm Curtis Thunderbird," he added and shook my hand with a smile.

"Whatever is the best," I said enthusiastically. "I'd ride all day if I could."

"Come up to the house over there, say, at eight tomorrow morning." He got in his truck and started to back up. "Close the gate when you leave, all right?"

Indians sure are casual and they don't seem to worry too much; what a wonderful change from the skeptical, doubting, stress-filled world of the white man!

I waved good-bye, took a long look at the river, gave the sweat lodge a smiling glance, and thanked Grandfather Black Elk for bringing me there. It was time for a ride and a meal. As I headed back to my camp I guessed I wouldn't sleep too much that night. Excitement filled me in anticipation of the new day to come.

The sun was lost in black clouds when I finished my meal. I gave the leftovers to the stray camp dogs and prepared for a restless night of wonder. Negative thoughts were filling my mind with images of what could go wrong with tomorrow's ride. But the guidance from Black Elk's Six Grandfathers has made my faith bloom like a flower. My faith in the Creator drove away the bad thoughts and brought peaceful sleep to me within minutes.

I awoke to a new day of knowledge and the unmistakable crack of thunder. No sunrise this day! Before my mind could slip into negativeness I recalled some age-old wisdom: Everything happens for a purpose. The *Wakinyan* would be riding with me this day. The thunder beings had greeted me with their rainbow sign many years before on my first visit. This was truly my spirit home and the acknowledgment was abundant.

A few minutes on the highway and I was at Thunderbird's door. He greeted me with a smile and peered out into the gray sky. "It's raining. You still want to ride?"

"You bet!" I replied. "A little rain won't stop me."

He walked around the house and into a small barn. Soon he appeared on a sorrel pony and trotted up to a horse trailer nearby. Within moments the horse was saddled and we were ready to go. "Got much experience ridin'?" he asked with a grin as he handed me the reins.

"Mostly on that beast," I said, pointing to my motorcycle.

"Well if you have trouble, just let go and fall off. The horse will come right back to the house."

Great, I thought, I'll be lying there—somewhere—on the snake-filled plains, with a broken leg, and the horse will be safe at home! Indian humor is sometimes hard to take, although the red people do have a wonderful method of teaching: If it's supposed to happen, it will.

I jumped on the *shuunka wakan,* waved good-bye, and galloped down the rode to the ford. A moment later we were in the water. Maybe I was at this place long, long ago. I mused my way into ancient times and rode up the east bank onto the plains of yesterday.

The *Wakinyan* were speaking all around me; the circle was becoming complete. Eleven years before I had seen the power of the Spirit, alive in the rainbows covering the Greasy Grass valley. Three years later I had slept alone with the *wanagi* on my vision quest. Now I was out there alone again, but this time on the holy horse. I felt alive and one with nature, with Mother Earth, Father Sky, the four-leggeds, the winged people, and *Wakan Tanka.* I remembered the teachings of the two hawks on my second journey and now the thunder beings were teaching me about my past, and about my future. They were my brother and sister, and from their power I would spread the teaching of *Hehaka Sapa,* Black Elk—the teaching of the Rainbow way and the Six Grandfathers.

I rode my relative-horse over the trails where Custer had marched his men to their fate. I sat on the four-legged and viewed the valley from the eyes of both worlds—red and white. I wondered why Custer so foolishly attacked, even when the quest for the presidency moved him so strongly. Glory has killed many vain people. It is sad that the white man's glory-seeking has resulted in death for so many beautiful, peace-teaching beings: two-legged, four-legged, and winged.

Never before had I felt so much at home. Riding a powerfully alive mount, under a sky of thunder and lightning, I was living the life of my former self—a past earth walk that had a tremendously powerful link into the present and into my current life. The spirits were giving me the chance to see "the other world" and find my way to the true wisdom of *Black Elk Speaks.* Within two years of this event I would be given the honor of brotherhood and adoption into the Oglala Lakota tribe. This gift, I believe, was brought to me by Black Elk himself, through the teacher *Wanblee Wichasha,* Eagle Man.

As I rode through the bottoms of Medicine Tail Coulee, I was overtaken by an incredible force of déjà vu. It was as if I had ridden into a piece of the past. All my peripheral vision synchronized with a holographic plate in past history. Energy flooded through my body, filling me with deep peace and understanding. I had been there before; there was no doubt now; this was too "real" to be anything but truth. *Wakan Tanka* was giving acknowledgment, to take away any doubt, to fill my soul with love and brotherhood— *Mitakuye oyasin.*

When I rode into that past dimension a wave of joy radiated throughout my body. Everything was so acute, unlike any experience I'd ever had. It was magnificent! I laughed out loud until I cried. Joy was penetrating my soul like an arrow from above. I stopped my horse and rode in tight clockwise circles. I happily proclaimed my thanks to the Creator with a voice as loud as the thunder.

After several minutes (which seemed like decades) I came back down to earth, or to this dimension, whichever is more accurate. The tears were dripping off my face and mixing with the raindrops that had been falling, unnoticed, for quite a while. I think I was in a state of shock; the energy within me was almost paralyzing. My mind was awakened to a new plane of thought. I realized, truly, for the first time, how we are all One.

My horse walked southward toward a lone tree upridge from the coulee. He seemed to have a purpose, and I was quite dazed, so I let him have his way. As we approached the tree I realized his mission. For the spirits had left a gift there for me. Up in the branches was a large, weathered nest. Below, on the earth, lay the remains of a winged hawk being. I dismounted and knelt in front of my deceased friend. I knew he had lived his life in freedom and that the Creator had left him there for me. I honorably took his feathers, claws, and skull. They would bring great power to my shields and pipe, and I would pray with them in many ceremonies in the future.

I mounted and walked my horse along a trail. Holding the feathers in my coat I drifted off into a dreamscape. When I regained my composure I realized that I had ridden up the high ridge to the south of Medicine Tail ford. There, I had a grand view of the entire valley. The cottonwood-edged river flowed north-ward below me; the lowlands to the west danced with the ghosts of the Lakota tipis; the hills to the north waved in the rainy wind, dotted with white grave markers from the century-old conflict; the coulee to the east stretched uphill into infinity; and the Bighorn Mountains of Grandmother Earth stood boldly on the southern horizon.

I gazed down to the flatlands south of the old village, to where Reno had attacked. The cornfields cut across the battleground like yellow patches on blue jeans. I longed for the old days and the "old way." My joy mixed with the pain of modern life. I prayed that it was not to late to save this Mother of ours. Respect, the corner-stone of coexistence, must be brought back to life. It must be taught and applied. I gave myself to *Wakan Tanka* and swore to be a teacher of respect, harmony, love, and peace.

The steep slope below me moved with life. Out of the green Earth Mother came the feathers of a winged one. First just a rustle, then bursting into full flight, the feathers soared upward and to the west. He was a beautiful adult red-tailed hawk, out for a rainy afternoon meal. He flew in descending circles over the ridge and softly landed on an obscure perch. This was surely home for him, and soon his mate peered through the brush-covered cliff. So there they were, again. My feathered friends, teachers from the past, rel-atives giving their acknowledgment.

My time at the Greasy Grass had, once again, come to a close. After a good talk with my new friend, Thunderbird, I headed east to the Black Hills. There my uncle awaited the news of my adven-tures. A few days later we headed for the Land of Much Water, and the thunder beings followed me all the way home.

At the end of 1988 I had the privilege of meeting an Oglala spir-itual teacher named Eagle Man. I met him at a Mother Earth Spiri-tuality seminar that he taught. Afterwards, I gave him a hawk feather from the Greasy Grass. It was a great honor for me to give a Lakota this feather. We became great friends and, in time, blood brothers, and he has taught me the way of the Rainbow Tribe. When he taught me the Sweat Lodge Ceremony he named me Thunder Hawk, after my adventures at the Greasy Grass.

The Great Spirit *Wakan Tanka* is everywhere. We are all one. *Ho hetch etu aloh. Mitakuye oyasin.* We are all related.

▼ ▼ ▼ ▼ ▼

Thunder Hawk is very serious about his spiritual obligations. Several summers ago, he underwent his first Sun Dance on a Sioux reservation where, surprisingly to me, many non-Indians were allowed to take part in a ceremony conducted by full-blooded traditional people. The following summer, I counted over 160 dancers at that very same Sun Dance, and close to half of them appeared to be non-Indian. Thunder Hawk's preparation in the basic ceremonies and his firm belief in Black Elk's vision led him to this culminating ceremonial experience that up to then only a few white men had experienced. This happening came as a great surprise to me because I had not expected these advanced ceremonial doors to be opened so suddenly. I mistakenly believed that it would take at least a decade for such to happen. Last summer, not only was an international Sun Dance held, but at least three Sun Dances took place, maybe more, where non-Indians were pierced and non-Indian women danced also.

Most Rainbow Tribe people will not have access to a tribal Sun Dance and I hope that they will not attempt to put on their own. I still do not want to see any inattention to Earth Day and Harmonic gatherings for world peace and working together. This focus should never be diluted because it has achieved many powerful results. Black Elk did predict that many colors will join together around the tree of life. This could be a gathering for a world event and not necessarily a Sun Dance tree. I have no right to tell anyone how to follow their vision, however. Time will tell on these matters.

SACRED STONES

Every Oglala who believes in the omnipotence of *Wakan Tanka* wears or carries a small, spherical stone carefully rolled up in a wad of sage and deposited neatly in a miniature buckskin pouch no more than an inch in diameter. . . . It is not necessary to carry these stones on one's person every day, but if one is about to embark upon some important mission, such as a trip off the reservation, or if one wishes to invoke the aid of the supernaturals, one carries the stone with him.

Inhering in each stone is a spirit called a *sicun,* understood as that aspect of the soul that lasts forever and is capable of being reinvested in another object, human or nonhuman, animate or inanimate, at one's death. . . . An individual's personal stone possesses a tutelary spirit, analogous to the Christian guardian angel, but with one important difference. Whereas in Christianity one guardian spirit may be signed to an indefinite number of people, each Oglala has an exclusive protecting spirit. During a crisis, an Oglala may pray directly to the spirit for aid or counsel. As long as he [or she] does not offend the spirit, he is guaranteed of its protection throughout his [or her] life. When he dies, the spirit leaves his stone and is free to inhere in another's stone.[1]

Horn Chips (1836–1916) was an impressive holy man, a close friend of Chief Crazy Horse, and a member of Chief Lips's band of Wajajes. The Wajajes were Upper Brules who joined the Oglalas in 1854 and later settled with the Oglalas when the reservation days began. A writer named E. S. Ricker who interviewed Horn Chips reported what Horn Chips told him about the great chief Crazy Horse, "Before going into battle [Crazy Horse] always threw a handful of dust over himself and his pony and never wore anything more than a breech cloth and leggings, a single hawk feather in his hair, his ever present small stone behind his ear, and another stone from Chips under his left arm."[2]

In a later interview by Eleanor Hinman with an Oglala named Red Feather, Chips's mentorship of Crazy Horse was corroborated. Red Feather told Hinman that

> Nearly every summer for the rest of his life, Crazy Horse went out on war parties against the Crow or Shoshonis. In 1862 or 1863 a medicine man named Chips, a friend of his youth, made him a special charm to ward off danger, a little white stone with a hole through it, suspended from a buckskin string that Crazy Horse wore slung over his shoulder and under his left arm.[3]

According to William K. Powers,

> Sacred stones play an important part in Oglala ritual and belief. The early chroniclers of Siouian religions make numerous references to the importance of sacred stones in a variety of rituals that predate Yuwipi (see particularly Densmore 1918; Dorsey 1894; Lynd 1864; Pond 1867; and Riggs 1869, 1893). What I think is significant is that the close asso-

ciation between Horn Chips and Crazy Horse identifies the former with particularly strong protective and curative powers. Since some of Crazy Horse's current popularity rests on his daring as a warrior in pre-reservation times, at least part of his magical powers are attributed to the *wotawe,* or sacred charms, made for him by Horn Chips.[4]

Powers has spent considerable time on the Oglala reservation studying Lakota culture and language. I respect both the man's research and his courage. The latter attribute sets him apart from many of his peers in the white man's sciences of archaeology, anthropology, and history. Long ago, before it was fashionable, Powers nobly noted the Sioux's tenacity for keeping their spiritual vision despite the forces aligned against us. Many paternalistic writers at that time severely downplayed Lakota spirituality and diluted it with Christianity, as if our Natural Way was doomed by the superiority of the nation's dominant religion. Unfortunately, some of these writers are still writing about Sioux religion and are still getting by with their dilution. One book claiming to explicate Sioux religion has far more pages devoted to the white man's religion than to its purported subject matter. Powers is one of the few who did not take this appeasing route.

I have had two stones come into my life. One I wore upon my person, in a buckskin pouch, when I flew 110 combat missions. My first stone was claimed by Bill Eagle Feather to have hit the Sun Dance tree when an airplane flew over it. Later, that same stone came into the *Yuwipi* Ceremony that Fools Crow held for me before I went to Vietnam. A subsequent chapter details that experience. (See chapter 9.)

The other stone, the one that I still have, came to me after I had pierced in the annual Sioux Sun Dance. I left the cockpit of my fighter bomber, and eight days later I was sitting in a university classroom. I have a new *wotai* now and it stands for a different purpose. Chief Eagle Feather predicted that my combat *wotai* would leave me after I found my second *wotai* in a Black Hills stream. This happened after I returned from the war and sun danced.

My present *wotai* stone flashed at me four times in a stream. My handsome nephew, Wolfie, was a small boy then and chased out a snake while we were getting ready to take a refreshing swim. The crawling one went right across my foot and scared me. It certainly got my attention and guided my eyes behind it when it went out across the stream. After the third flash I waded out into the stream, and when the stone flashed the fourth time I picked it up. It is a tipi canyon agate, lustrously colored, rainbow-rimmed, and crystalline-centered. It has many powerful images that it reveals whenever a person looks into it. I could show it to you and you would probably discover a new image that no one else has seen before, such is the power and the resourcefulness of this stone. When you find your own stone, made especially for you by the Creator, you will understand more of what I am saying. As an afterthought: Was the snake initiated by the spirit world to draw my attention to that particular part of the stream?

My warrior days are far from over, however. This new *wotai* is still a warrior's *wotai,* but it has a different power or, some might say, a new encouragement. Its rainbow coloration and many symbols could well be an influence that has led me to the Rainbow Tribe. I have a new fight, this one with the Blue Man of Black Elk's vision and his detracting and denigrating supporters. This time my allies are the Rainbow Tribe, as well as others of respecting and open-minded spiritualities and, of course, the many concerned environmentalists. A much more serious battle lies ahead for all of us. We do not face the conflict of superpowers but rather our whole planet is at stake. Oddly, our adversary is what we have allowed to be caused by ourselves—all of us.

Many personal stones are found near the bed of a lake or stream. But as in most things spiritual, this is not a hard-and-fast rule of the type that too many dogmatic modern American mullahs allow themselves to get hung up on.

I think that the power inherent within the stones can resolve some major conflicts that have surfaced of late regarding non-Indian usage of the peace pipe. With a simple stone, non-Indian people can beseech the six powers of Black Elk's message or whatever Higher Power concept they may have. A peace pipe need not be used, and both identities should be happy. To avoid conflict, I find myself beseeching in ceremony more and more with my *wotai* instead of my pipe. My stone did come to me in a very special and powerful fashion. I don't believe the six powers or the Great Spirit are particularly concerned about which item is used. Our prayers and spiritual attentiveness are more important than whether we are holding a stone or a peace pipe.

Let us look at a Rainbow man who has a good spirit and attitude when it comes to positive conception and identity in relation to a spiritual power identified with the stones. The following is an account of a Rainbow man who has found an important stone, his *wotai* stone. He takes a journey across the land and finds other stones and related spiritual experiences that have deepened his bond to the earth and his newfound tribe.

THE JOY OF MOTHER EARTH SPIRITUALITY

Ron Miller, Stone Man

The Rainbow Tribe of Mother Earth Lodge has awakened from a deep sleep. Their spirituality grows each day as their bodies, minds, and spirits become in balance with Mother Earth. Each of us awakens at his or her own pace, and the joy of sharing our growth is a powerful journey in human affection and consciousness. The Rainbow Tribe is very giving in a natural way when others have needs during their spiritual growth. There are no leaders, presidents, secretaries, treasurers, or chairpersons; there are only spiritually awakened human beings who are grateful to be from Mother Earth.

My spiritual-awakening journey began when I attended a "Black Elk Speaks" seminar. At first I was not awakened by the story of Black Elk's vision until Eagle Man talked about the healing of Mother Earth by the spiritual awakening of the fifth-generation children of the people who put the Native Americans on reservations in the 1880s. Then it happened! During the ceremonial instructions, Eagle Man passed some plain stones around the class. One stone, black with white lines and with a chip out of it, attracted my attention as I saw a warrior chief in full headdress. The next day when I took a second look at the stone I saw another Indian face, a face that expressed sadness. My spiritual guide had awakened me!

In the next few months I read *Black Elk Speaks* and *Rolling Thunder*. Then, in late April, I started going to garage sales looking for an extension ladder and something else that I would not know until I found it. One Saturday I went to a dozen or so garage sales and found nothing, but I went back about 4:00 P.M. to the first place I had stopped to buy a purple crystal rock for my wife. That is when I reached into the bottom box of three boxes of unpolished agates and found, under a bigger stone, my *wotai* (for which I paid twenty-five cents). That evening, Eagle Man called about a Sweat Lodge Ceremony being held that night, and before the ceremony I showed him my stone. He was amazed when he saw the four direction colors in the stone and said their representation in a single stone with many images was very rare. He called it a "tree of life" stone, because the stone has the four colors that are customarily draped on Black Elk's Sun Dance tree. It also has a human being on one side with the right hand touching the tail of a dolphin fin on the second side, the left hand touching a goose wing on the third side, the right foot touching a four-legged friend, an elk, on the fourth side, the left foot rising out of Mother Earth, and a line above the figure's head to a five-pointed star. The stone has the color black to outline the living life forms, the color white for the five-pointed star, and the colors red and yellow encircling the living life forms.

During the Sweat Lodge Ceremony, I received my natural or native name, Stone Man—*Inyan Wichasha*. In a short time I made another spiritual journey to visit the Pipestone National Monument. I acquired a red stone pipe made by Big Eagle, and also a red stone arrowhead made by Betty at the Little Feather Indian Center in Pipestone, Minnesota, on Saturday morning. Then my wife, Sharon, and I walked the Circle Trail on a path that winds along Pipestone Creek to the Winnewissa Falls, an area that is like an exceptional oasis in the middle of the prairie. I saw many faces in the stone cliffs and formations, and felt that the spirits were alive. We spent a quiet morning in this sacred land in no hurry to be anywhere else, only to enjoy the harmony that Mother Earth offered. I highly recommend a trip to this very special place that the Buffalo Calf Woman pointed out to the Sioux. The stones are very powerful there. Finally, we started back to the Twin Cities, stopping at two state parks to enjoy nature: the running water, the wind in the trees, a cardinal singing, the smell of wildflowers, the quack of a duck, a playful chipmunk, and the powerful quiet of a wilderness place. Pipestone, Minnesota, expands your periphery, your observance of nature to a great degree.

My spiritual journey continued with a trip to the West. On my way I planned to look for stones and visit a rock shop in Mission, South Dakota, near the Pine Ridge Reservation. A library book listed the rock shop as the best in South Dakota. When I arrived in

Mission I discovered that the rock store had been a funeral home for the last ten years! So I looked on the map for historical sites to visit and decided to go to the Sioux Indian Museum near St. Francis. What I found was a Catholic church, a mission right in the middle of the village with the museum on the church property. It had a small collection of Sioux artifacts, and some handcrafted bead items for sale. I purchased a beaded key ring in the colors of the four directions for a friend.

Then my spiritual guide led me to the Wounded Knee battle site. The map showed a road from Batesland straight west to Wounded Knee. The first four miles was a good gravel road, which turned into a hard dirt road for another six miles, and then into a two-wheel path up and down the rolling prairie hills. While on the path I became aware that I was on sacred land as I felt the presence of spirits. I turned off the air-conditioning, rolled down the windows, and opened the sunroof. As I slowed my transportation down to a walk pace, I breathed in a breath of sacred air. Visualizing of times past I was riding a pony up and down the rolling hills as I journeyed westward. I was aware of all the living life forms of the prairie, past and present, and was lost in a dreamy contentment of real-life time, not clock time.

Finally, I came over a hill and the path turned into a rough, hard gravel road, and I could see a village in the valley with a blacktop road going south. The road came to an end near the Wounded Knee battle site monument. When I reached the dry gulch where many of the women and children were killed, I got out and walked toward the monument, which was weathered and in poor condition as if the BIA or the national historical site agency built it long ago and forgot about it. A Sioux Indian called out to me and asked if I was a pipe carrier. I said yes and that I believed in Black Elk's vision. We gripped hands in the brothers' grasp. He said he was Owl Feather Man, and I told him I was Stone Man. We talked for a while as long-lost brothers. He said he had a drum for sale if I was interested. We worked out a deal for the drum, and he left for Pine Ridge. My spiritual guide planned for me to be at this place, at this date and time. We Rainbows call it "following your spirit" or "following the force." The drum is a healing drum with a six-pointed yellow star and eight red bear paws painted on one side, and a star shaped like eight white feathers with black stems painted on the other side on brown rawhide. Five strips of rawhide hang from the drum, and each has two pony beads of the colors found on my *wotai* stone: red, yellow, black, and white. A yellow feather is attached by a strip of rawhide.

I headed for Pine Ridge, which is a dusty western town in the middle of nowhere. Then I went north to Red Shirt Table with the Black Hills appearing to the left as I rode along a trail that divided the painted badlands to the east from the grassy prairie to the west. When I came to Red Shirt, I looked for stones under the bridge at Battle Creek. I did not feel any particular stone call out to me, so I cut some sage along the road and went on to Rapid City. As the Black Hills loomed larger on the horizon my iron pony worked harder, seeming to be drawn to the distant hills. I watched a beautiful red sunset as the sun slowly set behind the Black Hills. Once in Rapid City I decided to go on to Sturgis to spend the night so I could be at Spirit Mountain for sunrise.

I awoke around 4:00 A.M. and eagerly headed for Bear Butte. As I turned off Highway 34 with the mountain in full view it appeared to me in the dawn light as an expecting woman ready to give birth. Maybe that is why Bear Butte is also called Spirit Mountain: it gives birth to the two-legged spirit when it helps to awaken so many human beings who go there to do their vision quest. I felt joy in my heart and gratitude to be alive. As I turned into the state park entrance, I saw a sign listing the opening hour as 8:00 A.M. I stopped at the gate and got out to look more closely at Bear Butte. I saw the shape of the Indian woman as she is ready to give birth facing the west—the land where the spirits live and home of the thunder beings and life-giving rains. Four buffalo were grazing inside the park's fence as the sun brought forth a new day. I cut some sage as I walked along the fence toward Bear Butte. Two mule deer were grazing just below the tree line at the base of Bear Butte. All the animals appeared harmonious and drawn to the sacred land. I sat and meditated for a while before I headed back to the motel. New wisdom comes naturally in spiritual places.

After I showered, I went west to the Bighorn Mountains and an Indian medicine wheel. I spent an hour looking for stones in the Tongue River, which flows out of the Bighorn Mountains. I found several stones of the four colors: black, white, red, and yellow. Then I had a thought from my spiritual guide to take four stones to the top of the Bighorn Mountains and return them higher up in the river. So I stopped in the middle of a high meadow where the Tongue River crosses under the trail. There, where the river is the size of a creek, I placed the stones in the stream. I rode on to the medicine wheel at the western edge of Bald Mountain peak. The trail from the meadow at about eight thousand feet winds up a ridge for two or three miles to a plateau. The medicine wheel is at the high end of the plateau facing west, with the Bighorn River valley below the ridge. It is surrounded by a wire fence with barbed wire at the top to keep people from removing stones and defacing the medicine wheel.

Going first to the south part of the medicine wheel, I beseeched with my *wotai* stone to the power of the yellow south, asking the spirit of healing to remove the sharp pain like a bee sting from my shoulder, where the muscles had been strained by heavy lifting at work before my journey. I went to the west part and beseeched the power of the black west, asking the spirit beings of this sacred medicine wheel to join my circle and to give me thoughts during my journey of the good red trail I should follow in the future, and to guide me in my spiritual-awakening journey. I moved to the north part and beseeched the power of the white north, asking the Great White Giant to give me endurance and courage to set off on my own journey in self-employment, and the cleansing wind to blow away negative thoughts and to bring forth honesty and purity in my thoughts and deeds. I completed my circle to the east part, where I beseeched the power of the red east, the spirit power of knowledge, to replenish my mind with new wisdom as the daybreak star brings me another new day. I raised my *wotai* stone to Father Sky and thanked him for the clear blue sky that I might see the Great Spirit's wisdom in creating Mother Earth. I touched my *wotai* stone to Mother Earth and thanked her for all that she has given me to keep my body in good health and alive for forty-some years. I raised my *wotai* stone to the Great Spirit amongst the stars and thanked the mysterious one for the creation of the four directions, Father Sky, Mother Earth, all life, and for water, air, earth, and fire.

I saw a great white owl sitting in a dead lodgepole pine facing the west. I removed four ribs from a dead elk to make a whistle. Being out in the open, less-populated West was a time to meditate about my spiritual awakening. I would climb up to a ridge and sit facing west into the lodgepole pine forest and mountains. My spiritual guide gave visions of which human history has no recorded knowledge and thoughts that I could not have logically created with my limited education before my spiritual awakening. I felt as if new wisdom were replacing my old wants and values with the desire to seek out this new wisdom each day as it happens, and not to rush or expect to discover it every day. I returned to Minnesota to await my next journey.

I did not have to wait long. The Rainbow Tribe had started a weekly Mother Earth spirituality ceremony on Saturday nights at a local community church. My wife and I went together to one conducted by a woman who led a pipe ceremony, and I had a new feeling of joy and peace within me as she beseeched the six powers of the universe and the Great Spirit. I went almost every week thereafter.

It wasn't long before we of the Rainbow Tribe at Mother Earth Lodge faced a challenge regarding our way of conducting ceremonies. We had become a family. Red Dawn Coyote named us the Badger Clan of the Rainbow Tribe. We had our spirituality challenged as not authentic, but the spiritual growth we shared on the good red road was more powerful than the false prophet trying to lead us on his own road of prejudice and Stone Age myths. Later we found out that this interrupter also had a serious drug problem and obviously was not walking his talk. Red Dawn Wolf answered the false prophet, "We are but grains of sand on the beach, and who is to say who owns the sky above and the stars as the ocean waves mix the grains for all times." We told the false prophet to feel welcome at our lodge, but to respect our circle of positive energy as we respect the native traditions.

The next week I asked Buffalo Spirit Woman if I could lead ceremony and beseech with my *wotai* stone. I also felt that this could be a good means to avoid any conflict or criticism from those who believe that non-Indians should not use a peace pipe. She said I could lead ceremony with any special object of value to me or with no objects. My body, mind, and spirit were in balance as I faced the spiritual challenge from the false prophet with no anger, no hostility, no hatred, but with love and joy.

I arrived early at the church that had been generous to us. By 7:30 P.M., over thirty people had joined the circle. For the new people I told them of Black Elk's vision, and as the sage I had gathered during my journeys was passed around the circle to remove negative energy, I told the story of how I found a happy stone at Wall Drugstore in South Dakota. I told the circle I had extra joy in my heart and that if they needed some joy in their lives, to take some out of the stone or put some in the stone as it was passed around the circle while we meditated to flute music by Nakai called "Shaman's Call." Then Red Dawn Wolf drummed for a while before I started beseechment with my *wotai* stone. I beseeched the power of the west and the spirits of all the black, white, red, and yellow human beings to join our circle and bring their knowledge and wisdom into our thoughts. I told stories about Martin Luther King's "I have a dream" speech and Buddha's "I am awake" answer to the question of whether he was an angel, a saint, a prophet, or a god. I quoted from Black Elk, "Sometimes dreams are wiser than waking," and Shirley MacLaine, "Know thyself and that truth will set you free." I talked about our spiritually awakened teachers, Mother Teresa, Jesus Christ, Buddha, Confucius, and White Buffalo Calf Woman. Then I beseeched Father Sky, Mother Earth, and the Great Spirit amongst the stars to hear our prayers for the healing of our environment, which gives us all the elements of life. We are all part of the living Mother Earth; all our cells are hers.

After I had ended the ceremony I put out a box of stones from my travels and offered them to any who needed a *wotai.* One woman told me that when the happy joy stone came to her she thought it would be warm and moist, but it was cool and dry and she could hear birds singing as she held it and meditated. It was a joyful ceremony, and I am convinced that a special stone can hold as much spiritual mystery as any other object.

This is but a short chronicle of a Rainbow person. We have found our way to beseech, to acknowledge, to recognize through natural form, and to utilize the land, the created things, and ourselves to find our place in this universe. We have crossed over the bridge from a past with which we were dissatisfied. Most of us come from trails that were unfulfilled. We have found a new harmony that is backed by a powerful nature. It offers a closeness when we do ceremony together and a confident strength when we are out there alone. It is good and we shall endure.

Hetch etu aloh.

▼　▼　▼　▼　▼

And so we have an adventure of a Rainbow man who simply wants to be close to the earth and find a harmony with brother and sister beings. He has discovered a high degree of relationship to the *inyan oyate,* the stone people. This man would never support the past practice of boarding schools for Indian children to destroy our culture and spirituality. This man also will be there to support Indian treaty rights, civil rights, and tribal sovereignty. And so I say to any potential, narrow-minded detractors, do not be against the simple yet deep message of Stone Man's travels. Stone Man is a good example of the new people who have come to recognize the power of the Natural Way. I feel strongly that many will understand the true depth of his stone story, and that we will all continue to move forward to observe what Mother Earth has waiting for us if we only have the depth and wisdom to reach out for it.

8

RAINBOWS DISCOVERING SPIRIT GUIDES

Reincarnation is generally regarded as the belief that a person has had a past life and is now leading a present life with some connection to or atonement for the past. Many people, especially in North America, have a stirring inside indicating that they once lived as Native Americans. I am often asked about reincarnation in my talks across the country, and my standard response is probably disappointing when I do not give the answer that most want to hear. This subject is definitely a mystery, but I have found little supportive evidence to verify such a happening. I cannot discredit the reincarnation theory—but neither can I substantiate it. Possibly, however, I can shed some related insight on another concept of a past presence that manifests itself in the present. This concept or belief is called a spirit guide.

Rather than talking dogmatically like those Christians who theologically and philosophically deny the possibility of reincarnation in every case, or speaking fatalistically like those Hindus who theologically and philosophically assume the inevitability of reincarnation to all but the highest caste, the Lakota treat reincarnation as a thing that is possible, occasional, exceptional, and *wakan* [holy]. When a Lakota observer is faced with data that indicates experientially that one is dealing with a reincarnated personality, one tries to keep a respectful distance from that phenomena, and then

147

tries to live as sincerely, generously, and ordinarily as possible around it. In my mind the traditional Lakota position on this matter has a tremendous amount of wisdom and respect to it.[1]

One of my favorite historical authors, William Powers, has some worthwhile insight to offer regarding the Lakota concept of the various states of individual being:

> In the Lakota tradition all animate beings (the redundancy is intentional) are born and die. In the process they pass through what might be called by analogy four states of individuation. Each individual comes into a being as the result of (1) having a potentiality for being, (2) transforming this potentiality through birth into an essence that is independent of the body, (3) providing continuous evidence that this essence exits [leaves], and (4) finally providing evidence that the essence independent of the corporeal existence continues after death, therefore freeing its potentiality to inhere in another (potential) organism to begin the process all over, ad infinitum, in what we understand in English to be a system of reincarnation.
>
> When old Lakota medicine men spoke of these four states, they named them (1) *sicun* [immortal aspect], (2) *tun* [to give rise to—potentiality], (3) *ni* [breath, life; evidence that an essence exists], and (4) *nagi* [spirit] respectively. These four states have been described as consituting a belief in four souls, or at least four aspects of one soul. Most explanations have come from scholars whose own traditions require that each person have one soul and every other system is simply regarded as a variation on that theme. . . . If a Lakota were writing a book on euro-american souls, he might conclude that we were somehow deficient because we thought in terms of "one" soul without any reference to process—unreasonable by Lakota standards.[2]

What is a spirit guide? Is it some form of reincarnation?

A spirit guide is from the world beyond, and it finds its way to the present to be connected to an individual who recognizes it. From my experience, a spirit guide can announce itself in dreams or make its presence known through an image on a *wotai* stone. My *wotai* stone, which is described in the previous chapter, has a discernible indication of a warrior that I call Charging Shield. This image is as obvious as the silhouette of Fools Crow that is easily perceived when the stone is studied. Fools Crow's image was apparent while the venerable holy man was still living, however. Charging Shield's image is very dominant and expressive, like a warrior of old. This image conveys to me the spirit of this Sioux warrior who once lived and to whom I am related. I regard Charging Shield as my spirit guide and believe that his force, or the mystery connected with his image and the *wotai,* has allowed numerous adventures and experiences in the Natural Way. Possibly it is a force that is just allowing itself to be imaged upon the stone as a means of offering me the reassurance I need to undertake some of the tasks I have set for myself. When Black Elk went up into the spirit world, he saw far more powerful forces as Grandfathers—and, possibly, they were only imaging themselves in that way so that a young boy could better relate to them in order to comprehend the complex knowledge and prediction that they were about to impart. Black Elk's vision has reached out to many in this age of communication.

Since the *wotai* stone came into my life, it seems that my personal adventures have proliferated. I believe I have had far more adventures than most people. I also believe that Charging Shield's spirit or energy has been a driving force behind my writing about the natural connection and passing on my experiences with Eagle Feather, Fools Crow, and Ben Black Elk. Charging Shield's glaring image also gives me fortitude to stand up to any detractors who wish to challenge me upon my way.

I believe that Nicholas Black Elk, Fools Crow, and Bill Eagle Feather are also spirit guides. Fools Crow's presence was readily apparent right after his death when I was in the heart of writing *Mother Earth Spirituality.* At that time, certain books dropped off the shelf for me to open to gain new information. Some of my friends were also influenced by his spirit right after his departure, and they would call me or point out certain articles or experiences that were later included in the manuscript.

A Rainbow friend named Jim, who came from the East to distribute new coats and jackets to Indian children for the winter, stopped and told me that he had had strong indications of Fools Crow much of the time that he was traveling toward the Sioux reservations. Ravens and crows swirled around him a lot during his trip, and I saw three crows right after I talked to him. Jim said that

Fools Crow had a message for me. He stayed overnight, and that night I dreamed of Fools Crow and willows as well as of Bill Eagle Feather and Ben Black Elk. The next day we built a sweat lodge, and while we were below the hill at the river cutting our willow saplings, two golden eagles circled over the lodge site and remained there until we returned. The lodge was as strong as the ones that I had experienced with Jim and some traditional Indians from the Rosebud reservation earlier, indicating that we had put the lodge in the right place. It is an honor to dream of Fools Crow, Bill Eagle Feather, and Ben Black Elk. These three men who are in the beyond do come occasionally into my life, and I consider them valuable spirit guides. Their power still reaches into this world. All three men had a spiritual effect on one another. In a way, their presence is a form of reincarnation. They have lived before and now their presence is in this world and they are manifesting themselves, their thoughts, ideas, and suggestions through a present entity. This is certainly not an example of the popular notion of reincarnation, but if this observation is explored in depth, a degree of similarity between the two subjects, spirit guides and reincarnation, may be discerned. Where a presence becomes quite dominant, this experience may possibly be the indication that some people are mistaking for reincarnation.

For example, let us imagine that person A lived two hundred years ago in England, where he was very close to Celtic and Druidic beliefs. After A's lifetime, A became a spirit (as most of us believe we will) and influenced B, who lived as a Sioux holy person 125 years ago. B died and his spirit influenced C, who lived most of her lifetime close to Harney Peak in the Black Hills where B had vision quested many times. C, who was also very spiritual and fought to keep the area as a natural park, has just passed away. The spirit of C is now a spirit guide influencing D, who is presently living and is having strong feelings of having lived two hundred years ago in a certain area in England that she just visited. D is also intensely environmental and has an overpowering sense of reaching back into time when she finds herself standing at the crest of Harney Peak. D wonders why a certain part of England and a specific peak in the Black Hills should have such a nostalgic effect upon her. It is an age-old perception, "I have been here before."

A theory could be offered from the foregoing that each spirit left an impression upon the other to such a degree that A actually reached down to D through B and C. Another theory might claim that A reaches directly into D, no differently than Charging Shield is perhaps reaching from a separate past directly into my life. It is all mystery but human beings, who like to analyze and classify, call it reincarnation. Maybe a better answer lies somewhere between the theory of reincarnation and the concept of spirit guides.

We Indians have heard numerous theories from the white man, so I guess we should be allowed to speculate some on our own. Even if my spirit guide theory seems farfetched to you, it at least offers some food for thought. It is just simple, two-legged supposition based on the expansion of the mind, a *wotai* stone, ceremonial experience, and actual manifestation of spirit guides in *Yuwipi* ceremonies that I have observed. My supposition is also bolstered by the knowledge that native peoples did set some excellent humanistic and environmental examples. Therefore, I refuse to assign this knowledge some form of negativity. I have also been influenced by the harmony I have observed from the Rainbow Tribe people and the poor example I have seen from those who preached to us and scared us when we were children. I have been told things a lot more preposterous than my mere suppositions—for example, I come from a rib; we come from monkeys; you could only walk one way across the Bering Strait; I will go to hell or I won't go to hell, depending on whether I follow this missionary or that missionary. The Mormons tell us we are a lost tribe of Israel; they also say that there were ancient cities here in North America (no archaeological discoveries yet). Pat Robertson states emphatically that Hitler was a demon possessed, Karl Marx was a satanist priest, and the devil will be tied up for a thousand years pretty soon.[3] (We Indians do not have a devil to tie up, and I have yet to meet a rational two-legged who has ever met one.) Robertson's book is titled *Answers to 200 of Life's Most Probing Questions.* How egotistical! A Sioux, a Navaho, or an Iroquois spiritual person would never make such a claim. Traditional Indians may have many suppositions or "wonderings," but we would never make such presumptuous claims to have answers to what is obvious mystery.

▼　▼　▼　▼　▼

Some spirit guide indications are very strong and personable, as described in the following narrative. I met Hawk Who Hunts Walking several years ago. He is a generous person and a craftsman. The beautiful drum he made for me has endured many sweat lodge ceremonies and I am still using it. It manages to keep its tone even in the steamy atmosphere of the lodge.

LITTLE CROW—OLD FRIEND

Chetan Wahkamani, *Hawk Who Hunts Walking*

In the spirit world, the world of the above-beings, two spirits stand together at the edge of the cliff of birth. Both wear well the experiences of many former lives. One lived as a Native American trapper in the Great Lakes region of North America and as a warrior of the plains, a defender of his people, the Mdewakanton Sioux. He was called *Mahtogi,* Brown Bear. Next to my friend Brown Bear, I stand. I was a chief of the Mdewakanton Sioux. I chose, at first, a path of peace with the white man, but before I returned to the spirit world, I was called upon to defend my people, my starving children. I was called *Ta Oyate Duta,* His Red Nation, and also *Chetan Wahkamani,*[4] Hawk Who Hunts Walking, Little Crow.

I, Little Crow, turn to Brown Bear and speak, "Old friend, this time it is your turn to journey alone. Now, good spirit, prepare to jump to your birth and I will watch you descend. As is the way at first, you will not remember me, but I will be watching. I will whisper in your ear at your birth and when you are a child in your mother's arms. When you become a young man and then an adult, I will slowly awaken you to our way, our friendship."

Brown Bear turns to me and speaks, "Old friend, I am ready. I will pray to *Wakan Tanka* that my ears may be opened, that I may hear you." Brown Bear pauses. Our eyes meet. "Be patient with me and guide me well. Do not leave me. Be at my side often, old friend. I will find my balance with your words of counsel and with Mother Earth under my feet. We will learn together." With a parting glance, Brown Bear turns away from me and leaps to his birth. I kneel at the edge of the cliff and watch him descend. He is born to the parents he has chosen and named Steven by his great-great-aunt, One Who Helps.

One dark summer evening on the prairie at the house of his aunt, his mother asks him to go outside and gather the clothes that have dried on the wash lines in the backyard. The warm summer breeze moves over my face, as outside I calmly await his arrival. The young man is surprised by his mother's request. He peers out the kitchen window through the white lace curtains and sees nothing but black and feels nothing but fear. Without another word, his mother turns away from him and walks into the living room. It is obvious; there is no choice. He stands down from the kitchen stool and walks carefully to the back door. Holding his fear inside him, he opens the screen door and descends the three steps to the narrow walkway that leads around to the side of the house and the clothesline.

I, Little Crow, have taken the form of a coyote. I lie waiting for my old friend in the dark shadows of a pine. As his feet leave the last step and meet the pavement, I move out from the protection of the darkness and show myself to him. Immediately our eyes meet. He tries to speak, to call out, but he cannot. He is frozen in fear. We are frozen in time. As old friends we meet, spirit guide and *voyageur.* The seed of awakening has been planted. I disappear into the night.

Years later, in the forests of northern Canada, again in the form of a coyote, I walk into his campsite. In the full light of the midday sun, we stand and stare into each other's eyes. This time the *voyageur* has no fear. He is still and quiet. Our eyes are full and open. As cousins, we speak to each other from our hearts. I turn and vanish into the trees.

Gifts

For a few years now, I had been feeling quite annoyed by this sensation that something was pushing me, prodding me, like the touch of a stranger's hand in a crowd. What or who was it? I did not know. After much similar pushing and prodding by loving friends, I sought an answer to my questions. I relented and began visiting this remarkable person and, in time, a trusting friend, a psychic, who gave me her counsel and instruction. Clarity was her gift to me, and the seed of awakening blossomed; from within me understanding grew, and after much work and patience with myself, old friends were united. My spirit guide's words are clear. I listen within.

From this place of wholeness, of balance, every step I take is felt to be my own. It is a secure feeling to have good friends, spirit beings in bodies, and spirit beings out of bodies—above-beings. But it is one path and it is mine, for it begins within me; there is nowhere else to look for it and no one left to ask which way to go. I, and only I, know.

My spirit guide and I have worked together all our lives to gain a comfortable rapport. He has no quantity of time as I do. He is not limited by emotions but uses them as tools to teach. He possesses a fantastic sense of humor and always takes great pains to make me the brunt of his practical jokes. He cajoles. He teaches. At times he has purposely given me the absolute worst advice, which has taught me (as was his intent) to take counsel with others but, in the end, to listen only to my own heart. He often pleads with me to lay down the heavy baggage of old visions that I have allowed people to deliver to me and, instead, to ask to appear from within me my true self. He constantly advises me to be well grounded in Mother Earth. "Pay attention to your feet," he says. "Pay attention to your feet." I pray with the pipe to Mother Earth and to the White Buffalo Calf Woman that their energy may come up into my body through my feet and that I may be fully grounded.

Once, while out one winter evening listening for my old friend, I turned a corner on my usual neighborhood walk and saw about one block ahead of me a brilliant fire burning in the middle of the street. I was shaken immediately from my prayers and moved cautiously up to it to see what was happening. This certainly was very unusual. What was a fire doing burning in the middle of a city street? Moving closer to the fire, I felt the heat of the flames on my face. I looked into the flames and, to my surprise, I saw a pair of boots. Not just any boots, but boots identical to the ones I was wearing that very moment. I was struck. How strange! What a scene I made—one man alone, standing in the middle of the street, watching a pair of boots being consumed by flames. I looked up and absolutely no one was around. I became frightened and confused. That old, familiar, annoying feeling crept into me and then I knew, deep inside me, that this was the work of my trickster (heyoka) friend.

Slowly, I backed away from the fire and walked with an ever-increasing pace down the street. I slowed every few steps to allow a quick and secret glance over my shoulder to see if the scene was real or an apparition. Arriving at the end of the block, I turned to take one last look; around the corner came a fire truck. It pulled up next to the boots and stopped. A man jumped out with a fire extinguisher and put the fire out. He jumped back onto the thundering beast and disappeared down the street.

Silence once again filled the deserted street. A man emerged from a house. He walked over to what remained of the boots, picked them up, and vanished into his house. I stood in silence, staring at the boots on my feet. The boots! This play performed for my benefit deserved a reply. "Yes, old friend, I had forgotten. I must always pay attention to my feet—to my grounding. Thank you." I walked home. The snow crunching under my feet awakened every creature for miles.

Before I had heard my old friend speak his name, big black crows frequented our house. They stood, ever-present guests on our window ledges, and beat their hammering beaks on our window so often and so hard that we thought for certain they would shatter the glass. After my spirit guide spoke his name to me, the crows ceased hammering their constant message. They had finished their work and left.

Years before this remembering, I met a woman from Pipestone, Minnesota. Being an artist, I was fascinated by the beauty of the peace pipes, so I asked her to get me one, which she did. I lived with this pipe for many years. It was kept for a long time in a dresser drawer, and, eventually, it found its way to a glass case that hung on the wall in my bedroom. It was not till years later, after my first Sweat Lodge, that I took the pipe off the wall to examine it. Immediately upon touching it, I felt it to be a close and, until now, unappreciated brother. I examined the bowl of the pipe closely, and when I turned the bowl upside down, to my astonishment my old friend's name was etched into the base of the pipe—Little Crow! I took a deep breath to collect myself and ran shouting the news, showing the discovery to my wife. This pipe is the most sacred material possession I own. It is a gift from the spirit world, from the above-beings, from Little Crow.

In the sweat lodge I pray, "Old friend, may you be with me always. May all the holes upon my path be placed directly in front of me and, with your guidance and counsel, may I fall into them, to receive your many gifts."

Sweat Lodge

One Sunday morning I was paging through the paper and saw an article about a Native American medicine man. Little Crow shouted into my ear, "Go to him." So I did. It was the Year of

Reconciliation between the white man and the Mdewakanton Sioux. This Mdewakanton medicine man and I shared the same tribe, but in different lifetimes. With him I took my first sweat.

I was struck by the experience. The person I was, shattered into the many different people who I really am inside. They all stood before me. I shook with fear. I wept inside with remembrance and with happiness. This was a great turning point for me, a sacred timeless place in ceremony, a place to be with the ancestors, the above-beings. *Medakouye ouyahsin!* I spoke the Dakota (eastern Sioux) pronunciation. I am related to them all!

In time I was introduced to Eagle Man, with whom I have taken sweats and have learned much about prayer with the pipe, as well as humility and humor. In one unforgettable sweat I received my name. As tradition dictates, I was given the name of my spirit guide, Little Crow, *Chetan Wahkamani,* Hawk Who Hunts Walking.

During this sweat, the spirit of my old friend entered the sweat lodge and greeted us all with his humorous ways. Smiles lit on the faces of the circle of people as one by one he flew between us, to welcome each of us to this sacred place. Our hearts were filled with joy and remembrance and we prayed and sang, celebrating our kinship together in this moist womb of Mother Earth.

Before the door was shut the first time, as we sat knee to knee in silent prayer with our thoughts, a lone dog tried to enter the lodge. I knew the trickster would be near. The beat of the drum danced in our hearts as we became one with the ancestors. Prayers from each of us rose for thanksgiving as clouds of steam enveloped us, billowing from the red glowing rocks resting in the center of our lodge. The lights of many souls lit up our faces as we sang and prayed together. During the smoking of the pipe after the sweat, we all stood motionless, passing the pipe between us, the crackle of the campfire awakening us to the evening's stillness. Above us was another dome, its starry face looking down upon this small circle of people deep in tranquil thought. The blackness of the night warmed us.

I have since built a sweat lodge on our land in northern Minnesota, deep in the Superior National Forest. I worked, cutting young saplings from the thick underbrush, clearing a hilltop to make space for the sacred dome, bending the saplings in place and tying them together with string, laying soft grass and cedar boughs for our cushioned seat, gathering large stones for the fire to heat our lodge with the clouds of boiling steam.

The first sweat was taken with a friend. A spirit friend from her youth visited her as we sang together to the beat of the drum. Later that evening it snowed. The lodge sat silent in the dark, tobacco ties dangling from its curved domed boughs. Everything was sprinkled with a white, silvery sheen.

The Sweat Lodge Ceremony always brings a stirring to my soul. It calls me to once again awaken wholly to my true self, to seek guidance from the ancestors, old friends, loved ones, and to thank the White Buffalo Calf Woman and *Wakan Tanka* for their gifts and blessings.

Drumming

Little Crow has said that drumming is good for the blood. He means physically, the blood that flows within your veins—your health. I take it one step further to mean the blood of your family and the bonding of your life to others. The resonating quality of the sound of rawhide stretched over wood bears a great resemblance to the harmony of the hearts of many people—red, yellow, black, and white—beating together as one heart, in love, and with respect for one another.

Once in an early sweat, the drummer, who sat next to me, stopped drumming in the middle of a song and handed me his drum. "Take it," my old friend said, and I have been drumming ever since. With time and patience, I have learned obedience and chosen the way to travel. I have learned how to listen for the trees to call me to them from a cedar swamp, to choose the one who gives way to me and my work. I take the wind-downed trees and carve and shape them into a hollowed form resembling a pumpkin or a slice of bone, empty inside, without seeds or marrow. I receive fresh deer hides and process them into rawhide, or with cowhides, I cut and stretch them to make drums.

Their sound resonates in my home. My chest throbs with their vibration. People call me to hunt for their drum for them. I form the drum to their individual spirit, and on the face of the drum I paint their "face," their name, and their story. It is slow, time-consuming work. I know I have done this in many lives before, and with my old friend's guidance, I have remembered the way. I have also been asked to teach about drumming, to help people on their own paths to make drums for themselves. This I enjoy.

I will always make drums. The drum I wish to make, I have not yet begun. The drum I wish to play, I have not yet heard. It waits patiently in many forms to be called to give way to the beat of the drummer's prayer.

> Trust from within.
> Take the path of your own heart only,
> Live in mystery, rejoice! Let it flow!
> Love God, *Wakan Tanka*.
> I raise my pipe to you,
> *Hetch etu aloh!*
> Little Crow

▼   ▼   ▼   ▼   ▼

Little Crow's spirit guide reaches into many facets of his life while he is making his natural road. His journey is obviously enhanced; the relationship has facilitated Little Crow's confidence and insight.

Earlier I discussed the presence of Charging Shield, whose influence in my life is akin to the experience of Little Crow. I have another discernible image upon my stone; it bears a resemblance to a person who always seemed to open doors for me when I was a child, whether it was a trip to a trout stream or the purchase of a new baseball glove. Later, this person, my brother Russ, taught me how to weld and I found myself in a high-paying occupation that financed my college education.

The accidental death of my brother Russ exposed me to the close presence of a spirit immediately after a death. In my college years, I was a union ironworker and a certified welder, an occupation at which many Native Americans are gifted. Ironworking is a dangerous occupation, yet walking narrow beams far above the ground does not seem to scare Native Americans as much as it does most people. I was working in Colorado one summer, and on one particular morning I constantly thought of Russ, who also was an ironworker. We had worked together the previous summer on air base hangars in Glasgow, Montana. His presence was absolutely dominating and all that I did was think of him as I worked in the railroad yards near the Air Force Academy cutting the steel bolts that secured the steel beams that were being transported to the job site by railcar. After cutting the bolts with an acetylene torch, I helped a raising gang remove the beams with a crane. I constantly thought of my brother and even had a close call with a sliding beam because of my inattention. Just before noon, the superintendent of the project came with a very long face and my paycheck and told me my brother had fallen from the iron to his death at a job site in Rapid City.

Many of the ironworkers knew my brother well. The crane operator, who had been his close friend, took the rest of the afternoon off to console me and help me pack for my trip back to the funeral. After the funeral, where ironworkers were pallbearers, I was hired by the same company that my brother had worked for, since I was a certified welder and at that particular time union welders who could climb iron were not available in the area. I began work right where my brother was killed and stayed at that job site until I returned to college.

His presence, at the time of his death that morning, was absolutely overpowering. He was alone when he fell. He was welding down roof decking for new B-52 bomber hangars and his helper did not come to work that particular day. Russ backed off the edge of the hangar and fell about fifty feet to the ground. You could see the scratch marks of the welding electrode rod holder where it dragged across the metal hangar roof. It is believed that he might have been alive for several hours after he fell and before he was found. Maybe in his dying state he came to visit me at the job site in Colorado. We did share a camaraderie in our work. Or, possibly, his spirit came to me all of that morning after he had transformed. Regardless, his spirit was extremely apparent. Strangely, he rarely appears in my dreams now, nor do I feel his presence as I do the holy men's, even though my brother and I were quite close and he was proud of me for becoming an ironworker. Yet his image is on my stone, which makes his absence all the more perplexing. Could it be that, because he is not as knowledgeable as the holy men are, he is now somewhere in a period of learning? But then, again, the warrior figure, Charging Shield, has never appeared in my dreams either—although I do feel his presence at times when I am in the sweat lodge and especially when I bring the *wotai* stone into a ceremony. At this point, I would like to point out to any potential detractors that I did not put these images upon this stone, and it is free for all to observe and interpret. These images were placed on that stone by a far higher power than whatever a detractor will ever possess.

Unfortunately, my brother Russ was from that era of the reservation boarding schools in which Indian identity and especially our spirituality were denied and repressed. He lived in a time when

Indian people suffered abusive racial prejudice and severe social limitations. I recall, as a child, walking past bars on my way to school and seeing signs that read, *"No Indians and Dogs Allowed."* Indians would have bootleggers buy alcohol for them, and it wasn't until 1953 that Congress passed a law that allowed an Indian to walk into a nightclub legally. Indian men had served honorably in World War I, World War II, and the Korean War and yet could not legally socialize with their non-Indian comrades alongside whom they had fought. My brother Russ was a World War II veteran, and I am sure this situation was highly detrimental to his spirit. All of my brothers were veterans. Early restrictions and unjust treatment caused many Indian veterans to become alcoholics, and there was no Native American spirituality to counter such conditions, as is becoming available now in this era of communication. Russ knew little of our culture because it was not available when he traveled around from job site to job site. In Rapid City, his hometown, Indian culture was not as highly regarded as it is today. Young Indians should realize the limitations of the past and should endeavor to appreciate the many benefits that Native American spirituality is now allowed to provide for them.

Among the ironworkers, however, my brother Russ found a companionship with men who admired anyone who could climb the high steel beams. Friday evenings they had raucous socializing and he was included. I think he would have appreciated the many good Rainbows who lack prejudice and have a rich spirituality that is far more rewarding than the loneliness and emptiness of bars and nightclubs. He lived hard and drank hard, yet he was one of the most generous persons I have ever known. Completely lacking jealousy, he always appreciated the successes of his friends. For these traits and many others, I hope he has found happiness in the spirit world.

PART THREE

DISCOVERING THE
HIGHER MYSTICAL
REALM

Peace . . . comes within the souls of men when they realize their relationship, their oneness, with the universe and all its powers, and when they realize that at the center of the Universe dwells Wakan-Tanka, and that this center is really everywhere, it is within each of us.

Black Elk, quoted in Joseph Epes Brown, *The Sacred Pipe*

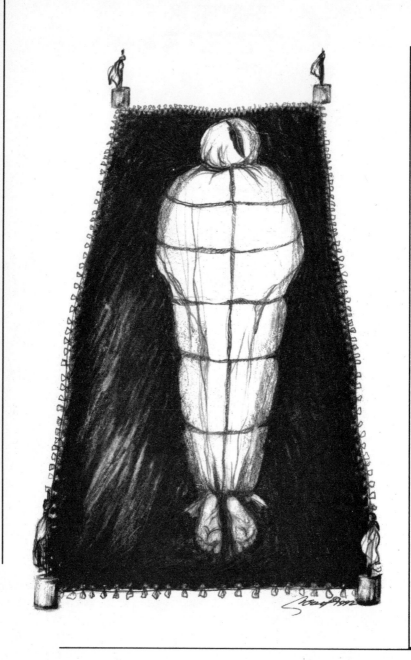

9

SPIRIT-CALLING CEREMONY

Entering the higher realm of ceremony, one finds a participation that is unique: the ability to bring ancestors of the past into phenomeno-physical form. Among the Sioux, the holy person demonstrates that he has this power or gift not through statement but through reputation. A holy man such as Fools Crow or Bill Eagle Feather never said, "I will do a *Yuwipi* Ceremony and Big Road or Gray Weasel will appear." Rather, he would simply state that a *Yuwipi* Ceremony was to take place and that he would try to help you.

Yuwipi means "they bind him" or "they tie him up." The holy man has his hands tied behind his back. Then a blanket, a special blanket with designs, is draped over the holy man and he is tied again. Both Chief Eagle Feather and Chief Fools Crow had an eagle feather sewn to the top of their ceremonial blankets in a way that it was positioned at the center of their head when they were standing. On the outside of the blanket, the holy man is tied seven times. The rope is wrapped and tied around the *Yuwipi* conductor, beginning at the neck with a noose and ending at the ankles. The conductor lies face down within a rectangular area set off by 405 tobacco offerings strung together. The lights are turned out, or blown out if kerosene lamps are used, and a calling song is sung. Soon, if there are no detractors present, the spirit helpers enter with a flourish that is startling to new initiates. To Lakota traditionals, it makes them proud and contented to be reassured that their spiritual way is indeed powerful.

It is important to realize that deep spiritual knowledge regarding ceremony is best learned from active participation.

> Once a person enters into the realm of the spirits, things tend to penetrate one another, and it is often inappropriate or impossible to make standard material distinctions. . . .
>
> In the Lakota prayer meeting there are many spirits, *taku wakan kin* [the mysterious thing], but yet there is only one Great Spirit, *Wakantanka*. The spirits addressed are many, yet all prayers are addressed to one Grandfather. As a person enters into Lakota spirit ceremonies, one must take upon himself the Lakota religious world view, in which the spiritual mystery of the "One and the many" is vibrantly alive and dynamicly [sic] present. Their world view is very holistic.[1]

Father Stoltzman, who has served many years on Sioux reservations as a missionary and educator, goes on to say that Sioux people are not analysts looking for the specific cause of a noise or spark that occurs at times in some ceremonies, in particular a *Yuwipi* Ceremony; rather, the Lakota participants see themselves as relatives looking for a cure or answer to their prayers.

> They have a holistic view which brings together everything material and non-material, ordinary and *wakan* to work toward a particular beneficial result. A medicine man in his ceremonies is judged *wakan* primarily by the surprising and beneficial results and actions toward the relatives. "By their fruits you shall know them." In many ways, the faith-filled Lakota is quite "indifferent" to the different physical phenomena that take place in a ceremony. If it ultimately accomplishes the healing or the goal desired, this is wonderful, mysterious, and *wakan*.[2]

I called Father Bill to discuss his writings, and as I did so a bald eagle with the morning sunlight illuminating its white tail flew by over the Mississippi River toward his church. That was a good sign from the natural world and Father Bill sounded pleased when I told him so.

Father Stoltzman describes the beginning of a *Yuwipi* Spirit-calling Ceremony:

After the spirit-calling songs have been sung, the spirits come in, usually with a flurry of sounds, rattles, and sparks. The medicine man tells the people which of his spirit friends or other spirits are there. Then the round of communal prayers begins. . . .

In the course of the meeting [ceremony], a person may be touched by a rattle, a paw, or a hand. One should not be surprised or afraid. The Indians call this a "healing." It is from "something spiritual" who is caring for that person, giving that person a blessing. One responds by saying, *"Pila-maya, Tunkasila"* (Thank you, Grandfather).[3]

You may be surprised that I am so friendly with a former missionary after all that I have said in previous chapters. Because of the horrendous oppression of the past I am a warrior and have to fight for what I believe in, but I cannot be a narrow-minded, overzealous one. Here is a man who obviously respects the Natural Way in his writings. He is not trying to harm our native spirituality. There is no way that I would attempt to take away the spiritual path that he has chosen. I will respect such a man and hope that I can be his friend.

According to Stephen E. Feraca,

Certain elements among the Teton have often tried to expose the *yuwipi* men as frauds, usually without success. Horn Chips, now dead, can be considered one of those *yuwipi* men who has greatly added to the cult's popularity. For one thing his spirits spoke in many voices, and all his prophecies are said to have been fulfilled. Some years ago, by order of the Agency Superintendent, who was in charge of Pine Ridge Reservation, Horn Chip's [sic] meeting was held in a lighted room. Indian police were present and the police chief himself carefully tied and wrapped the *yuwipi* man. Lights flashed on the ceiling. Horn Chips was untied when the flashing ceased. It is understandable that many Teton refer to him as the "real *yuwipi* man."[4]

Teton is a term used for the westernmost Sioux; it includes the Oglala tribe along with the Hunkpapa and Sichangu tribes and other bands. To observers, the *Yuwipi* experience is extraordinary and sensational. That some holy people have attained such power to reach into the spirit world is not amazing to me, however, for it is obvious that they have found their truth to a very high degree and have earned their power by preparing themselves through related ceremonies such as Sweat Lodge and isolated quests on mountaintops. In ceremony, spirit helpers come forth and cause some rather startling phenomena, possibly to bolster the confidence and respect of the more dubious participants and also to keep a keen interest going among those attending the ceremony. I was Chief Eagle Feather's helper for a crowded *Yuwipi* Ceremony held in the basement of an abandoned church. Many Hunkpapas attended this lengthy ceremony. The active spirit participation kept the crowd attentive.

We shall look at a *Yuwipi* Ceremony held on the Pine Ridge Reservation during the time of the Vietnam War.

FOOLS CROW'S *YUWIPI*

A gray Marine fighter bomber hung motionless in the clear Vietnamese sky. The high tail of the Phantom was decorated with a silver eagle above a red, white, and blue ribbon. In the forward cockpit the pilot's helmet was stenciled with a warbonnet of dull, camouflaged feathers. As the craft flew north the pilot keyed a radio switch on the throttle handle. "Ground Shark, Ground Shark, Yankee Echo Eight approaching target."

"Yankee Echo Eight. Hold ten miles. Report feet wet at angels' twenty," Da Nang control instructed.

The Phantom turned toward the South China Sea. When the coastline passed below, the pilot banked the aircraft before engaging the automatic pilot button. The plane dipped slightly, correcting its altitude as it circled off the coast. "Yankee Echo Eight. Feet wet. Holding at angels' twenty," the pilot reported, circling at twenty thousand feet. He checked his gauges and, through the intercom, told the radar officer in the rear seat to record a fuel estimate.

Alone with his thoughts for the moment, the pilot rested his head against the ejection seat. He had flown over fifty missions, and all that had been foretold in the *Yuwipi* Ceremony held at Fools Crow's cabin had come true. Spirit people had entered, predicting he would see the enemy many times. "Over a hundred times," they had emphasized. "Bullets will bounce from your airplane," they said.

He pictured Fools Crow waiting at the horse gate when members of his family arrived for the *Yuwipi*. He remembered that his grandmother's last request had been that he attend a *Yuwipi* Ceremony before leaving for war. In the centuries-old calling, Fools Crow would beseech the spirit people for protection. His mother had been with them that clear summer night as they drove from West River to the holy man's reservation home. His grandmother's prediction that he wouldn't come back if he failed to attend a *Yuwipi* had been enough to dispel the black-magic aura drummed into his mother by the missionaries. He wished his father and grandmother were alive to attend with them.

The tall, trim man held them for a few moments with that mysterious look, the penetrating stare of a hawk or eagle. Fools Crow was like a badlands hawk or an eagle—regal, keen, observant—alone and aloof within his own vast spaciousness, oblivious to the encroaching, crowded world.

Fools Crow spoke from the gate when they stepped from the car. "What took you so long? You should have been here earlier."

"We're sorry, Grandpa," my sister Mildred answered. "We stopped to get groceries." Grandpa is a respectful form of address for Sioux holy men.

Fools Crow had no telephone, so how did he know we were coming to see him, I wondered, as the holy man led us into his mud-chinked cabin. Kate Fools Crow stood by the wood-burning stove and welcomed us with her warm smile. Speaking in the rich Sioux language, my relatives visited and laughed together as the blue enameled coffeepot was filled, meat was cut and put in boiling water, dried *wojapi* (berry cakes) were set in a pan of water, and fry-bread preparations were made. I strained my ears trying to follow and envied my friend Sonny Larive, who was my age and held his own in the conversation.

I had been too long in the white man's world flying the big military jet machines to remember well the language that was spoken fluently by my Sioux parents. But Fools Crow did not hold my inability against me. I was an Oglala warrior in his eyes. He had seen me powwow dancing in the evenings and then watching fervently in the early morning hours of the annual Sun Dance. I had been one of the few young spectators when Bill Eagle Feather brought the piercing back into the ceremony. Bill is given credit for bringing it back out into the open, and Fools Crow was the Sun Dance chief who pierced him. There had been earlier Sun Dances, but they were held secretly out in the badlands for fear of reprisals from the government authorities and the missionaries who were in league with them. Both adversaries of our culture were very powerful in those times. Maybe Fools Crow read my future; for whatever reason, he was going to hold a ceremony to protect me for combat in a land faraway.

He had spread the word through the moccasin grapevine: I was to come down for a ceremony. And despite the meddling of the priests who dominated my mother and at times controlled my sister, when it was time for the youngest in the family to go off to war, they did as the powerful holy man had recommended. My mother had been in this position before. We were a typical Sioux family, and five of my brothers, her sons, saw combat. They all volunteered for the military in time of war and were not about to turn down the chance to serve in the frontline outfits.

I had volunteered for my combat tour although I had been accepted for law school at the university in my home state. With eight years of service, I had more than fulfilled my military requirement and did not have to go to Vietnam. But I couldn't think of spending my remaining years having to put up with my combat-experienced brothers. At that time, too, the Marines were short of trained pilots, especially fighter pilots. The Marine Corps had been good to me, allowing me to rise in rank and giving me responsibility. My country, like every human being I have met, wasn't perfect, but it gave me more freedom and opportunities than all the others. I owed a loyalty to both the Marine Corps and what my country stood for in the conflict in which we were involved. A lot of two-leggeds in this world have fled from what we fought against (totalitarian communism), and I do not see much freedom where it still remains, even though at the time of this writing most of the rest of the world has rejected and thrown off that yoke. Besides, my Sioux blood and my lineage wouldn't let me back out and pass up such an opportunity. As I have said in many ways, at times it seems that some Indian people have different minds; maybe there is an unbroken blueprint within the chromosomes that passes from generation to generation. The old Sioux warriors wouldn't think of passing up a good fight. I even had to go to the dean of the law school for his permission to be accepted for the following year so that I could do my combat tour. Ironically, at that time, most of the affluent within the dominant race would have bailed out had they been in my situation. The selection of Vice President Quayle was a poor example in my eyes. In the old Sioux tribes, he would never have been allowed to lead.

I do not want to be misinterpreted, however. I am proud that I fought against communism, but I certainly do not condone the puppet regimes that have been installed throughout the world to do the bidding of capitalist corporations. I am against the unjust interference that has been practiced against many of the South and Central American countries, especially the example set by years of military aid to Somoza, Noriega, Pinochet, and other dictators. What a shameful history we have in regard to these nations. We should find a leader with the courage and conviction to right these wrongs and truly bring to these nations the democracy of which we have long deprived them. We owe it to them for the centuries of neglect toward this hemisphere.

The laughter flowed within Fools Crow's cabin. Sonny Larive, my friend, also attended that dark night on the edge of the desolate badlands near a tiny town called Kyle. Mildred, my mother, Sonny Larive's grandparents, and Fools Crow's son-in-law, Amos Lone Hill, exchanged conversation in the "L" dialect of the Lakota Sioux. Blacktop, a bashful eight-year-old, sat fiddling with the damper on the potbellied stove near the west wall.

When Fools Crow went to the closet for his medicine bundle, it was a signal for the women to push back the furniture and draw the curtains. Sonny helped prepare for the tying ritual that would precede the *Yuwipi,* while Mildred unrolled a long string of tiny cloth tobacco offerings. The four directions were represented by red, yellow, black, and white flags placed in earth-filled bowls to form a square in the middle of the cabin. Mildred wrapped a string of tobacco offerings around the bowls, marking the rectangular limits of the spirit area. Sage was passed out to all participants, who placed some in their hair and over one ear.

The holy man entered the square and raised his peace pipe to offer an opening prayer. He then prepared an earthen altar by the stove and placed two leather rattles on the floor. Finally, he stood ready to be bound. Sonny bound his arms and hands behind his back with a strong cord and draped a blanket over the Oglala's head. An eagle feather hung from the top of the blanket that covered the holy man to his ankles.

Next, Sonny wrapped Fools Crow with a rawhide rope, beginning with a noose around his neck and then winding it six times around his body down to the ankles, representing the seven sacred ceremonies. While the holy man was lowered, face down, to the floor, Mildred took the place of honor with the peace pipe, behind the dirt altar, with her back to the stove. The kerosene lamp was extinguished.

Amos tapped a drum and sang a centuries-old call to the ancestors of the Sioux, the spirit beings. They came quickly, rattling the stove pipe and swishing the rattles through the room, as if they had been close by, waiting for the call.

We all prayed for answers. Would I return from the war? Would I be a prisoner? Would I be maimed? Fools Crow knew the spirits would tell the assembled people the answers and, if I prayed humbly and made a promise to give something back in exchange for my life, they would try to protect me. Tiny blue lights entered through the stove door behind Mildred while all of us prayed. They circled the room, flickered and danced with the heartbeat of the drum, ascended to the ceiling, circled the participants, and then, as the song ended, disappeared back through the stove door behind the pipe holder. The buckskin rattles that had accompanied Amos Lone Hill's song fell to the floor, silent.

Fools Crow's muffled voice spoke out in the darkness, telling how a stone had struck the sacred tree at the summer Sun Dance, while an airplane flew overhead. The stone bore the image of an eagle. He told of Eagle Feather's Sun Dance vision. "He saw the airplane land in a far-off place, and a warrior pilot walked away without looking back. The warrior walked toward the tree and stood with a boy. The stone was brought to the Sun Dance lodge. I took the stone from Eagle Feather and put it in my medicine bundle. It remained in the bundle only a short while and then it was gone." The group waited while the holy man took several breaths. He instructed Amos to strike up the calling song. The special song would bring forth a spirit helper.

Amos sang out. The drumbeat stirred the rattles and once again they flew around the room. The blue lights gave me a sense of pride—pride in my culture and its ability to bring forth such communication. In time I would understand more, but on that occasion I was happy with what I was experiencing and with my mother sitting next to me. I was very thankful that I had been born an Oglala.

A ghostly voice spoke from the center of the room. It spoke in Sioux to Fools Crow and the holy man answered back. They carried on a conversation.

"The stone has returned and is now among us here. Eagle Boy, you must pray hard so it will remain." Fools Crow spoke out in Lakota. I recognized my name, *Wanblee Hoksila (Hokeshila),* in the holy man's words. (After I returned from war, my name was changed to Eagle Man.)

My dominant mother jabbed me hard with her elbow. Tender and so loving when I was a small child, she treated me like a weaned warrior in later years. "Big Road is here. He is speaking to Fools Crow. Tell them you will do something so that the stone will help protect you," she commanded harshly.

I answered quickly, "Grandfather, ask the stone to stay with us. Tell the spirit people that I offer myself for the Sun Dance. I will live for the Power of the Hoop."

A shrill tremolo pierced the darkness, followed by a chorus of "*hau*'s." The tremolo cry, *"Le le le le lah. Le le le le lah,"* came from the women to honor a warrior who would go off to battle. It would be repeated when the warrior returned, or at his grave.

Then Fools Crow spoke with uncharacteristic volume and excitement, "The eagle on the stone is for a warrior who will fly with the winged people. The young man in Eagle Feather's vision is one of us. Eagle Boy, you shall take this stone and wear it as your *wotai.* When you are across the ocean, you shall carry it. As long as you wear it faithfully, the bullets will bounce from your airplane. You shall see the enemy many times. You shall not fear battle and shall laugh at danger." My mother often repeated this interpretation to me and to her friends who respected traditionalism.

After a long pause the holy man spoke more cautiously, "There is no guarantee, however, that you shall return and become a new warrior to stand beneath the Sun Dance tree with Blacktop, my adopted grandson. Your protection will depend upon your respect and truth for this Way."

Fools Crow paused and coughed, weighing what he would reveal. The rattles buzzed. He coughed again, stilling the rattles. "*Chan Wiwanyag Wachipi* [the Sun Dance tree]," he said. Later, after several Sun Dances, Bill Eagle Feather explained to me. My circle had begun. In the old days it could cost the sacrifice of a warrior or several warriors who would pledge to live for the Spiritual Hoop, as I had just done. The trials would be difficult, but the reward would be whatever the warrior wished, if he succeeded. A Sun Dance is similar. The trial is difficult but a sun dancer usually gets his wish if he succeeds. If I left my trail tomorrow, I would have to be thankful for having received more adventures than a dozen men of my time.

The rattles clashed, each shaking a different rhythm, their discord breaking the stillness. "*Ohuze Wicasta* [Mystic Warrior], *Changu heh.*" Fools Crow began his statement and drew deep gasps from beneath his blanket. The paired rattles stirred again, this time in unison. "A warrior of the eagle hoop, a warrior of the four-colored circle . . . a Mystic Warrior. You will stand beneath the tree with a small boy. *Changu* is my adopted grandson, here. You two will stand off from the tree." Bill told me at a later time what Fools Crow spoke from beneath the blanket. "If you make it to the Sun Dance, you will fulfill part of your mission. You will fight the one who would destroy our way. Remember to respect this gift or you will be punished. *Ho hetch etu aloh.*" I was to respect the *wotai* and what the ceremony stood for.

A concluding song was sung—the untying song. The kerosene lamp was lit. Fools Crow was sitting up untied. His blanket was neatly draped over the stove. The tying rope was wrapped in a tight ball. The rattles, without handles, rested beside the dirt altar in front of Mildred. No one, including Fools Crow, had moved during the untying song.

My *wotai* was on the dirt altar resting on a buckskin leather pouch. It was a smooth, olive-drab-colored stone about the size of a fifty-cent piece and about three times thicker. It bore but one symbol buried deep within its military-colored grain. It imaged the symbol of an eagle. (Note: This was my first *wotai* and obviously was for protection in combat. A few years later, I received a second *wotai* and the first *wotai* disappeared soon thereafter, as Chief Eagle Feather had predicted it would.)

This *Yuwipi* Ceremony illustrates how advanced spiritual communication can become. The Rainbow Tribe people are at their beginning, and how much they will evolve depends on the depth of the truths that they will cultivate. The Great Mystery is obviously Truth. How close a people can come to the Creator's harmony will decide the reach of the power within a ceremony. Fools Crow was an extremely truthful being.

I look back at Vietnam and realize how fortunate I was to come from a culture that could prepare me for war. The *Yuwipi* Ceremony gave me great confidence while I was engaged over a hundred times in combat. I also had a culture that I could return to, one that respected a warrior's role in combat.

My combat *wotai* helped the spirit world protect me in Vietnam. At the very least, it gave me a tremendous psychological advantage (if I were to attempt to explain it in white man's terms). But it went far beyond this academic description.

What relationship does the war in Vietnam have to the Rainbow Tribe? Plenty. It begins with knowledge. We must learn from our mistakes there and apply this knowledge to the global environmental war we are involved in now. This war will last for some time to come, and its impact will be much longer lasting than the impact of Desert Storm. There are many beneficial lessons to be learned and applied to the environmental war we are now facing. Most of the Rainbow Tribe people I know do not have the egotism that hampers an understanding of what can be gained at times by actually losing. They have pointed this viewpoint out to me many times, and when I apply this philosophy to what happened in Vietnam, I can understand more fully what they have been saying.

Recent events in Eastern Europe and the disintegration of the Soviet Communist empire need no explanation. What I fought against in Vietnam, millions have fled from in search of freedoms that past regimes would not offer. Millions would flee from or change the dictatorships on both sides involved in Desert Storm if they had more knowledge.

My Rainbow friends were right. In defeat we can still learn valuable lessons. The Vietnam war, unlike Desert Storm, we could afford to lose. The aftereffects of Desert Storm still must run their course, but if we lose the environmental war, we perish. Fools Crow has departed now. We could use his valuable communication with the spirit world to help us with the environmental war. Fortunately, there are still a few communicative holy persons who contact the spirit world through the power of the *Yuwipi* Ceremony. Rainbows are progressing as well into the higher realms of spiritual communication. Whether they will ever achieve the high degree of communication exhibited by the Sioux holy men, only time can tell. It must be remembered that these ceremonies have been tempered and tested by generations, and that fact alone may mean that it will be a very long time, *if ever,* before certain Rainbows can even presume to obtain that power. I can only hope that some of the traditionals will carry on this power, and it does appear that they are maintaining it, especially among the Oglala and the Sichangu.

Some ceremony that is unplanned can also bring forth spirit appearances. Let us look at an experience that a friend and I had at the end of a trip to see the daughter of John Neihardt. Since it was such an uncommon experience on my part, I asked my fellow traveler to relate what took place to allow another's viewpoint and observation.

As the time drew near for me to submit my manuscript for *Mother Earth Spirituality* to the publisher, I knew I would have to make a trip to Nebraska to see the daughter of John Neihardt, the author of *Black Elk Speaks.* Hilda Neihardt is her father's literary executor and I needed to secure releases from her for quotes I had used from *Black Elk Speaks.* I asked my friend Molly, who had contributed a considerable amount of proofreading for the book, to come along. I felt that the trip would be memorable and wanted another person's observations, especially Molly's, whose advanced age had in no way affected her discernment and astuteness.

PTA (PEYTA) WIGMUNKE, FLAMING RAINBOW

Molly Poets, Raven Horse

Truthfully, being in my seventies and having recently had a bout with a cold, I didn't have a lot of spare energy to be taking a trip, but when I was invited I couldn't let the chance go by as long as it represented an opportunity to learn something more of Indian culture, and Black Elk in particular.

We left from Ed's house on a moderately cold day. It was late in the afternoon before Ed finished some last-minute work, and when we went out to the car, there was Rex, Ed's aging and well-loved pheasant dog, firmly attached to the back seat, panting gleefully, eager for the wheels to start turning. The poor four-legged creature gave new meaning to the expression *hangdog* when he had to return to the house.

We drove until quite late that night. Since the countryside was mostly prairie, and snow-covered, there wasn't much to look at along the way, so the conversation drifted to some ideas for books that Ed was thinking about writing. One in particular I thought was highly loaded with possibilities; I was impressed anew with the range and scope of his imagination, even though I'd had lots of opportunities to see it at work. Three plots were described and I could see them all developing into books I would really enjoy reading. It was a very entertaining means to pass the time.

We stopped and got a good night's rest, and the next morning we dressed up to meet Hilda Neihardt. About mid-morning we arrived at her house in Bancroft, Nebraska, where she cordially greeted us. This house originally was her grandmother's; it was the house in which John Neihardt had lived for a number of years and where many of his works were written. It is owned now by Hilda and furnished with antiques of the period. Ed's manuscript had been mailed to her earlier and she seemed very interested in what he was doing, even though quite reluctant to do anything that would detract from the honor due her father, John Neihardt, and Black Elk. She is within my age range and is without doubt the most fiercely loyal to, and the most respectful toward, Indian tradition and people, of any person I have met, red or white.

The remainder of the morning was spent by Ed and Hilda with many questions as to his goals and purpose in writing his books. I sensed a special appreciation from her for Ed's Oglala ancestry and the fact that now, finally, a traditional Sioux who firmly believed in Black Elk's vision was writing and being published. In the course of their learning about each other, many interesting tidbits were dropped and of course I was "all ears." She spoke not just of her life, but recounted how her family had lived on the reservation for two summers while her father was gathering the material for *Black Elk Speaks*. It seems that some of the members of the two families became lifelong friends.

After lunch we walked from her house to the Neihardt Museum nearby. On the way we visited the small cabin that Neihardt had used as his studio, and where *Black Elk Speaks* as well as his other work was written.

One of the first things called to our attention after meeting museum personnel was a magnificent bust of John Neihardt done by his wife, who was a student of Rodin in Paris at the time they met. After a correspondence courtship, she left Paris and they were married. Unfortunately, she never captured the images of any of the Indians, to my knowledge, but there must have been a number of strong faces to choose from at that time on the reservation. Perhaps Indian beliefs and their nonconceptualization by the

dominant religion of the white man in those times had some bear-
ing on the fact that she didn't.

We spent some time looking at articles that had been Black
Elk's, including his drum and his pipe. The sense of loss was overwhelming to me, not because one man was gone—that is inevitable—but because a tradition so valuable to today's world had
been so systematically wiped out. Thanks to Great Spirit, enough
was salvaged to rekindle the natural flame that seems to be spreading so advantageously to us all.

Leaving the museum we walked back to Hilda's home and on
the way Ed found two hawk feathers, which were saved. Bancroft
is but a small agricultural town near the northeast corner of
Nebraska, seventy miles north of Omaha, and it is conceivable that
a hawk or an owl could spend an evening or two unnoticed in the
tall elms and cottonwoods that allow a vantage point to the nearby
fields and meadows. Maybe that is how the two feathers could
have been placed there, or maybe the spirit world left them for
acknowledgment. Who knows?

Hilda insisted on taking us out to dinner. Shortly before we left,
a friend of hers stopped in, so she accompanied us. We had a
remarkably good dinner considering the size of the town, and the
caliber of most small-town restaurants.

Since Hilda and her friend both had some health problems, it
was decided to include a holistic healing in the ceremony Ed
planned for the evening. We prepared ourselves as Ed incensed the
perimeter with smoking sage and sweetgrass. It was wintertime
and darkness came early. When the lights were turned down and
as the pipe ceremony began, Hilda exclaimed, "Oh! there's someone here." She shrieked shrilly, "They are here!" Her last exclama-
tion startled Ed, who was in the center of the room with the peace
pipe. He thought Hilda was afraid and asked her if she wanted the
lights turned on. "No, no," she retorted, "absolutely not." And a little later, "The room is full of people," and indeed it was. Their presence was almost palpable and very real. Then the holistic-healing
beseechment was done for Hilda. After that, work was done for
her friend, and Hilda drummed as she said Black Elk did—with a
very rapid, rather soft, even beat, not really like any other Indian
drumming I've heard. The beseechment was an appealing to the
six powers of Black Elk's vision under the one Great Mystery, with
a special appeal to the medicine power of the south power, *Itokaga*

ouye, as it is this power that is attributed to the growth of the plants that are utilized for most of the world's medicines.

At that time my eyes were drawn to the right, and close by me stood a tall Indian man in a long wraparound robe. He just stood there, watching and impassive. Not quite believing my eyes I looked away, and off to my left, a few feet, stood another robed figure. The room was in darkness so the faces were indistinct, but I looked back and forth several times to be sure I was actually seeing them. Who these figures were was a matter of speculation to us, and no doubt each of us had his or her own opinion. The figures themselves gave no clue as to approval or disapproval but the feeling was good, and the mere fact of their presence indicated to me that what Ed was doing was approved. An unmistakable feeling of power pervaded the room, and as the ceremony ended it was hard to reclaim the present reality as I felt emotionally drained, yet renewed.

Hilda had invited us earlier in the day to spend the night, and after her friend left we all retired. I had a guest bedroom next to the living room. Ed told me that he had quite a vivid experience soon after we bedded down. Hilda had insisted that he sleep in her bed and she slept on the couch in the living room. The bed was an old four-poster antique that would make collectors drool. I wonder if it could have been her father's at one time and I should have asked. As long as I have known Ed, I have observed that he is quite reluctant to do certain ceremonies unless it is the right time and for a specific need. He is also careful not to exaggerate in the realm of phenomena. His stone came to him in a special way and he had a particularly strong vision in one Sun Dance. This, he flatly states, he cannot lie about or downplay, but he has always been careful to avoid overstatement in this area. On this night, he said that just before he fell asleep, or possibly as he fell asleep, the clear shaft of a rainbow appeared at the foot of his bed for a few moments. He stated that it was but a small portion and not an entire arc of a rainbow, but the colors were very vivid in the dark room. He said he was wide awake as he stared at it, and if he had been dreaming it certainly left him wide awake. Could this have been the spirit of Flaming Rainbow?

Awakening the next morning rested and refreshed, and after a good breakfast prepared by our gracious hostess, we set out for the museum grounds to do a second ceremony.

Close by the Neihardt Center is a circle that represents the hoop of the world, with paths leading from each of the four directions to a tree. This symbol, the centering tree of life that is spoken of as flowering with singing birds, is of course demonstrative of Black Elk's vision. Ed prepared for the ceremony. Hilda was again drummer, and I took pictures as the four directions were invoked, accompanied by Ed's eagle bone whistle. I understood that it was the first time a Native American had done ceremony there, and, as part of the ritual, a wooden cup that had been made by Black Elk and presented to John Neihardt was used to water the tree. The cup was so old and cracked that it had to be refilled several times, for it leaked its water rather quickly. Light snow swirled down and carpeted the pathways of the large sacred hoop symbol centered at its hub with a real tree representing the tree of life. This powerful, moving edifice is tucked away, almost hidden in this tiny Nebraska town, and I would presume that most of the town's inhabitants have never and will never read *Black Elk Speaks*.

A significant number of the rest of the world has read the epic, however, and will continue to consume its many reprintings. Life is that way. A powerful word, an extremely meaningful recording will go on, sweeping around those who are most immediate and yet do not have the ears to hear. Reliable sources estimate that over one million copies of the book have been sold, and it is being reprinted in foreign languages, even Japanese. Snowbirds hopped about during the very moving ceremony. I watched while two beings who had been in close contact with the mystical Oglalas carried out their beseechment and acknowledgment. It was so quiet and peaceful there, bringing home the fact that we don't hear our Mother Earth's cries; they are constantly blotted out by our airplanes, cars, air conditioners—all the things we think we can't do without.

A modern-day Oglala warrior who had experienced as much combat as many of his forebears of old and who had been close to the son of Black Elk, offered his pipe to the onlooking six powers of the world-reaching vision. The daughter of the courageous writer who would not alter the old prophet's powerful vision for the sake of appeasing the dominant and closed, two-legged powers of the time held a cup of water while the winter songbirds did their part and danced upon the tree. Her heart must have ached for her father whose book sat so long upon the dusty bookshelves of time. John Neihardt paid a heavy price for his truthfulness in a time of untruth, deceit and religious narrow-mindedness, bigotry and racial supremacy. Those days are not completely over with but they have diminished, and that gives me great hope. The previous afternoon, Hilda was distraught with a weak-willed, finger-to-the-wind, appeasing kind of writer who had just been published and had misrepresented somewhat, in her opinion, her father's works and the innate and obvious spiritual preference demonstrated by the old prophet Black Elk when he climbed to the top of Harney Peak with Neihardt to pray traditionally. Was it the spirits, the ghosts of these two men, who made their impression the previous evening?

This was a new day, however, a new red dawn. And a renewed appreciation for the works of Flaming Rainbow was in the wind as the birds gathered. New, yet reflective "talk making" was about to begin out of the bloodline of the people John Neihardt had so dutifully recorded. Amid feelings of fulfillment on both spiritual and mundane levels we voiced our thanks and said good-bye to a lovely lady who remembers Black Elk in a way that none of the rest of us can.

▼ ▼ ▼ ▼ ▼

10

HEALING WITH

CEREMONY AND MEDICINE

Ceremonial healing can take place in many ways and might begin when you least expect it. On my way to a national religion and ecology conference, I stopped to visit the Vietnam Memorial in Washington, D.C., and found myself involved with ceremony.

HEALING AT THE WALL

I was wearing a worn Marine Corps flight jacket and carrying a seabag. A POW/Missing in Action booth appeared in the distance between me and the memorial. I noticed that several men, obviously Vietnam veterans by their dress, were donating their time to the management of the booth. One wore an old army field jacket and the other's open shirt revealed a T-shirt that read "Vietnam Veteran and Proud of It." They spotted my jacket with its squadron and Phantom patches and greeted me warmly as I drew closer. I was no longer a stranger among the hundreds of other strangers who had been floating by on that spring day. After taking a sharp focus on my jacket's 100-missions patch, one of them asked where I had been stationed in Vietnam.

"Chu Lai," I replied as I relieved myself of my baggage. I asked if I could leave my seabag in the booth.

By this time they had read my name and rank on my flight jacket and replied, "Certainly, Captain. We'll watch your gear. Take your time. We'll be here when you come back." I was concerned for my belongings that were to be used at the religion and ecology conference. My drum and my pipe were in the bag and also my eagle bone whistle. I took out my eagle bone whistle and my buckskin pipe bag that contained my peace pipe. I placed these items in the travel case I had hanging from my shoulder. The men looked at the fringed pipe bag but did not comment. I thanked them for watching my seabag and walked toward the wall—where my past waited.

It is a compelling experience for a Vietnam veteran to take the walk before that long black wall. To me, the spirits of those who made the supreme sacrifice are ever present. If you have come back from Vietnam, one resounding aspect, like thunder on a lonely mountain, is the realization that you are here and alive when, but for the designs or the generosity of the abiding forces, your name could just as easily be on the wall. It is overwhelming, and few combat veterans, if any, have the ability to stop their welling tears, especially when they draw close to a familiar name.

A veteran approached at the beginning of the wall. He had just walked its long reach from the opposite end. His eyes were red. He gave me a brief glance and painfully looked away. We passed by in silence. It was now my turn to walk the long gauntlet.

A great deal of anguish and lament can be found at the Vietnam Memorial. Fortunately, I am one of those who returned to a tribe that honored its own. My tribal chairman, Enos Poor Bear, even had me carry into battle the American flag that had flown over our Sun Dance. I put it, folded, under my ejection seat when I flew a mission. When I sent it back to the reservation, Fools Crow, who was Sun Dance chief, had it flown again at the Sun Dance, and a recognition ceremony for those who served in Vietnam took place.

At the wall, I looked for several warrior acquaintances of the past. One was blasted out of the sky and another crashed at sea. A third barrel-rolled into the ocean on a return mission. Others disappeared on long, dark nights. There is Brook, and Richard—and Roger, drowned under the whirling blades of a rescue chopper. Oddly, as I walked away from Roger's name, there stood a woman on the walkway who looked almost exactly like his wife. She is from my generation. The woman has aged somewhat, but she is dressed like a pilot's wife and is still attractive and probably always will be. I watch for her reddened eyes to discover Roger's name but she glances by. She recognizes briefly the wings above my name patch on my flight jacket and walks on. Is it a ghost or an apparition? I ask myself. I look the other way, down toward the bronze statue of the three veterans who hold themselves with calm dismay against the capital's skyline. I turn and look for the woman, expecting her to have vanished, but she is still there and intently reading the wall.

Memories flood back. Despite the tolling of time, combat memories and the ones you were with, living and dead, never seem to fade.

The skies of flak and missiles come back and so do the black, lightning-streaked, rainy nights orbiting over the South China Sea. Waiting to streak inbound to strike and be struck at. For me, the prolonged waiting at the very edge of fire-strewn skies was more disturbing than the actuality of combat itself. I can see the plane captains as we started our engines, the frenzied bomb crews rushing to reload us when a Marine battalion was being attacked by a dauntless and efficient enemy fighting for a cause they believed was honorable.

The wall makes memories so strong, it even carries me back into the times that directed my destiny toward the fields of war. I can still remember the names of people in boot camp and my tent mates in Korea, back in my enlisted days, long before we even knew there was such a place as Vietnam.

I reached the opposite end of the wall and my eyes were red, no different from the veteran I had met at the end of his journey and the beginning of mine. I looked over at the statue of the three veterans and went in that direction. The hopeless stares of these figures in bronze made me think of a complaint I have heard on more than one occasion coming from a few Indian people. A Hispanic, a black, and a white are represented but the American Indian is missing. Despite our high volunteer ratio in combat units during times of war, we are not depicted. In my opinion, the Native American does not have to be represented in this particular statue. Indian veterans were honored by their tribes when they returned from war, and to me, this statue symbolizes a belated (although gracious) attempt to honor. If someone wants to erect a statue to the American Indian veterans, however, I will donate to it. We do have the highest volunteer rate for combat units. (This statement is based on a study conducted by Senator Inouye of Hawaii.)

I remember a touching scene when I was in law school and fly-ing helicopters part-time for the Marine Corps Reserves. I took a Reserve helicopter back to the Hunkpapa people and helped honor their dead. Since this was during the time that draft-exempt college students were demonstrating, my non-Indian copilot was amazed by the moving ceremony that took place far out on the Standing Rock Reservation. We circled to land and were met formally by a marching contingent of Sioux warriors who were members of the American Legion and the VFW. We changed quickly out of our sweaty flight suits into our dress uniforms in the belly of the heli-copter. A recruiting staff sergeant in dress blues was also with us. We were told to march at the head of the contingent into the gym-nasium. The assembled crowd cheered when we entered the build-ing. Warriors spoke and women tremoloed. I had to speak to the packed gymnasium. I told the excited crowd that it was an honor to return to a land of tribal people who appreciated the sacrifice of their warriors. I told them how they had salved my spirit with their honoring medicine and how this medicine was deeply appreciated by all the living who returned. My nervous copilot, surrounded by a cheering, tremoloing crowd of Indians, had to speak also. I advised him, when he asked, to tell them that he appreciated a peo-ple who know how to honor both their dead and the living who return from a war.

After the speeches, we went outside. Close to the gymnasium were several rows of young cottonwood poles that had been planted in the ground. At the top of each pole a pulley was attached and a cotton rope hung down. Young Indian men and women waited with an American flag for each pole. Many Sioux warriors from this Hunkpapa and Minnecoujou Sioux reservation had been killed. A drum rolled and we stood at attention, holding our salute for a long time before the flagpoles. A flag for each departed war-rior was raised on its own sapling staff, and the Sioux anthem and our national anthem were played. A singer chorused an ancient fight song while the Sioux women tremoloed. In the background, draped from two taller poles, the American flag and a tribal flag waved. It was an extremely moving scene cast upon the computer of life.

I left the Vietnam statue and went out toward the sidewalk behind the wall. I did not want to pass the wall again, although that would have been the shortest distance to my seabag. For some vet-erans, one trip past the wall is enough. I saw the lady I had seen earlier, sitting on a park bench, looking forlorn. Her eyes trailed to the emblazoned gold wings stamped on my faded leather name patch as I drew closer, and at that moment a wisp of a smile blossomed briefly. There was nothing that I could do but walk on. I imagined that I conveyed the appearance of a street person looking for a home, judging from the way I was dressed—jeans and my old flight jacket. The lack of a morning shave, the brief scattered stubble lightly sprinkled on my part-Caucasian face, didn't help my appearance either. On the street, in unfashionable traveling attire, I do not resemble a passive and gentle person. I surely would have scared her, had I spoken. No doubt, she would think that I had stopped to panhandle for a cup of coffee or some cheap wine.

I collected my bag and asked the veterans if my hotel was within walking distance. As I was returning my pipe bag to the seabag, one of the men asked me if I had done a ceremony at the wall. I shook my head. He asked how long I was intending to remain in the capital, adding that he had worked on several Indian reservations and had been a corpsman with the Marines. The other, who wore the army field jacket, chimed in, and we were soon engaged in reminiscences and discussions of places where we had served and fought during the war. Several other veterans stopped by. The conversations grew.

It was a welcome relief from having just been to the wall. Suddenly, in the midst of our conversation, the former corpsman asked, "Captain, you have a peace pipe, don't you?" When I nodded, he bluntly requested, "Captain, we come here all the time. Could you do a ceremony for us or some kind of honoring?" He turned toward the wall. "Could you take a bunch of us down to the wall and do something like I saw them do on the reservations?" He turned back to look me straight in the eye. "Name the time, Captain, while you're going to be here. We'll be waiting."

I didn't hesitate or fumble for the conference schedule in my shoulder bag. I was talking to combat warriors. *These men were never honored.* I spoke sharply. "I'll be back at ten o'clock. I'll be back at ten o'clock, the day after tomorrow morning." I hoisted my seabag to set off for the nearest intersection to hail a cab. After taking a few steps, I turned and told them to bring four solid-colored pieces of cloth—red, yellow, black, and white.

I can still see the light in their eyes. It is almost as vivid as my image of Bill Eagle Feather standing before the Sun Dance tree, tugging and pulling backward with his arms lifted to the skies. That was, and always will be, my most vivid, living memory. *We will finally be honored* was spoken out through their eyes.

I walked back past the park benches. There sat the woman. This time she threw me a startled look and turned her head away quickly as I drew closer. Maybe she thought I was some kind of bum who had inexplicably latched onto her. To her, I had probably come across the flight jacket in a surplus store and had added some patches to complete the impersonation. No doubt, to her, I was a fantasizing Walter Mitty, of whom there are many. I tucked my head against the ugly seabag like some kind of embarrassed, lumbering turtle and not a fighter pilot as I walked by.

My seabag is a disguise, however. This container can do what fancy suitcases cannot. It can hold a thick round drum or hide a valuable buckskin, a beaded warshirt, heavy beaded belts, a bone hairpipe choker—gifted items that money cannot buy. No one yet has attempted to walk away with this rugged canvas that also contains an eagle bone whistle and a personally carved peace pipe that took me many hours to make. (I do not subscribe to the myth that you have to be given a pipe and cannot make your own. The positive ceremonial activity I have been experiencing with this pipe reinforces my belief.)

In my travels I have yet to lose my seabag that looks to the world as if it contains nothing worth taking and also diminishes my appearance—if I were to worry about impressions.

I picked out a bench near the intersection to briefly rest my load and contemplate. I was in that war and I guess I am as qualified to express an opinion based on my observations as is George Will or other "intelligent" pundits who never saw combat duty over there. Being in the nation's capital, my thoughts turned to leadership. Leadership is desperately needed in this land because of all the past untruths. Truth is reflective of nature. We all know that nature has a perfect working order. The sun comes up every day and all things work in truthful harmony. Nature does not lie. Truth is an essential part of a genuine leadership, which has to reach far into the future in order to help those generations yet to come. Truth is not just for today or for the cheering moments when a cowardly politician full of half-truths has just been elected by his party.

The Vietnamese people under the leadership of Ho Chi Minh wanted their own country, first and foremost; that is why they fought so hard and so well. Their desire for nationhood ran deeper than any fear of Communist repression. The Vietnamese had thrown out the French, and they saw the Americans as another white foreign power. They were not far wrong in their estimation when you consider the way our CIA interfered and began to install pro-American puppets. America had a chance to negotiate with Ho Chi Minh long before the war started, but our foreign policy was so Eurocentric that we couldn't comprehend or respect the seeds of worldwide nationalism; we had forgotten the revolutionary aspirations of our own past. Our State Department and our presidents failed to understand the meaning of the four races of humankind. Had they been familiar with and respected the powerful philosophy behind *Mitakuye oyasin* (We are all related), that tragedy might never have happened. Instead, they saw Ho Chi Minh as some little brown, bearded upstart, and this ignorant, racist attitude cost the United States dearly. It cost our American boys who went to Vietnam, grievously. Manifest Destiny still lingered on, way beyond its time.

The Vietcong and the North Vietnamese soldiers were exceptionally brave and tenacious fighters. It wasn't just the stringent military discipline that made them stay in the ranks and follow orders. Besides the fierce drive for nationalism, they fought well because they experienced a higher degree of fairness than what they saw taking place in the ranks and the streets of their counterparts on the other side. During the war, they looked around the streets of Saigon and saw the sons of the wealthy in civilian clothes, driving motor scooters and convertibles. In Hanoi, even the sons of the political leaders were in the frontline units. This has a lot to do with your loyalty, determination, and staying power at the height of battle. The North Vietnamese were underfed, had a scarcity of ammunition at times, had no air cover, and had to make most of their movements at night, yet they still pressed on to success. Many times when they were wounded or suffering from disease they had to heal themselves in caves and underground tunnels, yet when they recovered they went fearlessly back into battle.

Compared to the North Vietnamese troops, with their combat zeal and staying power, the South Vietnamese troops were unreliable. American commanders could not depend on the South Vietnamese in combat operations. They relied more and more on air power, but this was ineffective in the dense jungle and for night fighting. We bombed a lot of trees but were not allowed to touch the military warehouses or the receiving docks of Haiphong harbor where our NATO allies were unloading their profitable war cargo. On the home front, politicians clamored for limited truces. Eight-day truces were granted to the North Vietnamese in order that military cargo might be unloaded and hauled openly down Highway 1 connecting the north to the south. We fighter bomber pilots could go aloft unarmed to observe, but bombing of the mile-long convoys loaded with fresh ammunition was not allowed. On the day following an eight-day truce, the ninth day, we suffered heavy casualties.

The Defense Department's refusal to invade North Vietnam has been offered by many historians as the simple logistical reason why America lost the war. The secretary of defense was Robert McNamara. Whenever we flew north we could look down and see a huge swath of land bulldozed out and defoliated. McNamara, who used to be called the Whiz Kid, actually had a so-called electronic fence built on the DMZ (demilitarized zone) that was to somehow smugly eavesdrop on North Vietnamese troop movements. Like the "impregnable" French Maginot Line put up against the Germans, it was easily outflanked. The North Vietnamese military commander General Giap simply went around it and later blew holes through it. We called the ineffective gouge across the earth below "McNamara's folly." The North Vietnamese must have laughed at it every day. The lesson to be learned is that you cannot have an egghead, who lacks common sense, run a war in which your soldiers are suffering needless casualties. Politicians can cause many casualties as well, especially when they or their offspring are not up on the front lines with the rest of the tribe's warriors.

Once the American troops realized that it was mostly the poor and the minorities in the frontline units and that the rich and the politicians had their own offspring tucked away for years in colleges and graduate schools, their spirit began to fade. Toward the end of the war there was a high incidence of fragging and disobeying orders by our troops in the field. (Fragging is the grenading of your own officers, usually at night and undetected.) This sign of revolt happened more than the U.S. armed forces will admit. This is odd. You would think that the military would want to make the politicians understand that unfair conditions spawn a reluctant, inefficient fighting force.

As far as I know, not one chief (a United States senator or congressperson) had his or her son in a frontline unit. I have no evidence of any of them being on active duty at the time of the war. Maybe a few will be discovered after this is written, but I am sure it will not be enough to invalidate my point. The Bush administration's vice president, Dan Quayle, hid out in the National Guard, and his selection for high office was extremely detrimental to the morale of Vietnam veterans. Recent presidential and vice presidential candidates either avoided the front lines or, if they did serve in World War II, had their offspring tucked away from active duty in later wars. This is not the mark of a true tribal leader. We should have new laws that leave no loopholes for the barons, the lords, the aristocracy. Actually, we should have a law that simply states: When war is declared, all able-bodied offspring of nationally elected officials will serve immediately in frontline units—Marine Corps, Army Infantry, Airborne, or Armored. If Congress can enact special banking privileges to cover its members' checking overdrafts, it can certainly pass this type of law. Desert Storm statistics show that the poor and the minorities were disproportionately exposed to combat in the Middle East, just as in Vietnam. I respect the way the desert war was fought, however. No truces allowed resupply, and we went on into Iraq to end the takeover of Kuwait. We ignored those Iraqis and Kurds who fought for freedom immediately after the main battle, however, and Hussein went free.

This country still has the best system available compared with other countries I've been in, and we seem to be making improvements as communication and knowledge progress. Introspection might be painful but it is a great aid to true progress. A nation is little different from a person. Introspection, whether for an individual or a nation, can be very revealing at times. A reader wrote to me, "If I don't admit my fears and imperfections, then they own me." It is obvious that introspection did occur regarding the needless dangers that Vietnam warriors were exposed to, because Desert Storm did not needlessly expose our warriors. Truth—it all gets back to the natural need for truth. It becomes more difficult to hide the truth in this age of communication.

There is always hope that fewer wars will come into being, at least on the scale of Desert Storm, Vietnam, and Korea. We now know of the millions who died in the "killing fields" of Cambodia and Laos. This country had to pretend that these mass murders were not happening because there was no more fight left in our troops, who were aware of the inequality at the draft centers.

Starvation and slaughter rampaged in Cambodia and Laos. The victors from the north began an era of repression that caused thousands of boat people to flee.

Ten o'clock came two days later. Four of us from the conference stepped from the cab. Two women and a black veteran, who had insisted on paying the cab fare, were with me as we walked to the ragtag group that waited.

The four colored cloths were placed on a table within the booth. I walked over to a stand of trees and plucked four branches for sticks. I tied a colored flag to each stick and passed them out to two warriors and to the two women. I took my pipe from its buckskin container, assembled it, and hung the eagle bone whistle around my neck. I was wearing my buckskin warshirt under my flight jacket and could feel the warmth of the muggy day that was beginning.

In my pocket was my *wotai.* I squeezed it hard and told it to give me the strength and the distance of a mountain lion. My blood sister, Jamie Sams, told me that a mountain lion is a lesson in the use of power in leadership.

Mountain lion stands on its convictions and leads you where your heart takes you. Others may choose to follow, and the lessons will multiply. You are never allowed to be human or vulnerable, if you call on the medicine of mountain lion. The pitfalls are many, but the rewards are great. You must always be aware of keeping peace. However, you can never make everyone happy unless you lie to yourself or others. Therefore the first responsibility to leadership is to tell the truth. Know it and live it, and your example will filter down to all within the pack.[1]

I had to be the mountain lion that day and show no human emotion. For added assurance, I called on my spirit guide, Charging Shield. His past consideration with me was a perfect reference for the moment. "You, oh stern, heartless-looking warrior, let me now be like you, without emotion. I will not cry. I will not draw forth tears. Although I was among these warriors and fought within the fire and steel of these modern battles, I shall be of that white man's steel, emotionless, while I do this ceremony."

I thought of the eagle who allows only one chick to live in times of overpopulation, the buffalo herd that turns out the aged leader, the fox that casts out the deformed kit, and related harsh decisions made by the old two-leggeds who chose to walk into the blizzards or onto the ice floe rather than prolong their burden and loneliness. "I shall be you, Charging Shield. You who would never bend or cry," I called out to the four winds. I took on the scowl of one of the major powers within my stone. "Fall in," I yelled out harshly.

We assembled in a military manner. I was already beginning to sweat in my buckskin shirt. One warrior was heavy with tattoos and was comfortably attired in a black Harley-Davidson T-shirt and brown patent-leather vest. The vest bore his Vietnam ribbons and a motorcycle pin on one side, and on the opposite side a POW/MIA patch was sewn. I admired him for putting his ribbons on his vest. He reminded me of another warrior who had his combat ribbons attached to a leather plate on a Harley motorcycle that I saw in a parking lot. I felt good that whole day even though I never met that warrior.

"Fall in." I subconsciously repeated the command that was decades old in my memory. The group assembled in two squads. "Forward march," I called out like a drill sergeant.

The motley group obeyed commands from long ago and marched forward to halt at the beginning of the long black wall. We milled about for a few moments, and the other people on the walkway started to step back and stare at us. Such an odd sight we must have appeared. A ragtag band of veterans sprinkled with two women and led by a sweating Indian wearing a buckskin, beaded shirt underneath a pilot's jacket and carrying a peace pipe.

After a brief pause I led the group forward on the walkway. I was halted by a call. "Captain, here's a name." I turned and watched the burly, toughened man in the motorcycle shirt step forward to reach out to the wall. Looks are deceiving. He caressed the stone of the wall lovingly and began to cry. I feverishly called out to the spirit of the mountain lion and Charging Shield. I was the leader and would not cry at that moment. I would do all that later, but not at that particular moment. "Resolve!" an inner voice yelled at me. "Resolve! You shall show no emotion and not even be human at times. You are not allowed to be two-legged or vulnerable. . . . You shall not be vulnerable." Somehow my eyes stayed dry and my voice did not crack. It was a miracle that my voice did not choke at that moment. Such a strong, powerful man, unafraid to exhibit his feelings. Unafraid to reach unabashedly into his past with love and concern. When you watch such a strong man cry, you have great respect and admiration but it is very difficult not to release and cry with him. How fortunate it was that I had had my cry two days before. I stared at the Harley-Davidson eagle until the man looked at me and said, "Captain, here it is. This is my cousin. My real cousin. We played together when we were kids." The eagle, my natural namesake, fortified my resolve at this complex moment. He said the words so emphatically and innocently, as if they were still children playing. "He's here, isn't he? Captain, he's here?" he pleaded.

I said calmly, "Yes he is, he is here." My spirit shuddered at the powers that he so desperately wanted me to have. I called on my rock-hard spirit guide. "Charging Shield," I demanded in a warrior's voice. "Assure this spirit. Assure him that his cousin will be with him or I will cast you and my stone into the Potomac." I looked at the crying warrior squarely, unable to believe that I had to become a mountain lion. I took the stone from my pocket and walked toward him. I caressed it slowly across the name on the wall. Each letter I touched with meaning. I looked at him directly, fighting back the tears that wanted to well up when I saw the river flow from his eyes. "Mountain lion, Charging Shield, . . . blizzards, . . . fox," my words came out disjointedly as I fought to keep my leadership. The warrior began to sob when I took the stone from the wall and touched it across his shoulder blades. Such a strong warrior he was. He reminded me of my vigorous and dynamic Vietnam friend Jim O. from Ohio. "My friend," I said, "your cousin is now sitting upon you. Now let us proceed."

Within a few paces, another name was called out and the procession stopped again. "Captain, we have another comrade who must be recognized." The corpsman came forward and cried out the name of a companion. I took my *wotai* stone and did the same as I had done for the Harley-Davidson warrior. The corpsman cried and this time it was easier for me not to cry. We went on, with each veteran in turn stopping the procession. Each time, I asked the spirit of the warrior to come into my *wotai* stone in order to do ceremony at the end of the wall. As we proceeded, the people on the walkway stood back with reverence and respected the dignity of our meaning. It was all too powerful and real for anyone not to understand the depth of what we were doing. When we reached the end of the wall, we made our way through a group of high school students and marched toward the three figures cast in combat uniforms and bearing the arms and equipment of the Vietnam warrior.

We stopped before the statues that seemed now to be alive. I placed each person who carried a colored cloth in the position of Black Elk's colors—red facing east, yellow facing south, black facing west, and white facing north—and afterwards I gave a brief talk. Strangely, the high school students assembled and looked on with intense interest. Several black people, what looked like a Hmong couple, and whites from various walks of life gathered quietly. I offered my peace pipe to the four directions, down to Mother Earth, up to Father Sky, and lastly to Great Spirit. I cradled my pipe back into my arms and said:

> We are gathered here today as warriors, warriors who fought in a war that many of us did not fully understand. We fought in a time when politicians' sons were not in the front lines with us. Neither were the corporate heads nor their sons, or the chiefs and the sons of the chiefs of the many bands and groups that run this land. Some of us volunteered, some of us were drafted, but none of us came from the leadership of this country—political, religious, or economic leadership—and yet we were the only ones to go forth into battle. This long black wall is testimony to those who have gone on into the spirit world because of this battle far away in a foreign land. These surviving warriors who stand here are not of Native American ways and were not honored when we returned from this war, and that absence has been a severe handicap and hurt for us who have lived.

I stopped and took out my stone. "Within this stone," I began, "lies the spirits of those who have gone beyond and whose names are inscribed upon the wall. We have just taken them from the wall." I waved my *wotai* in a semicircle and called out in the direction of the wall, "Oh, you warriors who have gone on, help us here in this land where you once were. Become spirit guides and descend upon the shoulders of your comrades to guide them in the wisdom and knowledge that you have gleaned from your new realm."

I brought my *wotai* down and waved it over the assembled warriors, then walked among them touching the rainbow-rimmed agate to each man's shoulder. Returning to my position between the warriors and the statue, I continued: "Long ago, in the old days of leadership, and I believe a much more prudent leadership, the chiefs and their sons were the first in battle. This was a great detriment to foolish war. It is a lesson to be learned from the just people who are the ancestors of the land. When warriors went forth for the tribe and came back, or did not come back, they were honored—so that the people's way would live. Let all who are here today, let us honor these warriors who stand before us."

I placed my stone in my pocket and handed my peace pipe to one of the women before speaking to the figures in bronze. "We do not have time to lament, however. For the world has fallen into serious trouble from overheating, overpopulation, and pollution. In time, many millions of world citizens can be imperiled, and eventually, ultimately, this earth could become a black shell of life-lessness. Therefore, it is a new war that warriors must embark upon." At this point I turned back to face the assembled group and waved my hand at the wall. "The spirit warriors who surround this wall are no doubt aware of our planet's situation and no doubt would like to see those who are living channel their energies toward a new beginning. I call on you veterans to remain warriors, but to become new warriors, warriors for Mother Earth. I call on the spirits we have taken from the wall and placed upon the shoulders of these new warriors for Mother Earth to lead them toward a new environmental awareness. Take your past lament, your bereavement, and channel this energy toward fighting for Mother Earth, and let your spirit guide help you. *Ho.*"

The woman who carried the red flag spoke after she had subdued her tears. "Please forgive me. I was on the other side." She looked at the red flag of knowledge and almost cried again. "I was a demonstrator. I was a protester and now here I stand. I never knew what you have gone through and now I know and I am so ashamed." Her tears began anew and lasted for some time. The veterans stood silently and some shared their tears with her. I turned away and shared a few of my own.

"Please forgive me," she repeated emotionally. "Now I know and understand so much more."

The warriors nodded solemnly. The ceremony was over. The crowd stood stunned. It was as if time had stopped. We all became brief statues of dismay looking toward the White House, then walked away. We would change this world with a duty of our own.

One last echo comes to me from that ceremony. "Captain, I sure do thank you," the black man spoke in a southern drawl. "I am released and got new direction. A bad, hurting weight has been taken from me." He gestured toward the statues where we had done our ceremony. "I thank you, Captain, and whatever tribe is out there that kept it all alive."

▼ ▼ ▼ ▼ ▼

Most of us have suffered from a lost love or a parting relationship, and indeed it is one of the most painful experiences to be encountered upon the trail of life. Wolf Runner made a positive effort to utilize the natural powers to heal. They helped him find a happier trail.

THE NATURAL WAY BACK
Wolf Runner

I leaned into the steep hillside and pushed the sharp briars aside. Soon, I was deep in the hollow where my play had been endless as a child. I selected a proper site and thrust my shovel into the clay soil. With much effort, a shallow grave was made ready.

The workshop instructor had sent us into the woods to do a special task. With the smell of the just-turned raw earth in my nostrils, I gathered grapevines, leaves, twigs, and grass. In my hands, a mask of myself took shape. Gently laying it into the grave, I stepped back and looked at my likeness lying there. With one match, the mask was ablaze. When the last smoke ascended, I began to shovel the dirt back in. Then, I awoke.

For a week I contemplated the dream. Putting the past behind me and letting go of the "old me" was clearly the message. There was much to let go of in my life. I was on the eve of taking a major step in that process. My family and I were moving a thousand miles away to a new life together. Thus my realization that there were some things that needed to stay behind, in this soil, right here.

In *Black Elk Speaks,* Black Elk tells of the importance of taking one's vision and bringing it into its power by acting it out here on earth. This dream seemed to be pressing for expression. As a psychologist, I had worked with hundreds of people, helping them grow and heal through the messages of their dreams. Only they could determine the meaning of their dreams. Only I could engage the power of this dream, and learn from it.

I made preparations and hiked deep into the beech and maple forest near our Ohio home. After crossing a shallow creek, the path led back into the old virgin-timber stand where the giant grandmother/grandfather trees lord over all. The site was to be a special place with privacy, where my own ceremony could be done according to my dream. In between giant maples and a few oaks, by an old fallen log, the setting was found. I dropped my pack and got out my folding shovel, my abalone shell and sage, and four groups of yarn in the sacred colors: red, yellow, black, and white. In each of the four directions were saplings far enough apart to make a circle about thirty feet across. Each sapling was then tied with the yarn of the four colors, which created the boundaries of my ceremonial site. In the shell I lit the sage and sweetgrass and sent the smoke out beseeching the six powers of the universe: to the east, to the south, to the west, to the north, to Father Sky above and Mother Earth below. My request was to the force that moves through all things, the Life Spirit, the Creator, to hear my prayers and bless what I was to do this day at this place. Mother Earth was asked her permission to dig into her and told of my purpose. Smudging the entire area and myself as well, I began my digging.

The soil did not yield easily. I labored intently, avoiding some tree roots and, apologetically, cutting through others. Soon the grave was open before me. My choice was not to make a mask of myself for the grave, but instead to bring with me much that represented the "old me." Those things painted a picture of me as I had been and of the life already left behind.

On the bare earth, in the center of the grave, my small fire was built. Eleven years of appointment calendars flowed out of my pack and, page by page, into the fire. I flashed back to each of those years, saw the faces of clients that went with the names, felt some of their pain once again. My thoughts recalled the vacation trips, the special moments, the highs and the lows, joys and regrets. Into the fire went an old address book, filled with names of people who no longer stayed in touch. Into the fire went photos of my ex-wife. The flames consumed the images with no malice, and none was felt in my heart. There was much in my life that was now in the form of ashes, there to fertilize the growth that was to continue for me.

The ashes smoldered slowly, the last sparks dying. Many feelings had gone through me as I burned my old life away. My thoughts became aware of how right it felt. Splashing water on the embers, picking up my shovel and beginning to return the soil to its home, I felt strength and pride arise in me. I realized there was *nothing* to feel ashamed about. My life had been lived as a warrior of the heart. I had acted with courage, faced danger, made mistakes, and "counted coup"! The proud spirit of the eagle was with me; the strength and endurance of the wolf; the self-respect, validation, and confidence of the moose, elk, bighorn, and deer all were with me. The old part of me was now released to the light. I left it behind, there in that forest, vowing to act with more determination in my life.

Sweat Lodge Night

A ladle scraping a metal bucket was the only sound as everyone hushed to listen to the hiss of the steam rising from the glowing rocks. Well water found rock it had possibly filtered through many years ago, and brought the heat out for all of us to feel. Prayers from our hearts rose with the steam and mingled with the sweat from our pores.

In the moments of silence, I marveled at the path that had brought me to be sitting there on mulch from aspen trees, under an ancient apple tree by a Colorado foothill, inside a domed structure I had helped build, leading a special ceremony. Here I was, a psychologist, Ph.D. and all, working together with people in a group in an entirely new way. My work had included facilitating hundreds and hundreds of hours of group-counseling experiences and thousands of hours of individual therapy. Workshops were led and courses taught, all aimed at helping people become more aware of the potential within them. The stories told to me of pain and suffering far exceeded what authors of fiction imagine and write down. Through self-exploration I had delved me into much of my own pain; it was that exploration that enabled me to be here now.

In this lodge my presence was not as psychologist or counselor. I was more of a facilitator/participant and less of a leader. There, with dipper in hand, my presence was to give structure to a process that held its own power, created its own leadership. The process of the Sweat Lodge Ceremony was giving each of us the opportunity to connect with a vital part inside of us and bring it out to offer up for union with something greater than ourselves.

In the darkness I traveled back in my mind to a steep hillside overlooking the Ohio River, *Ohio-se-pe,* the Beautiful River, as the Shawnee called it. My being sat inside this black ball of energy that seemed ready to burst. When I called out to signify the end of one of four durations, the sweat lodge door whipped open. Moonlight, fire glow, and fresh air poured in, filling our eyes, lungs, and souls. A realization occurred of my having been "reborn" many times, Mother Earth breathing life back into me when I seemed stuck and slowly dying. The healing power of regular contact with the natural world is felt on physical, emotional, and spiritual levels simultaneously. There are many paths to healing and higher consciousness, but for me nothing seems so real as getting out into genuine contact with the earth.

Sigurd Olsen, in his classic north country work *Listening Point,* says that mountains give us strength, but water speaks to our soul. Feeding our souls was the unspoken motivation that began drawing my son and me to the north woods after my divorce from his mother.

On the Arctic Watershed

North of Sault Sainte Marie, north of Lake Superior Provincial Park, we turned east at Wawa, named with the Ojibwa word for wild goose. We drove through rugged, rocky land that gave way to the expanses of the northern boreal forest. At one point on the highway, a large sign decorated with a bull moose and a bear announced that we were entering the arctic watershed. On that barely perceptible divide, the water runs either south to the Great Lakes, or north to James Bay, Hudson Bay, and the Arctic Ocean.

We had entered a land of lakes and thick forest. Thick, that is, where it had not been cleared—cut by loggers. Where the trees stood, I felt united with old friends. Northern cedar was there, its scent jogging my olfactory memory back to fishing cottages my parents rented during our summer vacations. Paper birch was there, with great sheaths of bark that made the concept of birchbark canoes seem quite feasible. Flying out of the spruce at one of our campsites, a female peregrine falcon screamed as she tore across the sky. Flotillas of mergansers patrolled our shores, diving for fish again and again. Loons called their wonderful calls, waking us at night and tempting the belief that, yes, we were hearing wolves. The Blackfoot people call the loon *matsiisaipi,* "handsome charger," for its great displays of skimming across the water like a proud warrior going into battle. We couldn't think of a better name for this beautiful bird. Hearing its wings cut rhythmically through the air, when the only other sound is the slice of a canoe paddle's wooden blade, brightens the heart.

For three days and nights the rocky northern point of a secluded island was our solitary home. Ontario's provincial bird, the mosquito, usually drove us into our tent early in the evening, but one night we were up late panfrying filets of a magnificent great northern pike that had given itself to my son that day. The fish was hooked deep and probably would not have survived had we released it, as we did all the other pike we caught. The cooking tasks kept us up late, and we sat in awe watching the northern sky show us millions of stars. It was about eleven o'clock when we saw two early arrivals for the Perseid meteor showers. My son was amazed by their speed while covering such tremendous distances. As we settled into the celestial special, we began to notice a faint blue-green light filling the sky around the horizon. As we looked unimpaired across the lake, huge misty curtains began to flow upward. Then, brilliant, stationary laser beams broke the darkness and reached right in front of the Big Dipper and Cassiopeia. Wave after wave stunned us with their beauty. We gasped, cheered, and shouted, announcing the new displays to each other from west to east. Science has its explanations for the phenomenon, but here, far from any city lights (and I do mean far), in mercifully clear air, and at this latitude, the aurora borealis reached down into our souls.

Experiencing events like this, and fairly often, surely is a major reason why we find so much spirituality in the original Native American way of life. Number one, *they were out in it*. If the northern lights were happening that night, they usually saw it. The recently departed Edward Abbey used to admonish those who were working for the environment to spend 50 percent of their time on such work directly, and 50 percent of their time "out in it." Armchair traveling will not get you there. Number two, *they were open to it*. It was part of Native American culture to see "the force that moves through all things" in all that was around them, and in themselves. The process of growing as human beings seems to depend so much on our degree of openness. Are we able to see and accept change in ourselves and others? Are we able to integrate new and different ways of viewing the world into our present thinking? Can we see how science serves us with what it knows, and limits us with what it does not understand? Psychologist Gordon Alport once said that "what we know is but a drop, and our ignorance a sea!"

For my son and me, on our island of "pure peace," the healing was taking place. As much as I have helped people with "talking therapy," I have come to believe even more in the power of experiential "therapy." Silently, pulling the weight of the same canoe together, we shared a strength that did more than put us miles down the lake. We gladly shared daily tasks that at home would have been called chores. The time together had no distractions. There was no television, no radio, no busyness, nothing to get in between our contact with each other and the world around us. Out of the comfortable silences, words of meaning and substance arose from the heart and found a voice.

For days we were alone with the loons and the great "lake wolves," the northern pike. We came to realize, especially that brilliant night, that we were also there with *Gitchi-Manitou* (the Ojibwa's way of saying Great Spirit or Great Mystery). The wilderness has a way of showing us how subtle that spirit is, how often it is experienced not as a humanlike swirling image in the sky, but as the whole experience, the gestalt that is greater than the sum of its parts. Wind rustling through white pines, waves lapping on a rocky shore, bathing ancient granite, mergansers disappearing beneath the lake's sun-speckled surface, all speak together in one breath, a breath that on this island we call *Gitchi-Manitou.*

Earth-centered Wellness

Our relationship with the natural world has a healing potential that works. When I became active in the wellness movement in the late seventies, there was acknowledgment of the environmental dimension of wellness on a theoretical level but little understanding of how to work with it. I saw the wellness movement as reshaping the way we looked at health. Instead of viewing health as the mere absence of illness, this was a holistic look at both prevention and potential. Why just survive, when we could thrive? Enlightened companies were seeing how they could hold down health-care costs by helping employees to remain healthy.

Though holistic in concept, most wellness programs began doing little more than physical fitness programming. The more enlightened ones soon added programming in the areas of nutritional awareness and stress management. The idea was "risk reduction." Seat belts were strapped on, along with jogging shoes, and cholesterol was vilified. As the movement evolved, the importance of family, career, and even spirituality became recognized. We also learned a tremendous amount about what works and what doesn't when it comes to helping people change their health behavior. Improving the health norms of one's peers proved far more effective than scare tactics in modifying modern life-styles.

Soon it became increasingly obvious, though, that we could cut out the cheeseburgers, run three miles a day, meditate, and learn to really communicate our true feelings all for naught if our planet was dying. If we went out our doors into a smog-filled, overcrowded, toxic-laden world, all our wellness efforts would be meaningless.

There can be no personal wellness without earth wellness. Improving human life-styles is perhaps the single greatest thing we can do to improve human health. Improving human life-styles as they affect the environment is also a key to improving the health of the planet. It is our consumer choices, our energy use, our way of relating to Mother Earth, and how we value her that determine to a great extent the nature and degree of most of our environmental problems.

Fortunately, a lot of the choices we make to improve our health help the earth as well. This is the basis of what we call "earth-centered wellness." When we switch to eating foods that are free of pesticides, preservatives, and so on, we create a demand for food produced by agricultural methods that do not harm the earth. When we exercise more, we may become fit enough and motivated enough to walk and ride bikes more often and drive our cars less. If we are getting outdoors as we exercise, we are regularly making contact with the natural world and valuing it more. We protect what we value. The connections are many.

More and more of these connections were made by me and were reflected in articles written and workshops presented on the environmental dimension of wellness. At the same that I was so involved in being "well," though, my personal life was going through a great deal of emotional pain. I was into personal growth but was only kidding myself. Until the emotional and spiritual healing inside took place, I could only go so far. Not caring enough about myself had allowed me to endure a marriage in which my needs for love and affection went largely unmet. I held myself back creatively and professionally. Although I appeared to be doing fine on the outside, my soul was dying underneath.

During those years, the natural world was used as a place to escape. I distracted myself from my pain for many months by planning and carrying out a fifty-two-day trip to Alaska and northwest Canada that involved driving ten thousand miles. I grew a beard on that trip and discovered a wilder part of me there. I shaved the beard off upon returning, but then grew it back, realizing that a significant change process had begun. Allies supported me in my growth. It was hard work catching up with my elusive feelings. Now I realized how I had, and how I could, use the natural world as an ally in my healing process.

I discovered that the world is speaking to us all the time, if we only listen. The messages are there, cloaked beautifully in metaphor. Our dreams use this process nightly to speak to us. Sometimes the messages come during our waking hours, all around us. This is the story of such an experience.

Don't Push the River

The river had been rising all night. I stood on the stream bank and considered the cold, brown surge before me. "One more time! Just one more try!"

For two days I had walked and waded, stalked and crept along and through Shaver's Fork trying hard to seduce a trout to strike my offerings. I had floated flies, spun spinners, drifted worms, and even lowered myself to the banality of tossing salmon eggs, cheese balls, and kernels of corn. Rainbows, browns, brookies—none responded to my pleading invitations.

The day before, other anglers had plopped their bait here where the stream widened, just below the frigid swimming hole, and the fish had given themselves to them. The men smiled warmly as the sun sparkled on the water. They were pleased with their catch.

My companion was on his way east over the Alleghenies this morning, headed home. Home for Alan now was his parents' home, where he had wisely retreated with his five-year-old daughter after the separation from his wife. She had spent better than 80 percent of their marriage as a depressed and suicidal mental patient. Now he was building a new life for his daughter and himself. Twenty-year friendships are rare and precious. Alan and I had been assigned to room together our freshman year at college. I had the record player and he had the albums of Bob Dylan and Buffy Saint-Marie. We kept sharing music and experiences right through Jimi Hendrix, Crosby, Stills and Nash, friends on bad trips, protest marches, and short and long romances. Now we found an annual May rendezvous to be just the spring tonic our lives needed.

A year before, we had walked in black bear tracks along a rhododendron-shrouded Forest Service road up a beautiful wild valley. A raccoon scrambled over the rocks and out of sight; a doe and fawn crossed the road ahead, curiously observing us who walk on our hind legs. The rocky stream gave Alan the gift of his first rainbow in a small pool under a tree. My hooks found another rainbow and my first brown trout as well. The water spirits had smiled on us. In camp, a glow of firelight and satisfaction on our faces, we talked from our hearts as men who are closer than brothers sometimes do. We both spoke of the laughter and love of our children and the loneliness of our marriages. Alan had always been the bold one, the experimenter, the risk taker. I was always more cautious, more likely to set a goal and persist and endure. Now we were coming full circle. Alan had settled down and become an unbelievably responsible father in a virtually single-parent household. I had outgrown my old patterns of adapt and survive. I was ready for change and growth, ready to put my own needs first for a change.

Now, a year later, I was still trying to make it work at home, without much change. Back at the stream again, neither of us caught any fish and we tried so hard. Worst of all were the golden rainbows that we could see in the clear water under the hemlocks. Nothing could induce them to kiss a hook. "That's the funny thing about fishing," my father had often said. "You can spend a lot of time without catching anything." The worse our luck, the more effort we put out. We couldn't strike out! The long weekend went quickly and we passed up opportunities for pleasing hikes in the forest. We let product supplant process. It seemed like that next pool would yield a fish. God, what a beautiful riffle behind that boulder! Ease that spinner in there. Another perfect cast! Nothing. Maybe around the next bend . . . maybe next year!

Now I had one morning left to test my fortune. It had rained all night. The forest was damp and cool, the river misty. Nothing was clear anymore. Light brown silt obscured the rocky bottom. Monday morning. I had the whole place to myself, alone again. Have you ever wanted someone to do something with you or for you that he or she didn't want to do? Regardless of the outcome, it is never satisfying. Maybe I could forget this truth and push the river just a little, one more time.

My rubber-coated feet moved like the fingertips of a novice braille reader. Places I had stepped before easily were now under more of the cold water than yesterday. The icy wet fingers of the river slipped in over the tops of my hip waders and bathed my thighs. I scrambled for a higher rock. Casting. Retrieving. Putting it out there. "You can't catch fish unless your line is in the water." Rejection, rejection.

Few things are slicker than silty sandstone. My left foot began slipping to the left. I shifted my weight to the right and that foot began its glissade down to the left as well. I spun and put my back to the current and righted myself but not before being soaked to the waist. Pants, shirt, underwear, and everything they covered were immersed in the frigid, muddy water.

Messages could be ignored no more. It was time to quit. Much more sad than angry, I had not even engaged in my usual attempt at anesthesia through profanity. I was disappointed, heartbroken, as I wrenched the hip boots off and poured gallons of Shaver's Fork back onto the bank. "It is *so* hard for me to know when to quit," I said to myself as I sat forlorn on some tree roots.

I trudged back up the hill to my camper and peeled off the soaked clothing, dried with a towel, and dressed for the road. The dry cotton helped, but I knew I really needed more than my own energy to warm me. How many times had I been here before? How many times had I needed that loving touch, a word of soothing empathy that was not forthcoming? Perhaps I needed to cast my efforts into a whole new stream.

I took that message to heart, and it became a truly transformative point in my life. Strength was found within to leave that relationship, and courage initiated the journey of recovering access to my numbed feelings. Traveling that new path, I began to find what was needed in many areas of my life. Eventually I discovered Nancy, or Sparrow Hawk, a partner who shared many of my visions and my passions.

In the warmth of a healthy relationship, I grew as never before. Creatively and professionally, I held myself back less. A realization came that I had long outgrown the work at the university counseling center. I was thinking in global wellness terms, not just in terms of how many clients could be seen in one week.

Sparrow Hawk and I realized that the time had come to do the work that we really felt needed to be done in the world. Human health and environmental health were one and the same. We needed to spread that message and create a merger of the wellness and environmental movements. With the encouragement of Jan Hartke, then president of the Global Tomorrow Coalition, we formed Earth Awareness and Restoration Through Healing (E.A.R.T.H.). Eventually we became a nonprofit organization, dedicated to motivating people to care about themselves and the earth.

Through my presentations at the National Wellness Conference, the E.A.R.T.H. project attracted the interest of corporate wellness programs. The opportunity to reach people where they worked and to make the personal wellness/earth wellness connection a programming reality was very gratifying. We saw that motivation was the key. People needed to care about themselves before they would take even the first step to improve their life-styles or to care about the earth. It is all interconnected. We also wanted to reach environmental groups with the message of how to help people change their ecologically related behavior, based on what we in the wellness movement had learned.

It was a great leap of faith, but it felt entirely right. Leaving my full-time work at the counseling center enabled us to devote our full energies to the E.A.R.T.H. project. We then decided to move from Ohio to Colorado to find more fertile ground for our efforts. In retrospect, both were excellent changes. We wanted to relocate where our dreams of an institute for human healing and earth healing could be realized. We needed and found the support of other like-minded people. Getting here required conquering our fears and doubts and placing our fate in the hands of something larger than ourselves. We had both had many ways of holding ourselves back, many ways of selling ourselves short. Belief in our own ability came, in part, once again from the messages our spiritual life brought us through our experience in the natural world.

Once, out in the mountains of Colorado, a regal, ten-point stag deer walked close to me and even gave me a scrutinizing look. When I described this encounter to my Lakota friend, Eagle Man, he took it in with little surprise. "He's telling you that what you're doing is good," Ed said.

I felt acknowledged. I felt recognized by a creature who was saying to me: "Brother! I, the white-tailed buck, the ten-pointer, salute you! The Great Good Spirit gave you the maturity, the power, the strength, the grace that you see in me. You too are a ten-point buck. Give yourself credit for what you have done and are doing now. Move through the world with harmony. Be at one with the woods and at peace with yourself. Then go back to the civilized world and take that pride and peace with you. Remember the look in my eyes! *Ho!*"

▼   ▼   ▼   ▼   ▼

We have experienced a healing of the mind, so to speak, in this chapter, first in the revelations regarding Vietnam veterans and then in Wolf Runner's account of moving forward positively from a breaking relationship. Now let us explore the recovery of several individuals from a critical infliction of the physical body.

ATHEIST IN CEREMONY
Loren J. Hynes

I was undergoing chemotherapy for cancer, specifically rabdomyo-sarcoma, and I was told by the doctors that I wouldn't be expected to live. I found out on October 26, 1985, and it was in the spring of 1987 when I was at my worst that I met the Rainbow Tribe. They were cheerfully gathering flowers and fresh grass in a meadow that was just outside the fence line of a horse pasture. Within the pasture there was a sweat lodge tucked beneath a partially fallen beech tree and surrounded by a grove of ash, elm, and maple.

I was too weak to walk very far. John parked the car next to the fence line and I walked from there to the lodge site. It was still daylight and the Rainbows were placing the fresh grass in the lodge to sit upon. The first of the season's flowers were brought in for their pleasing fragrance. My cancer had destroyed my sense of smell. You notice flowers more when you lose a part of you that was designed to appreciate.

At the time I was an atheist. I didn't believe in anything. Despite my lack of belief, Eagle Man's daughter, Julie, and his son John invited me to the Sweat Lodge Ceremony out by Lake Minnetonka. I had attended the same high school as they and we had loosely kept in touch. They had gone on to college and I had joined the working world. I would run into them occasionally at some of the old hangouts when they were not at school.

They were both aware of my deteriorating condition and told me about the sweat lodge ceremonies that were being held. I was pretty weak when Eagle Man took his first look at me. I read his thoughts. Later, he admitted that I "looked like death warmed over." I didn't have any hair and weighed eighty pounds on a six-foot two-inch frame.

John told his dad that I was an atheist, but that I still wanted to go through the ceremony. At my stage in life, I was willing to try anything.

Eagle Man took me for a walk and asked me some questions. He downplayed any conception I might have had that he was a healer, but instead emphasized that he was a teacher. He doesn't want anyone calling him a medicine man. He told me that reservation holy men never run around saying they can heal or cure people. He remarked on a person who isn't a Sioux but is always boasting that he is the chief medicine man of this particular tribe, although he hasn't cured anybody yet. I could tell that Eagle Man didn't want me to get my hopes up when he started talking about the death philosophy of the old Sioux warriors and how they were not afraid to die. He suggested that I should start thinking about dying like a warrior of long ago. He said it would probably be a little different for me since I didn't believe in a spirit world. He wanted to give an example, I guess, and the closest he could get was his combat experience when he was a fighter pilot. Even though he was not too encouraging he gave me a ray of hope. What he said came through to me. He said that among the pilots he was with in Vietnam, those that didn't seem to care one way or the other were the ones nothing ever seemed to happen to. "In combat, everyone wants to live, " he stated, "but if you just leave it up to a higher power and go on doing your duty you'll increase your chances."

He told me an Indian doesn't like to tell anyone what to believe when it comes to a spiritual concept, but in my case he was going to make an exception. He said that he had seen some pretty strong evidence of the spirit world in the *Yuwipi* ceremonies he had been privileged to attend. Some of these ceremonies were real strong ones conducted for various reasons by two Sioux holy men to whom he had been close. He said that he himself would probably never come close to conducting a *Yuwipi* Ceremony but that he had been experiencing some strong spiritual evidence in the sweat lodge. He gave me hope when he told me about a little girl dying of leukemia. She too had lost her hair. She went into a sweat lodge and got a new lease on life. Eagle Man told me he couldn't turn anyone away from a ceremony if they had a good heart and he could sense that I meant well, even if I was an atheist. I was told that I would have to respect everyone else's vision, however. This respect Eagle Man insisted upon; otherwise, the ceremony probably wouldn't work for me.

I sat next to Julie. She is quite spiritual, very spiritual in fact, and since then, we have been very close friends. I kept thinking that I had to respect everyone else's vision inside the lodge. Those were Eagle Man's instructions and I concentrated on them; of course I didn't have to concentrate very hard that I wanted to live.

The outcome of the ceremony was a definite change in my lack of belief. I firmly believe in a higher power now. There is another thing I firmly believe. If I hadn't met John and Julie and Eagle Man, I would be a dead man today.

The Sweat Lodge was on a Saturday night. I received almost immediate confirmation that higher powers were working for the good of those who attended.

John had told me about Malcolm, his graduate school professor at the university. His professor attends sweat lodges occasionally and had been fretting and worrying over John's motorcycle riding to and from classes in heavy traffic. Occasionally, Malcolm and John rode their bicycles to classes as they do not live far from each other and they are good friends. As we rode home together that night, John told me that he had heeded Malcolm's words and prayed specifically for his own safety in the sweat lodge. He also said that he had accidentally stepped on a peace pipe at the sweat lodge and had broken the wooden insert that goes between the pipe stem and the pipe bowl. He told his dad, however, and his father fixed the pipe with a spare stem that he had in his pipe bag. On Monday, John was in a motorcycle crash that could have seriously maimed or killed him.

John was driving his motorcycle on the freeway from the university to his mother's home when he hit an oil slick while going around a curve. He was wearing a leather jacket with a backpack strapped on containing a tape recorder and a metallurgy book. On his feet were tennis shoes. The motorcycle went out from under John and he found himself at fifty miles an hour on his back sliding across the pavement. He arched his back so that only his backpack and his feet were in contact with the abrasive pavement. A driver behind the accident told John that the scene was like it had been choreographed by a stuntman in a James Bond movie. When John came to a stop, his backpack was in shreds and his tennis shoe soles were almost ground away. John did not have a mark on him and was uninjured due to the shock-absorbing effect of the book and tape recorder in the pack. The driver behind the scene was so excited that he offered to drive John to his mother's home. The driver described what had happened before his eyes as analogous to underwater ballet. He said that time seemed to almost stand still and the whole scene seemed to play in slow motion. In fact, he added oddly, since no one was injured, it had a strange quality or sense of beauty to it. Maybe it did if the spirit forces of Mystery were there at the scene to answer to what John had called for in the sweat lodge.

Since that time, John has bought a car and uses it as his means of transportation, much to the relief of his parents and Malcolm, the professor.

John's accident gave me a newfound respect for prayer inside a sweat lodge. John asked for safety and was spared what could have been fatal. I wanted to live and I was spared. I now weigh 160 pounds and my hair is long enough to braid. I took some natural medicine recommended by a reservation holy man and I developed a different attitude toward life. I have been working at a full-time job and no longer take treatments. It is possible that I could regress back into the disease—anything is possible—but I certainly have enjoyed and appreciated my life since that humble but powerful little ceremony out by Lake Minnetonka.

My spiritual belief is now along the line of the Indian Way. I talk to Julie a lot and she has become a very dear friend. She has really helped me. Most of all, I know there is a Great Spirit, somewhere and everywhere, that can hear even the prayer of a once atheist.

> *Pilamaya,*
> *Pilamaya aloh.*
> (Thank you, thank you very much.)

▼ ▼ ▼ ▼ ▼

We will hear from another person who was once afflicted with the same disease as Loren Hynes. She is an older lady who had cancer of the liver. I understand that people seldom recover from it.

RAINBOW GRANDMOTHER
Molly Poets

Early in this century, I grew up in the most racist state in the union, South Dakota.* I don't feel as if I received a traditional South Dakota upbringing as far as attitudes about races are concerned.

My parents lived on what was part of the Sioux reservation near DuPree when they were first married. My mother was acquainted with the Sioux but couldn't speak their language. They did have a certain interplay though. Whenever she baked bread there was one Indian man who always sat on her doorstep until he got his loaf of bread and then went on his way. Their path from the reservation went right by my folks' door.

So my parents were not racist people. We were never taught that Indians were any different from us. When I went to school it was a different story, however. I heard about the poor little savage babies who had to be taken to Indian School so they could get something to eat. But I think the first training you get is probably more important and my first training was not racist.

We lived in a traditional German settlement. It probably could have been transplanted into Germany and you'd never have known the difference except for the language. However, we were taught German in the schools even when it was forbidden by law. Some of the Benedictine nuns who taught at our school also taught at the Indian School. I think they also taught at Rosebud Reservation but I'm not sure.

Indian tradition always felt right. I felt that there was a link there of some sort. I was always drawn to the Indians even though I didn't know much about their ways. My daughter Margaret and I

---

* This particular view is not shared by the author relative to these modern times. The State of South Dakota, led by a concerned governor, and with the participation of nine tribal chairpersons, established a Council for Conciliation in order to heal old racial wounds. The author, like all minorities, has suffered prejudice at times, but not only in South Dakota. I went through a nepotism ordeal in Minnesota that I don't believe South Dakotans would have allowed. I have met numerous concerned and conscientious South Dakotans. As you travel across the state, think of its citizens as wanting harmony far more than they seek disharmony. Positive efforts and recent gains should not be diminished. However, there are many Indian people who agree with Molly's view.

went to Ed's Native American culture class and everything fell into place. It felt so right, so familiar. From there on it just developed. Then, when I got sick with cancer about two months later, one of the first things I thought of was to have Ed do a healing, which he did. It was probably one of the first positive things that happened in the whole situation.

He did three ceremonies for me. Before he came to do the first one, my daughters Janet and Margaret and I did a Blue Star meditation to prepare ourselves. We meditated and mentally put a blue star on different parts of our bodies. This relaxed us and opened us to the healing energies of the ceremony.

Before Ed came to do the healing there was a tremendous buildup of tension as a storm was approaching. I was feeling just horrible. He was late because of the storm too. I've always had an affinity to storms. I feel the weather and am very sensitive to it. The storm released a lot of the tension that had built up. He did the ceremony for me and all that horrible stuff that I was feeling just fell away and I was all right. It seems a little presumptuous for me to say the storm was just there for me. It was part of nature that day and because I am part of nature I was open and susceptible to it. I was reacting to it.

First he did a sage ceremony and used the pipe. I sat in a chair in the center of my living room. Four stones were around me on the floor—red, yellow, black, and white stones for the four directions. Directly beneath my chair was a crystal for the Power of All, the Great Spirit. I don't think he drummed. My daughters Janet and Margaret helped. He beseeched the six powers of the universe and, of course, the Ultimate Power. It was a very simple ceremony. Ed talked about my having work to do and that I needed to be here and alive to do it. I was very moved that he felt I had something to stay here for. I wasn't sure of anything at that time. I had no purpose really. As far as I was concerned I didn't have a reason to stay other than to be here for my family, and I didn't see how I was doing them much good.

The sage has a power. It is the healing herb mentioned in Black Elk's vision. Just the smell of it when you are having it incensed all around you conveys what I can only describe as a beneficial effect—a power. I felt cleansed of a lot of negative thinking. I remember feeling really good about the ceremony. I don't know how to describe it except that it felt so right. I'm sure that the healing process was starting from that time. Releasing the negative thoughts opened me to a more positive way of thinking, or at least gave me the opportunity to make the choice.

Ed left his pipestone pipe here after the ceremony. It was the one he had carved himself with the eagle head. Jan took it outside the next morning and smoked it. After the ceremony we went out to get something to eat and we saw three rainbows. I mean three different ones. I took it to be a confirmation and I felt much better.

We all oohed and aahed about the rainbows and we were sure they were good omens. Everybody felt that. At the time we were not knowledgeable as to how nature works with Indian ceremony, so this was a natural reaction on our part that was Indian and we didn't know it. We felt that the rainbows were an acknowledgment and a promise. Nature was acknowledging.

Later on in the summer Ed did a second ceremony at his house on the deck overlooking the lake in his backyard. Ed had told me about a medicine that Fools Crow had shown him some years before after a Sun Dance. The holy man had cured cancer in different people with it, and Ed said that he himself had used it once before to heal a cancer victim and it worked. Ed said that he waited a long time to use it because he didn't want to be thought of as some kind of a medicine man. With all the ceremonies he and Thunder Owl started doing with the Rainbow People, he finally decided to use it after Loren's attitude was changed about there being a Great Spirit after experiencing the Sweat Lodge. He said that Loren was so far gone that it was the ultimate test of whether it worked or not. He never insisted that I should use the medicine—this is not the Indian way—but in my case he wanted me to feel comfortable about it if I should decide to ask for it. My cousin Bob was here from California when I decided that I should try it, and Margaret drove Bob and me across town to Ed's place. The ceremony was much like the first one. Ed went out into his yard and picked some sage and used that. I don't remember whether he smudged or not. (I am getting older and I wondered more than once why Ed had made such a special effort to get me Fools Crow's medicine. He had gone all the way out to the reservation to pick it and then had dried it.) Bob drummed. I remember thinking at the time, "Boy, I bet Ed's neighbors wonder what is going on . . . if we are having a powwow over here or what."

There was no nature acknowledgment that day as I recall. This ceremony didn't seem as important to me as the first one. I believe that first experiences are always more memorable. It was more like a continuation of a process that was already going on. I think this second ceremony was for an entirely different purpose, although we didn't know it at the time. It was only a matter of months after that second ceremony that Bob was diagnosed with lung cancer. I think that he was there for that reason, although we didn't know that until later after his diagnosis. I think that is why I didn't feel as strongly about it—because it probably wasn't primarily for me.

Spirit was opening Bob to the potential of ceremony. Everything is so related. Bob is now using the medicine. Time will tell. There are no accidents.

After the second ceremony I began to take Fools Crow's tea. It is a special tea made from purple flowers. The first couple of times I drank it I got a real buzz. After that I didn't experience any light-headedness. I remember Ed being surprised that it was purple. He drank some before he gave it to me and his eyes dilated. He said that it was pretty strong and he had to test it because he was a little worried about it being too powerful for someone of my age. He had been drinking it out of a black cup and had not noticed the color.

For the third ceremony, he brought one of his students along to observe the proceedings and the tea. He made some and we all had a cup. He did a pipe ceremony by himself. That was different from the other two times. Each one is different. This was just a brief ceremony.

It took two months from the first talk with the doctor until the final diagnosis. During that time the old debate about whether to live or die—to go or to stay—went on. I wasn't sleeping or getting any rest day or night. I couldn't seem to get away from the question. I couldn't decide which to do. My family was supportive and assured me of continued support whatever my decision would be.

I hadn't really thought about the issue until Ed said, "You have things to do to stay for," but on a subconscious level, my feeling that I wasn't serving any real purpose is what probably caused me to get sick. I didn't think I had a reason to stay here. Everything is a part of a process. That was too.

I wasn't really aware of a lot of fear, except I did think about the fact that there was going to be a lot of pain and I'm no longer good at handling pain. I guess few do that scenario well.

So a lot of my feelings I can't even describe. It seems like a gray cloud to me now. There was probably all kinds of gunk in that cloud, but I wasn't aware of how loaded down I was with it until it was over. I did know that I was going through a lot of feelings that I couldn't describe. It surely was a relief when they were gone. And they were gone—poof! just in an instant—after a dream I had.

It was in ancient times and we were traveling on this hot, dusty road. We were barefoot and dressed in biblical-type clothes. A couple brought this little boy and we were casually visiting. Soon the couple was gone and the boy was still there. They just disappeared! I thought how strange it was that they would leave their small child with a perfect stranger and not be worried. I understood that I was supposed to take care of this child. I asked him what his name was and he said: "Jesus." That's when I woke up laughing, and my decision was made and clear. I felt as if I could get up and conquer the whole world. It was really a very simple dream, and I don't know to this day on a conscious level what it meant. But when I woke up, everything was settled. There was no more fear. I knew I was going to get well. Everything was okay.

It probably was a recognition of the God spirit within. I don't particularly think of myself as Christian, yet I was brought up in that tradition. Those things are deep inside you, part of your early patterning.

I think it was acknowledgment or confirmation that God is within each of us. All we have to do is take care of that part of ourselves and we are okay. It also meant to me that we all have a little child within us, and that has to be taken care of. That is something that has always been hard for me to do. That's as near as I can interpret for now.

At the time of the dream, I didn't feel the need to try to understand it because I just felt so good and I knew everything was going to be all right. I didn't feel the need to try to interpret it then. I suppose on some level I understood; otherwise I wouldn't have felt that good about it.

Besides the three Indian ceremonies and the dream, I had all kinds of prayers from different groups, including a Wiccan ceremony. The Wiccan ceremony was an Essene healing that used a crystal for its focus. Wiccans are more misunderstood than the native peoples when it comes to religious history. I believe a lot of the falseness spread about them is because most are women and they are following a simple nature-based beseechment and communication with a Higher Force, which in itself is nothing new—unless it happens to be women who have taken it upon themselves to provide their own religious leadership! Some pretty vicious "history" gets written by the masculine world when that happens.

It is significant to me that the Gaia hypothesis—that the earth is a living entity—reiterates the Native American teachings. This belief was held by the ancient Greeks as well as other ancient cultures. The Native American teachings are probably just as ancient. The old native tradition of taking only what you need and leaving everything as you found it is important. We are not following that tradition, and that is what will do us in eventually. We keep raping the earth and not giving back to it in balance.

Let's take a commonsense look at the situation. We can all see the condition the world is in. All we have to do is open our eyes. We don't need any authority to tell us that we are in trouble. If we use our own good common sense we can see it all around us. We need to look at our lives with some common sense and then make changes. This applies not just to Western materialists. It also applies to the American Indians. We can never move backward in time. Some of the old traditionalists (and some of their young followers) have been heard saying, "Don't let the white man have this knowledge; it's not for them." These Indians are not being wise either. The truly wise holy people who have walked their talk, such as Fools Crow, Black Elk, John Fire, and Bill Eagle Feather, wanted this knowledge to get out to the world. "These ceremonies do not belong to Indians alone. They can be done by all who have the right attitude, and who are honest and sincere about their beliefs in the Great Spirit and follow *Wakan Tanka*'s rules." I like that wisdom stated by Fools Crow, and I am certainly appreciative that Black Elk told his knowledge to John Neihardt so that the world could understand the six powers of the universe!

These ancient wisdoms and teachings are the only thing that will save them, as well as the white man. We'll all go down together if it doesn't. This knowledge and wisdom do not belong to the red people alone. If they would listen to their own teachings they would know that they cannot keep it to themselves. The two-leggeds are not just red, although I can understand their animosity after what the white man has done to the Indians. I am not discounting what the white man has done to the Indian, but we are all new generations now. The white man almost destroyed all the old native societies that had so much wisdom. They had real wisdom.

Now that times have become so different, as Joseph Campbell says, we probably need a new mythology for this land. What that will be we won't see in this lifetime. It takes many generations to work out. The true mythology for this land was in existence and was right for this place at that time, the time before the Europeans came across the waters. Mythologies evolve with civilizations, so the old mythology now has to evolve into what is right for this land now. We became so tied up with materialism that we discounted mythology to the point that it has lost its validity for most people. That's what we need to get back. I think there is no other place to start but with the Native American traditions. That is what we have. That is what is the base for our mythology.

When you really touch into the essence of yourself, you are touching Great Spirit, Great Mystery, and that is very moving. This is the essential ingredient within the whole spiritual process. I don't understand how we got so far removed from what we really are in our society. You can't divorce spirituality from life. It is a basic ingredient in life. It's no wonder we have such a sick society. We have eliminated spirituality from our lives. We have separated ourselves from Great Spirit, and, sadly enough, I feel we have done it with religion.

▼   ▼   ▼   ▼   ▼

The Rainbow Tribe is very appreciative of Molly's extended stay because she has been a sagacious Grandmother to many. She brought new vision and knowledge upon my trail, particularly by introducing me to the works of Campbell. Her commonsense wisdom has been very valuable as well.

PART FOUR

❧❧❧

RAINBOW FIRE— RAINBOW SPIRITUAL LEADERSHIP

We should have been told that genocide and geocide went hand in hand. . . .

To change this—and it must be changed, or we perish—we must seek the counsel of Native peoples to find the way back. The way of harmony and respect for Nature and her children that we lost in the dim childhood of our culture. The people of the dominant cultures across the world must first ask forgiveness and healing, and then request to be taught the ways of the Earth by Earth's peoples in order to save our Mother and ourselves. This is an endeavor of spiritual and ecological justice.

Dan Turner, *Creation Spirituality* magazine, October/November 1991

11
GATHERINGS

Rainbow Tribe people are gathering worldwide. They are building sweat lodges at weekend retreats and hearing lectures from those who are close to the Natural Way. Gatherings are the beginning for many Rainbows.

A Rainbow woman opened up her own land for ceremony and took action to utilize the Nature Center nearby to impart Mother Earth wisdom. Fruitful lodges took place because of this woman's generosity, and many lives were richly enhanced. If you have a few acres of privacy, then consider sharing it to the degree that an occasional ceremony can be held. You will be helping others to reach into the earth, and they will then go on and be stronger earth supporters. In the end, your children and the generations unborn will benefit from their positive endeavors.

WATER SPIRIT'S WISDOM
Water Spirit Woman

I shared a naming ceremony with my close friend Tayja Wiger, who is part Oglala Sioux. Even before the ceremony began, I felt the welling up of ancient knowing—a kind of pressure from that mysterious place underneath my conscious mind, that place that is open to my Mother and my Father in a way too big in space, too big in time, extending into mystery. As I walked beside Tayja toward the arched bridge to the island at Carleton College, I felt kinship from shared roots into the past. Carleton was also my alma mater.

When we arrived at the sweat lodge on the island, beautiful garlands were placed on our heads. The wreaths were strong with the stems of woven vines and soft with the gentle blue-green of sage. Bright lilies showed the red way of the east and the yellow healing south, and our crowns were speckled with black—mysterious spirits of the west. The truth, strength, and endurance of the north were present in the delicate baby's breath. "Two warriors put baby's breath in your garlands and lost nothing in the process," Eagle Man said with a smile, recognizing the delicate power of love. I was glad Eagle Man's friend Thunder Owl was there, as I had felt the beauty and power of his *Inipi* ceremonies too.

Thunder Owl opened the ceremony. The rocks—the bones of Mother Earth—had taken Sun's heat into their being, and steam poured from their glowing energy as Thunder Owl dipped water to them.

Buffalo Spirit Woman gave her prayer, her words going into the intimate dark. "I feel as if I've been here before," she began. Her beautiful prayer for growth and healing for our Mother and all of her children continued, ending with ". . . Let light come into the darkness." Immediately there was an answering shower of lights rising like sparklers from the rocks. It was clear that our names, Crystal Eagle Woman for Tayja and Water Spirit Woman for me, were as right with the spirits as they were with us.

As the drumbeat echoed through my heart I felt like an embryo of Mother Earth listening to my own mother's heart. With others in the lodge, I went to that place in the rainbow of colors where purple rises toward the invisible world of spirits, where our physical eyes see only black. There in the womb of Mother Earth I learned what Eagle Man meant by regarding the earth as a bible for each of us to read for ourselves, needing no intermediary.

The signs leading Eagle Man and Thunder Owl to my name clearly showed us her language as she spoke it through our relative, Beaver. The afternoon of our naming, before Tayja and I arrived, the tightly furred one came to them while they stood on the wooden bridge to the island of our *Inipi* Ceremony. The chain of man-made lakes was bordered by mowed grass and frequented by people—hardly beaver habitat. Yet, as Eagle Man and Thunder Owl stood on the bridge asking for my natural name, a beaver swam close to them, paused in front of the low bridge, then gave his sign by swimming in four circles, one for each direction, in front of Thunder Owl and Eagle Man. His message completed, he acted like a normal wild beaver when he saw us coming. He was frightened by our approach and swam away.

When Eagle Man told me this story, it reminded me of a time the previous summer when Beaver had entered into my life. As was my habit, I had been swimming around May's Lake, where I had learned to swim as a child. It was evening. I had gone about half a mile when I noticed a silver wake on the water. When I got a little closer, I made out the dark form of a beaver's head. Surprisingly, the beaver allowed me to come so near that I had a close-up view of his large teeth! Then when I had come as close as I dared, he slapped his tail on the water, bringing it down cupped so that the sound echoed like a drum, and dived. Like Beaver, Great White Heron, Turtle, and other creatures of the lake speak to me, telling me secrets of the water. My natural name is part of me, and I feel it always has been, ever since the magic of my first days in a canoe with my father. Thank you, Beaver, for carrying Great Spirit's message.

The earth speaks. It speaks in a big way, so big that the sweep of its language is usually beyond our human understanding. We are like blind babies who can touch only a small part of our giant mother. For me the Natural Way has always been a part of my life; ever since the umbilical cord to my physical mother was cut, my umbilical cord to Mother Earth has been nourishing me just as it nourishes all my relatives. Sometimes I feel very humble to be such a small part of such a gigantic universal plan; sometimes I feel very proud to be included in such a grand design.

My acquaintance with this giant Turtle Island on which we live began very simply. When I was a small child, my father often took me turtle hunting on a small lake where we spent the summers. He taught me to know what I was seeing, not by telling me but by helping me to see the signs. He would point to a small dark protuberance among the water weeds tipping above the surface. If we paddled our canoe slowly and quietly, we could sometimes get close enough to catch an occasional mud turtle. It looked easy when my father did it. I wanted my turn. I saw a dark tip showing above the water, and I pointed. Dad followed my direction, guiding the canoe so that from my seat in the bow, I could reach the "turtle." But when the canoe slid within a father length (six feet) of my "turtle" my eyes distinguished, instead of a turtle head, the green feathery tip of a weed. Soon I learned to be as proficient at spotting as my father. He, with his quick hand, could sometimes flip the turtles into the canoe with his paddle. My skill was in springing over the bow and groping in the soft mud for the telltale stone-hard shell. When one of us did catch a turtle, we would turn it over, admire its beautifully painted dorsal carapace, then let it go back to its watery home.

The "voice of the turtle" speaks in many languages. In the physical world of my childhood a small physical turtle came from a small physical lake. There is another turtle, the turtle of the dream time, the turtle whose back forms the turtle island of North America. This island emerging from the ocean-womb of Mother Earth speaks less simply, and as I grope in the mud of my mother's flesh searching for the firm shell of a turtle, I am like a blind person feeling an elephant. My mind cannot conceive the whole of my Earth Mother or of this universe of which I am a part. In this river of life I am still learning the language of turtles, little turtles of the dream time who sometimes become weeds and sometimes become Mother Earth herself giving me the direction of my life. She asks me to be like a little turtle bobbing with the current, not attempting to direct it and not clinging to the bottom like a rooted weed.

Mother Earth had something to tell me through my Rainbow friend Bruce. He brought me a hollowed circle of maple cut by a beaver, perfect for a drum. Mother Earth's message is very clear. She wants me to have a drum, to listen to her heartbeat. The messenger she has chosen is Beaver, the brother who told Eagle Man and Thunder Owl my name. He cut the tree for my drum, and Bruce hollowed it out for me. In this way the *Wigmunke oyate*—the Rainbow people—work together within a wisdom too large for any one individual to understand.

Earth is a living being, and we are her children. This idea is older than we know. The Native Americans, who tell us they have always been here, have always thought of her personally. Now we moderns are beginning to catch up with them. Medical doctor and chemist James Lovelock proposed the Gaia theory. This theory explains the Earth as a living being much as a tree is living, even though 99 percent of it is "dead." Just as our hair and fingernails and bone can be called "dead," so can most of the earth. Yet the sum total of inert parts can be understood as being organized into a living being in us, in a tree, and in the earth. A conventional scientist might have called his theory something like "biological cybernetic system with homeostatic tendencies," but Lovelock had enough sympathy with ordinary mortals to call it "Gaia," after the Greek goddess of Earth.

For me the *Inipi* Ceremony opens a powerful channel to hear what this Mother/Father of us all wants us to know. When Eagle Man introduced me to the Sioux ceremony in the lodge in the woods at the edge of our pond, I felt my living bond with Mother Earth as I never had before. It was spring, a time when Earth should be bursting with new green growth. But this spring was different. We had had no rain for over a month, and our Mother's flesh was parched.

We had heard Eagle Man's explanation of the ceremony. One of the things he told us was that Father Sky has daily communion with Mother Earth. He told us in words I understood as one understands an explanation of sex when one is too young to experience its beauty. But the Sweat Lodge showed us living Earth in action, and she became a live being in my heart. In the lodge our living juices lost the Victorian meaning that deodorant ads try so hard to maintain, and it was easy to change one little letter and think "sweet" about the sage-scented lifeblood we shared with our brothers and sisters and with the sweet rain from Father Sky.

Bernie forks the glowing red stones into the central pit of the lodge. Eagle Man dips water onto the rocks, the ancient bones of our Mother; and steam boils forth, soon blending with the life juices—our human sweat; upward the blend carries our prayers for rain to Father Sky.

He answers. Twice a flash of white light sends a beam across the top of the obsidian-black dome of the lodge. Then, when the last prayer is ended, the drumbeat of thunder makes Eagle Man's drum sound like a whispered echo of the Great Spirit's power.

As we come out of the lodge, rain—over an inch and a half—pours to the Mother, giving her the fluid of life, and from her moist womb plants can grow again.

Three ceremonies followed in June, and within three days of the first two of them, rain followed, but only one-fifteenth of an inch. To the thirsty plants the hint of rain was like tears. I thought of the rain forests we were consuming, I thought of the ozone layer we were destroying. The universe seemed to be crying, "I hear you, but you must do more. You are killing your mother."

Another sweat ceremony I took part in was in the same place but led by Joe Thunder Owl, Eagle Man's Sioux brother. The circle of relatives took their places in the lodge, already warm from the previous sitting.

I watch the first stone forked on top of the others. Instantly I see an Indian face looking at me from the rock, the eyes shrouded in dark mystery, the lower half of the face illuminated, glowing red. The mouth is a strong straight line of brilliant red. Thunder Owl is not satisfied with the first position the rock took, and with his tongs he shifts it until the red line of the Indian's mouth takes the direction of a red road leading straight away in front of me. Silently I thank the spirits. Prayers for cleansing and endurance, wisdom and healing work their transformation within us.

The ceremony is over. I crawl under the lifted flap into the light dry air, newly born into a beautiful world. My body still steaming, I walk through the smooth mud of the shoreline, wade past the water grass, then swim beyond the lily pads to where the water is clear as crystal. I swim on my back looking up at Father Sky. I feel the child-wonder of camping trips with my earth father. Then I look at the dipper in the sky. As the dipper in the lodge held earth water, the star dipper holds spiritual water in its limitless space. That night I was aware of Earth's language in meaning without words.

At Carleton College, Eagle Man held up his own *wotai* stone and also a participant's crystal as a beseechment article for the first time. Then, at the sweat by the edge of our pond, many of us used crystals or *wotai* stones, offering them to the four directions. I thought of the earth of the pipestone giving birth to the tobacco, and the fire energy turning it to smoke as we gave our visible breath up to Father Sky. Then I thought of the crystal I held drawing down the energy of the sky and giving a rainbow to Mother Earth. It completed a cycle, making the energy move again.

Many sisters and brothers asked for rain, for the drought to stop. Before I prayed, I saw a red light come over the rocks, the light of understanding from the east. Then I felt something like a mild electric current. Later Eagle Man said that he saw the red light go over me when I prayed. I believe that light stayed with me to help me later. I asked for knowledge to be connected from the head to the heart so that I could understand what I needed to do and be open to receive the help I needed.

The following morning I received four signs. The first was the rain—over one-fourth inch, enough to cleanse the Earth as we had been cleansed in her womb the night before. It held hope, a promise for the future.

The next three signs appeared to me when I was sitting back in a lounge chair close to sleep. I saw three images. The first image was a small dog that darted onto the road in front of me with an offering in its mouth. It stopped facing me, looking up with beseeching eyes. The dog is a symbol of faithfulness, and I knew its offering was to be taken seriously. What it was presenting to me was a totally dried up frog, its four legs making a square as they reached out to the four directions. The frog is a changing animal like the moon, and like the moon its meaning is feminine. Also it represents in its amphibious life the transition from the element of water to that of earth and vice versa. It is cleansing in its power. But, as the dog held the frog out to me, its changes were stopped in all four directions—it was totally stiff, certainly not a power for watery cleansing. What was I supposed to do about it?

The next image showed me a tree: a dead skeleton standing in a dried-up swamp. The tree of life appeared dead, and I thought of the Judeo-Christian capitalism that prevails over this Turtle Island, drying up its natural roots. But on the top of the tree, very much alive, was a woman in a pink dress (a color usually symbolizing love), her arms and legs reaching out to the four directions. In contrast to the frozen position of the frog, she was spinning rapidly, reaching to the four directions and also up and down to Father Sky and Mother Earth. In the speed of her movement, she looked like a circle of pink light. I saw this image, not from the Indian point of view, but as an illustration of what white society had attempted to do to the Sun Dance tree. By outlawing the Sioux Sun Dance, our government had taken the water of life from the Natural Way that had worked so well for many centuries. But the spirit of love as personified by Buffalo Calf Woman is still very much alive and will bring the tree to full flower as Black Elk has prophesied.

The fourth sign, the final image I was given, was of a wide straight asphalt road leading away in front of me. On that road was a huge black earth-moving machine. How it worked was not clear to me, but I did notice that it came in black, so it must be from the spirit world. I knew that it was of the good red road when I saw it piling red earth down the center of the road, covering up the asphalt. The image brought back to my mind the image of the red road I had seen in Thunder Owl's lodge.

It is such signs that make our way clear and let us know that we are working in harmony with the spirits and with each other.

I thought of the task my friend and I had begun, a weekend seminar in "Mother Earth Spirituality." For that we had been given a strong sign. When we went to Belwin Nature Center, where we hoped to hold it, we saw an "eagle feather" welcoming us in front of the door. Actually it was a Canada goose feather, which told us to go to Canada for our sponsorship. We got an okay for our project the next day from Spiritual Science Fellowship based in Montreal, and then got permission from Belwin Nature Center to use that beautiful facility.

So four days later a weekend date, place, and sponsorship had been arranged, and the spirits were offering powerful help along the good red road. Since then we have been teaching Mother Earth spirituality from Santa Fe to Pittsburgh and in Canada as well as locally. It is as though there were a giant turtle buried under the flesh of Mother Earth, and everywhere we dig, people feel the protective shell of Turtle Island like the bones of our Mother. The people in our classes are like crystals reflecting the rainbow back to us magnified. Many of them are now conducting ceremonies, and the power grows. Now they are meeting on a weekly basis to simply beseech the six powers. They gather in an old church and beseech, acknowledge, and recognize the natural connection. After their ceremony they socialize and discuss the ways they can help the Earth.

Earth Day was coming. We believed a global ceremony of celebration would bring the water of life to the flowering tree, teaching us that every day is "Earth Day." The date of Earth Day is a practical one for planting trees. You want to do this before the sap starts to flow. We will "Earth think" and plant trees, taking those in clusters and those beneath the mature oaks, maples, cottonwoods, and elms. Those little seedlings that would never have a chance to grow skyward—we'll plant them in open places and look after them. We're going to focus on cottonwoods and other trees that can endure a dry spell, just in case the earth starts to heat up. We're concerned about the vanishing wetlands. The good-old-boy politicians have allowed millions of acres to be drained, and the diminishing flocks in the skies are telling us we're harming nature. When Beaver looked me in the eye, he said, "Mother Nature put us here to hold back the water." When Bruce brought me the maple drum frame, Beaver was telling us to drum forever this message. When the dog held forth the dried-up frog in my vision, I was being told that we will be in for some dry times unless we take action *now,* and I must beat the drum to stir that action. I see the farmers crying for rain. I will have to tell them over and over, "Listen to Beaver. Your greed to harvest more land has you draining the wetlands. Don't you know? When the water is held back, more of it evaporates into the sky and you get more rain!"

Maybe the huge black machine in my vision is an earth-mover to fill back the drainage ditches. Maybe it is black because by filling in the ditches it will be bringing back the life-giving rains that come from the black west of Black Elk's vision. Why have drainage ditches when you are actually creating a desert? What is that doing for the generations yet to come?

We have enough spring seedlings available to make a continuous line of trees all across the southern half of Minnesota and on to reach through tree-denuded Iowa. Wouldn't that be something? "Roads" of trees covering the asphalt of harmful greed and stretching for miles. Our defense establishment could make itself worthwhile with such a project. The soldiers could modify their tanks to become earth restorers. They could convert their gas tankers to carry life-giving rain from the spring runoff and look after the seedlings. Our earth is starting to heat and they would be coming to our defense. All things considered, it would probably be a better project for the local people to take upon themselves. Instead of "grass roots" we could call it "Rainbow tree roots," because it would help bring back the rain and a rainbow follows the rain. The Red Road of Knowledge tells me that these things have to be done. Mother Earth's drought and the vanishing wildlife are telling us they have to be done.

BEGINNING A RAINBOW CLAN

Clans have existed down through time. Other than the immediate family, clans were the primary identification with the broader, extended family. The *tiyospaye,* the extended family, was the backbone of Sioux tribal structure.

How do you begin a Rainbow clan?

I believe the easiest way to spawn an assemblage of Natural Way–minded people is to hold a weekend gathering. You can start on a smaller scale by having a speaker come in for an evening session or an all-day Saturday or Sunday session. Some organizers have taken a weekend at a camp or retreat center that offers an optional arrival on Friday evening for participants who will be traveling a long distance. A good practice to follow is to have speakers and conference staff arrive a day or at least an evening early in order to assure availability and preparedness, especially if a medicine circle or a sweat lodge has to be constructed.

Once a clan has been established, a monthly or bimonthly newsletter is a nice form of communication. Postage and supplies are expensive, however, and these costs can be borne by a subscription fee. The mailing list will grow at a healthy pace once activities develop.

Weekly or biweekly (semimonthly) gatherings are the best way to keep a Rainbow clan functioning as the number of participants increases. Many people are dissatisfied with what organized churches offer and are looking for a spiritual service that has a deeper meaning. Once your Rainbow service gets started you will be surprised at the amount of new people it will attract. Most Rainbows seem to come from a church background and have attended church services regularly; therefore the weekly services seem to fit in rather comfortably.

In Minneapolis, the Badger Clan of the Rainbow Tribe found a broadly based church that did not mind having the Rainbows use the church facilities on Saturday evenings at a scheduled time. This church's congregation is so open-minded that it rents office and facility space to spiritual groups whose beliefs may diverge widely from the congregation's predominantly Christian perceptions. The Rainbows take a collection during their Saturday evening beseechment service and donate to the church for heating and electricity. A portion is withheld for newsletter costs. The weekly service begins in the evening and promptly ends within an hour. After the ceremony, there is a time set aside for socializing in the church basement. Future sweat lodges, vision quest trips to the Black Hills, Lakota language classes, crafts and spiritual arts events, and related activities are planned and talked about or brought into being. The latest on new movies, books, tapes, and other forms of information is also made available by the age-old means of two-legged communication—the coming together of the tribe. (If Saturday evenings do not work out as well in your locale, choose another day, maybe even Sunday morning.)

A typical beseechment service will find the Badger Clan gathered in a circle in a large carpeted room behind the main assembly hall. The Rainbows started out sitting in the church pews but the atmosphere felt rather foreign to them, so they chose to sit in a circle on the floor in the adjacent room. One person usually conducts the ceremony, although several helpers such as a drummer or an assistant may be present. The assistant usually smudges the participants with sage, cedar, or sweetgrass at the beginning, takes up the collection, and ushers latecomers to seating spaces.

Initially, peace pipe ceremonies were held, but there has been an increasing trend for the Rainbows to use their personal *wotai* stones as the beseechment article for their calling to the six powers of the universe and of course to the Great Spirit, who is regarded as the Ultimate Force responsible for the powers. Occasionally, a peace pipe will be used, especially if a Native American conducts the ceremony, and occasionally a crystal will be used instead of a *wotai* stone.

The conductor is free to begin the service with an initial beseechment or calling to whatever direction he or she chooses. Most conductors begin with either the east direction or the west direction, however. The west direction is the predominant beginning direction among the Badger Clan because they are familiar with Black Elk's vision and recognize that it was the west power that first spoke to Black Elk. It is also practical because then the ending beseechment direction is the south power—making healing and growth the final subjects of the focus on the four directions.

The Badger Clan is reluctant to load up on a set of restrictive rules and dogma, except that they are adamant that the role of woman in ceremony will never be limited, will not be diminished or become dominated by the male role as reflected in organized churches, as well as in many tribes. Badger Clan Rainbows prefer that, at the very minimum, half of their ceremonies be led by women. Nature is equally balanced with both gender powers, and the Rainbows intend that they will reflect the truthful teachings of nature, without distortion. They feel strongly that the input of woman is an essential ingredient for needed world peace. They also prefer that no particular individual or set of individuals dominate or form a hierarchy within their group, and these stipulations have cultivated a harmonious gathering of like-minded people.

Let us take a look at a representative weekend gathering centered on "the spirituality of nature." This particular gathering did not form a Rainbow clan then, but later a meeting group established the Deer Clan. The setting was a YMCA camp outside of Cincinnati, and the conference was uniquely named "A Gathering." The camp has roomy cabins that border a spacious lawn. The Ohio River flows beside this green space that is larger than several football fields. Enough outdoor classrooms are available for several activities and presentations to be going on at the same time. A dining hall capable of feeding several hundred at a sitting is a popular place and is frequented for coffee and tea in the evening hours. The cabins offer dormitory-style living. The participants at this event were mostly from Cincinnati and Kentucky. Native American culture and ceremony was not the only focus. Other topics by speakers were also brought to the gathering.

> Using nature as a backdrop, the weekend offers a wide variety of experiential programs, with topics such as addictions, relationships, science and mysticism, and Native American spirituality. The teachers are international and extraordinary, many drawn through synchronous events to share their perspectives. Included are Native American spiritual healers, teachers and elders. Their perspectives are usually very traditional, and some have never taught off the reservation before. We join them in a humble way, respecting their ways. The ceremonies—most often Lakota—are powerful; the mystical becomes the reality; we have the opportunity to move from an ordinary state of consciousness to new states of awareness.[1]

The camp along the Ohio was an added treat for me because four other Sioux had traveled from the Rosebud Reservation in South Dakota. I met a good friend, Gilly Running, who built the sweat lodge. Gilly's father is Elmer Running, a medicine man who also conducts Sun Dance ceremonies.

After the lodge was built, sweat lodge ceremonies were held in the early evening and on into the night, since so many of the gathering's participants wanted to attend this stimulating ceremony. Many participants attended the Sweat Lodge several times to experience the manner in which the various lodge leaders conducted the ceremony. There is a basic commonality in Sweat Lodge Ceremony, but I do not know of any two individuals who conduct it exactly alike. Most of the "sweats" were mixed gender and conducted by the Rosebud Sioux and me. But a Rainbow woman also conducted several all-women lodges and they were well attended.

The Full Moon Clan gathered within a few weeks after the gathering at Cincinnati. In southern Michigan near Watervilet, and a convenient drive from Chicago, a hundred participants spent a weekend that was called "Native Wisdom" at Camp Ronora. Camp Ronora has similar characteristics to the YMCA camp near Cincinnati, except that the land seems to have an added spiritual context. At least some of the Rainbows seem to think so, especially after some strong ceremony acknowledgment. The agenda for this Natural Way gathering was similar to the one in Cincinnati. Books, tapes, art, crafts, beadwork, and nature-based jewelry were also available in the main meeting hall. A capable and congenial person from Chicago, Matthew Sweigart, was responsible for organizing this coming together.

The agenda at Camp Ronora focused on four teachers: Tarwater, Charla Hermann, Kathleen O'Sullivan, and myself. Tarwater lectured on Native American symbolism, arts, crafts, and traditions. He also displayed handcrafted drums that drew my admiration. Charla Hermann, who was reared in Wyoming and nurtured in the native ways of the Lakota and other Plains tribes, offered a lecture entitled "Discover Woman's Spirit." Like Tarwater, she is an excellent craftswoman and sings Lakota and other tribal ceremonial songs. Kathleen O'Sullivan lectured on women's issues and conducted women's sweat lodges. As at Cincinnati, mixed-gender lodges were also available. Kathleen drew from her work in Native American spirituality, alternative healing, metaphysics, and facilitating nature-based ceremony. I spoke on the six powers of Black Elk's vision and also conducted an Indian necklace–making class utilizing bone hairpipe, pony beads, polished stones, abalone, mother-of-pearl, and cowrie shells as the major materials.

It is interesting to note that no one spoke about converting the Indian tribes to do things the Rainbow Way or about setting up boarding schools. No one was condemned for not belonging to the majority religion of the land, and no one tried to convince the audience that Indians are a lost tribe of Israel. But there was considerable unspoken agreement that a lot of mystery surrounds all things spiritual and that no person or group of persons, be they Christian, Native American, or Rainbow Tribe, has all the answers.

I first met Tarwater at Camp Ronora when he was laying out the dimensions of the sweat lodge that turned out to be picture perfect. He had driven his pickup truck all the way from Alabama, and although Camp Ronora had adequate tools available, I was deeply impressed by how well equipped he was for building the lodge and obtaining firewood. Not only did the lodge turn out aesthetically appealing, but it was well insulated for the cool fall evenings. It also excluded outside interfering noise, even overflying airplanes, once you went inside. He is so experienced at lodge building that we even had towel and clothing racks to hang our clothes on before going into the ceremony. Old dead logs were provided as well to sit on around the fire. I had heard a great deal about Tarwater in my travels and knew that eventually we would meet.

After we were introduced I eagerly joined the rest of the early arrivals to search the woods for saplings and other lodge-building materials. I find that one of the most relaxing activities for my own personal enjoyment is to help build a sweat lodge. I like it especially when someone like Tarwater or Gilly Running is in charge of the construction. I had always thought of a sweat lodge as being a simple structure to build, but after being around these two spiritual men, I discovered that it can also be a work of art.

I was promptly distracted during one of my sapling forays by a tall stand of sumac. Never before had I seen such large sumac. The saplings were over three inches in diameter and were the height of small trees. I returned to the grove after the lodge was completed and cut a straight piece for a new peace pipe stem. I had always wanted a large enough sumac piece to work with so that I could carve four symbols on the stem. Two of the symbols are symbols that Eagle Feather's pipe stem displayed. A fatter piece of wood is needed when you set out to carve symbols. Sumac is a soft wood not much harder than balsa. It is much prettier than balsa, since it has so many shiny and varied hues. The pith is very soft and a hot wire can easily penetrate it to make a passage for the smoke. In the old days, Indians used hot pebbles to make the passage; it was a long and tedious procedure.

Tarwater also built a medicine wheel enclosure at the edge of the spacious lawn at Camp Ronora. A rectangular enclosure was constructed using thicker saplings at the corners for posts. After an entry gate was made, string was tied around the rest of the posts to enclose the medicine circle. The string was also used to hang tobacco offerings to the spirit world during the conference. As was done for the sweat lodge, the colors of Black Elk's vision were utilized to mark each direction of the wheel—a black cloth on the west corner post, a white cloth on the north post, a red flag on the east, and a yellow flag on the south.

A unique closing ceremony was held at the medicine wheel on the last day. After a concluding talk by the director, a gift session took place. Before the closing ceremony all participants had been invited to place a gift in the medicine wheel enclosure. At the end of the closing, all participants gathered in a line and went past the gift area to take a new gift for themselves. This is a wonderful way to end a conference or a gathering; it instills a special family feeling in all who have taken part and touches back to the old Indian way of giving in the *Otuha* or Giveaway Ceremony.

The Rainbows adapt what is best from the old ways. What I like about Rainbow Tribe philosophy and practice is that they do not depend on a guru to lead them. They are all leaders. Rainbow men and women of all races are regarded as equal leaders.

12

THE CALL TO LEAD

It behooves all who are upon the Natural Path to extend courtesy and understanding to Native Americans. Many Indians are reluctant to trust the newfound interest in their culture by outsiders. Past history and ongoing racial abuse by the dominant society give Indians reason to be skeptical and suspicious. Let us look at a Rainbow encounter that turned into one of harmony and relationship. We will find a pair of Rainbow Tribe women purchasing some gifts that became very meaningful. A good lesson in reserve and propriety comes forth from this observation.

LIVING BRIDGES

Buffalo Spirit Woman

We stopped in a Dakota town to do some tourist shopping and found several interesting shops. One was Indian owned and sold Indian-made jewelry. I purchased a porcupine-quill medicine wheel for a special friend of mine. Three weeks before I had given him one made by an Indian woman in Pipestone. He had used it in a veterans' acknowledgment ceremony and had given it to one of the vets in attendance as a remembrance of the occasion. At another shop my traveling companion, Marg, bought an elaborate beaded necklace for her mother. Pleased with our purchases, we continued on into the West, drawing closer to the dark mountains looming out of the plains, far out on the horizon.

Michael, and the rest of a group of seven women, met us at the information center parking lot. Since they had arrived an hour earlier, they had already proceeded to set up their tents in the area at the base of the mountain.

Many other people had chosen to vision quest this particular weekend and, consequently, the parking lot had only one space left when we arrived. Marg, Michael, and I walked across the camping area to a group of Indian men sitting around a campfire and I inquired about the availability of the empty sweat lodge next to their camp. They were evasive and noncommittal in their answers. They definitely gave us the impression that they did not want us there. After several attempts to get information, I was cut off with, "You'll have to wait until the elder awakens. He is very tired and probably will sleep for a couple of hours."

The three of us began walking over to the empty sweat lodge to see what was needed in the way of stones and wood in case we would be able to use the site later. A man came from behind one of the tents straight toward us. He offered his hand to me and said, "Hello, my name is Albert." I shook his hand and immediately felt a bit more welcome.

"My name is Kathleen O'Sullivan. I am here with a group of young people who have come to pray and do ceremony at this sacred place."

He looked directly at me and said, "This is a sacred place and is for all who wish to pray."

Encouraged by his warmth I added, "We have come with respect and would like to do ceremony this evening. Do you know if this sweat lodge site is available and if it is, may we use it?"

Again he spoke of the sacredness of the mountain and that all who wish to pray may do so. He thought the site was open and that we were welcome to use it for our evening ceremony and prayers.

Michael, Marg, and a couple of the other women began to clean the lodge site and brought wood from the parking lot area. I noticed as I walked across the campground that several of the five young men I had first approached were in different parts of the campground talking to other people and looking rather serious as they glanced our way. My mind was racing. I felt responsible for the group, as I had agreed to teach a class and do ceremony for them. I realized I was still feeling a sense of not being welcome. Before I knew it, I found myself in my car driving the short distance to the information center, where I was greeted by Chuck, a ranger who has a degree of Indian blood. We had met a year earlier on another vision quest weekend, and three weeks earlier we had talked when I had been there again, experiencing my own *Hanblecheya* ("crying for a vision").

After the preliminary greetings, I explained our experiences and our feeling that perhaps we were intruding. I said, "Chuck, we have come here to respectfully pray and do ceremony, but if we are in any way disrupting or causing any difficulty for the Indian people who are here to pray on their sacred lands, we will leave and go to the campground down by the lake."

A warm smile held his face in silence for several moments before he gently but firmly replied, "You have traveled a long way and have come with respect for the sacredness of the mountain and the people. You go back and do your ceremony. It will all work out. Don't worry, it will all work out."

When I arrived back at the site, Marg and a young blond man were squatting on the ground in front of the fire pit. He was drawing a picture in the dirt with a stick, and I overheard him saying that we had built the fire all wrong and we would have to let it burn out and do it over in an appropriate manner. I crouched down next to Marg and told him that we would certainly be glad to learn his way as we had come not only to pray and do ceremony but to learn whatever we could. He then proceeded to show us "his" proper procedure for building the fire.

Just as he finished his teaching, another man who had been at the sweat lodge site about half a block away came down with his power saw. He asked us if he could cut our wood for us, which he proceeded to do in very short order. We had been trying to break it in half by stepping on it and hacking at it with a rather dull hatchet. It must have looked pretty silly to him to see us struggling. We appreciated his humor about it and his help.

We had a blue tarp with which we were going to cover the sweat lodge. Our new friends felt it would not do the job, so three of them helped us to remove all the blankets and quilts from one of the other unused lodges, and then helped us to cover our lodge. I was beginning to sense a feeling of community building.

Marg explained to me that while the woodcutting was going on when I was gone to the ranger station, the blond man had begun talking to several of the women on a social level. She did not take part in the conversation until he said to the women, "I suppose you are going to use the sweat lodge as a sauna tonight." She realized at that point that he was testing, that he thought we were just there on a camp-out. She observed a change in his manner when she said, "Not at all. I have been fasting from food and water for two days and have come to do Vision Quest. I understand the sacredness of the experience."

The blond man again approached us, introduced himself as Singing Eagle, of Sioux and French ancestry, and from Montana. He told us his wife would like to explain to us about tobacco ties and sweat lodge. He also said that he would be happy to conduct sweat lodge for us. By that time the whole group was seated, waiting for me to conduct the lodge.

I thanked Singing Eagle for his offer and while he went over to get his wife, Maxine, I talked to the group. "This is a unique opportunity for all of us. These people are willing to share their spiritual teachings and to do ceremony with us—ceremony in what they perceive to be the right way . . . so let's learn." I quietly blended into the group and we listened to Maxine share her knowledge and wisdom. She was shy at first but began to open up as we laughed among ourselves about being "all thumbs" at our attempts to tie the tiny bundles of tobacco that are used as offerings to the spirit world.

At one point Maxine began to explain about the six powers and the colors used for each power. When she had finished, I took the opportunity to respectfully say, "The colors that are used by our new friends are different from the way we learned them from our mentor, Eagle Man, who uses the colors that Black Elk, the Lakota prophet, received in his vision as a young child. Tonight, out of respect, we honor our friends' teachings and use their colors as a valuable lesson that not all people's ways are the same, but we can learn from all people's ways."

The stone people (the rocks) were red-hot and ready to join us in the lodge, so we prepared ourselves by honoring the six powers and Great Mystery through prayer and by filling the pipe, which was capped with fresh sage and carefully placed on the altar in front of the sweat lodge. We filed into the lodge and sat cross-legged in a circle around the fire pit. Singing Eagle drummed on the new drum I had loaned to him and joked with us for a few minutes about how hot he was going to make the interior of the lodge. Then he got more serious and impressed upon everyone that it would be very moderate and that he would open the flap at any time if someone needed to have it raised to allow the cool night air to enter. He made a point of saying that he had been facilitating sweat lodges for over a decade and that during that time no one had ever had to leave. He believed strongly that the power of the circle was in staying in a circle and if someone had to leave that circle of prayer it lost some of its power. His next words echoed my friend Eagle Man's teachings, "We are here to pray, not to see how tough we are."

The flap closed and total darkness enveloped us as Singing Eagle sang the opening song to the four directions. His voice strongly carried the Lakota words to the four winds, and we knew immediately why he had been given the name of Singing Eagle. To my surprise, I knew the song and sang along in Lakota. Familiar streaks of light manifested for me as the spirits of the ancestors began to come into the lodge. Hearts opened and spiritual activity began.

With a pained voice, someone said, "My eyes are burning."

Singing Eagle took this as a natural time to take a break and had the door person open the flap to allow some cool air into the lodge. He also passed around a towel and some drinking water in a dipper.

The door flap was lowered and we were again in the womblike darkness. The song of the drum began slowly, then the sounds grew louder and the tempo quickened, carrying us deeply into our own beating hearts and body rhythms. Prayers were started to the left of Singing Eagle and I realized that Jason, a fourteen-year-old Indian youth from Canada, was in the lodge with us. His words of thanksgiving for being able to be in this ceremony were uplifting. Others who had never participated in this type of ceremony were experiencing new depths and strengths within themselves and were appreciating being able to express themselves so openly.

At the end of the prayer circle, a tall Sioux man from Canada began speaking. His prayer was particularly moving to me; he was thanking *Tankashilah* for the opportunity to pray with us and to protect us, his new friends. Not only had he been in the first group of men who had distanced themselves, but he also had been the least receptive to me when I was trying to get information about the availability of the sweat lodge. This was a definite shift in attitude. They had opened to us when they could see our sincerity. I was joyful and grateful for the change that I felt was taking place; energy was moving in the sacred circle of life, bringing us to a better *wookahnige* (understanding) that we are all friends and relatives and are living the concept of *Mitakuye oyasin* ("We are all relatives").

His beseechment continued and I was impressed over and over with the words that came to my inner consciousness, *You have something very special that really belongs to him—let this be your giveaway.* I realized that I strongly wished to give him the beautiful medicine wheel I had purchased for someone else. As soon as I made this decision I felt peaceful and knew that I would also gift Singing Eagle, Maxine, and Jason even though I had not come prepared to do so. I planned to talk to Marg after the ceremony to discuss what we could find as gifts for them.

"*Ho! Hetch etu aloh!* The ceremony is finished," was spoken and we began to crawl out of the lodge. I was just about out the door when I saw Jason sitting by the door in the position to leave last. I stopped and removed from my wrist the braided horsehair bracelet that I had purchased only a few days earlier and put it on Jason's wrist, telling him, "We have sweated and prayed together. This is a thank-you gift from me as a remembrance of this time." A broad grin covered his face and he thanked me.

While changing into dry clothing I spoke to Marg about gifts for Maxine and Singing Eagle. I told her how moved I was to give gifts to these people who had gone out of their way to help us. Unhesitatingly she said, "Oh, now I know why I bought that beaded necklace in Mitchell. It really didn't feel like it belonged to Mom, but I didn't know who I was buying it for. Of course, it belongs to Maxine!"

We finished putting on our dry clothes and walked to the car to get the necklace and something for Singing Eagle. I already knew I would give him a copy of a book that would broaden his vision and open him to new opportunities. Then I remembered a two-pound can of coffee to go along with the book. We returned to the warmth of the fire and the people who were animatedly talking about their experiences. The necklace, book, and coffee were accepted with surprised looks.

I looked for Sean, the new owner-to-be of the porcupine-quill medicine wheel. His handsome features and tall, lean frame were silhouetted in the firelight. I walked over to the other side of the fire pit and told him about my experience in the lodge during the time he was praying. I placed the medicine wheel in his hands and he became silent for a few moments. Tenderly, he put his arms around me and held me to him as if I were very fragile. He told me I wouldn't believe what he was going to tell me. On his way to Spirit Mountain, he had stopped at an Indian gift store and found a medicine wheel. He wanted it badly but had no money. He cried as he talked to Great Spirit and told him he really wanted it but he would be patient and wait, knowing someday he would have one. He released me and continued, "And here you are with one just about like it. Great Spirit, thank you and thank you, Kathleen."

The group began to go off to their tents for the night. The two who were prepared to vision quest, Marg and Michael, were almost ready to go up on the mountain. I was talking with them near the sweat lodge. Singing Eagle walked over to us and said, "Crazy Horse's spirit is here—he is buried on this mountain. There are other spirits here and not all of them are good. Earlier this week I was on the mountain and lightning struck very close by. Sometimes you can hear the ancestors chanting . . . there are rattlesnakes . . . this is a very powerful place and things can come at you in the dark. Are you afraid of the dark? Are you really sure you want to be in the dark by yourself all night?"

I listened, my own thoughts turning to the personal freedom and joy I have in my nature-based spiritual practices. I was born and raised in an orthodox Christian tradition filled with dogma and taboos devised by human beings to control the masses through fear of a man-imaged and man-illusioned devil. *It,* the Creator, has made nothing bad or nondynamic for the good. I have worked through these fears and taboos throughout my lifelong search for God, understanding, and knowing. I have no need for the taboos and fears that limited my life until I returned to the Natural Path, and I am not about to include a bunch of new ones upon my new path. I realized, however, that Singing Eagle was testing their determination and that he was concerned about any undue disturbance of the people from his group who had already been put out on the mountain a couple of days earlier. This was a very valid concern.

Michael stood in the background listening but not joining in the conversation; Singing Eagle directed his words of warning and testing more toward Marg. She answered firmly with, "No, I'm not afraid of the dark—rattlesnakes maybe, but I am prepared to spend the night on the mountain."

He began to point out the places where other people were fulfilling their vision quests and suggested that Michael and Marg stay on the lower part of the mountain, not too far off the path. With his flashlight he then illuminated the path for them to begin their climb. Undaunted and well prepared, the pair began to walk into the darkness of the mountain.

Since I was the facilitator of my vision quest group, I stayed down below, at the base of the mountain. In case a quester might decide to come down early or in case someone should fall or otherwise be injured, this is a good procedure. I hadn't put my tent up when we arrived earlier in the day, so I was heading back to my car to sleep when Sean called to me. He wanted me to meet the medicine man who had been sleeping earlier but had now awakened. He gave me a cigarette as an offering to give to him and instructed me to ask him to pray for "our people on the mountain." We wound our way through the tents to the far edge of the encampment. Sean introduced me to an ordinary-looking man and we talked for a few moments before I offered the cigarette and asked him to say a prayer. He had a humble, quiet manner and did not have need for a veneer or to prove himself. He thanked me and agreed to remember the people in prayer. I became quite engrossed in the strength of the energy he radiated. After our visit, Sean and I returned to the fireside and talked for some time.

Once in my car I fell into a very deep sleep only to be awakened by a light shining in my face through the window. I had been in such a deep sleep that I was disoriented at first, then I realized the brilliant light was moonlight. Misty at first but gradually taking shape, the moon was coming from behind the rocks on the eastern side of the butte, and the sounds of the ancients' chanting entered my consciousness. I heard myself say, "Thank you, Great Mystery, for calling me to this sacred place again."

The daybreak star was my signal to uncramp my body from the backseat and walk down to camp to await Marg and Michael, who would be coming down from their mountain experience. Marg was already sitting with Sean and two other men at the fire that they had kept burning all through the night. Marg commented about it being a "beacon" for her. They invited me to sit with them and offered fresh hot coffee. I didn't need much coaxing. We exchanged stories and experiences for about two hours before Michael came down. They laughed hard when they teased Marg about her fluorescent lime-green jacket, which looked like a huge curled-up caterpillar on the side of the mountain as the sun came alive for the day. They were waiting for it to roll down the side of the mountain.

Albert, the elder, joined us and the conversation took on a more serious note as he began to talk about his experiences in boarding school. He told us of having his hands, palms down, held on a hot stove because he spoke Indian. We knew from other Indian friends that cruel practices were experienced by almost all Indian children at boarding schools. It seems almost impossible that these inhumane and unconscionable acts took place for so many years without interference from the outside. But of course these practices, as well as other outright illegal acts, were never publicized outside of the reservations, and the recipients of the acts did not have the means to stop them.

We inquired about the large group of Indians who were at the encampment and seemed to be like one family from several parts of the United States and Canada. They told us stories about each group coming separately and how they had been brought together through circumstances over a period of several years and that now they meet at Spirit Mountain each year at the same time to be together. In good Indian fashion they let us know that we were now also part of that *tiyospaye* (extended family) and were welcome next year at the same time.

Daybreak was long gone and it was time to break camp. We talked about our time together on the mountain, acknowledging our unsure beginnings and the changes that had unfolded for all of us as we experienced each other's ways. We parted friends. No, we parted friends and relatives—each having a better understanding and respect for the other and knowing we walk similar paths on our way to Great Mystery.

▼   ▼   ▼   ▼   ▼

FOOLS CROW'S CALL

I received a call from *Honcoka Olowonpi,* Jamie Sams. A mutual friend of ours, Dennis Banks, told Jamie that Fools Crow, the Oglala holy man, had been very ill and was in the hospital and that I was to meet her in Rapid City. She is my sister through the Making of Relatives Ceremony and within a few days she met me at the airport and we went down to the hospital just south of the reservation. She told me on the way that the old man would pass on in but a short while, within seven hours or seven days.

I am usually adverse to the making of predictions, even by a close friend. Few people that I have met have an inside track on the future, but then again I have seen some powerful and very accurate speculations come out of *Yuwipi* ceremonies. Some of Bill Eagle Feather's sweat lodges were equally credible when it came to prognostications. In my estimation, Jamie is a medicine woman. She downplays her mystique, but I have been in a few of her ceremonies and it appears that the spirit world is with her. She severely startled a lifelong acquaintance of mine in a sweat lodge she was conducting. My friend reached back to high school and Marine Corps days. He almost jumped through the lodge when her mountain lion spirit-calling power came in. Jamie's prediction regarding Fools Crow was accurate, and I have since learned to respect her ability in this realm.

After driving south we discovered that the old holy man had rallied and had been allowed to return home. We went to his grandson's home. Everett Lone Hill is a relative of mine through his father, Amos Lone Hill. He is also the son of the late Marie Fools Crow Lone Hill, the daughter of Fools Crow. The old sage was close to a hundred years old and was asleep when we arrived. Most estimate that he was either ninety-eight or ninety-nine years old. Fools Crow never worried about his exact age or his birthday, something maybe we can all learn from. We enter this world and we shall all leave. Earning our eagle feathers is more important than birthdays.

I visited with Everett and his wife while Jamie sat beside Fools Crow and watched him with a pleasant smile as he slept. I was informed that my good friend Red Bow had been there the day before. Buddy Red Bow is one of the most easygoing people I've ever met but he also has his serious side. In the Sun Dance he is like Pete Catches. He never moves a muscle or twitches a single facial feature to exhibit pain when he is pierced. I wondered if Buddy, an Oglala songwriter who speaks fluent Lakota and travels the country doing Native American concerts, had made his long trip back to the reservation because he also had the same "mystery sense" that Jamie had.

Within a short time Fools Crow awoke and stared at Jamie. Because of his hearing impairment, Everett yelled both of our names in his ear before taking me by the hand to the aged man.

Fools Crow stared through me, but it was not unlike the stare I had seen in his powerful *Yuwipi* and during the piercing of the Sun Dance. Then his look changed and I had the feeling we wouldn't be seeing each other again in this world. I touched his hand briefly. I dislike saying good-bye to a mentor. I had helped to fight a good fight alongside the old man and this was back when he had been in his spiritual prime. He was King Arthur and Bill Eagle Feather was Merlin. An inquisition in modern form was out to erase our way, and I was one of the Knights of the Sacred Hoop along with Red Bow, Sonny Larive, Dennis Banks, Russell Means, Clyde Belle-court, Millie, Minnie, Pat, Wanita Lone Wolf, Eddie Loon, Lehman Brightman, Crow Dog, Eddie Benton, George Gap, Sam Stands Holy, Pete Catches, and others who came either to protect directly or to support the Sun Dance back when there were so few of us and the missionary-dominated tribal council had it diluted down to three days with carnivals and rodeos and a fourth-day mass. We could draw a parallel with the Round Table warriors of the Misty Isles in the time when they too saw an inquisition threatening, one that eventually decimated and destroyed their way. We Sioux warriors with the help of some Ojibwa warriors took our stand at the Sun Dance. (The term *warriors* has no gender.) This was before the young rose up, and there were but a few of us. Without the supportive stand of the young that followed, however, we would have lost to those forces that sought to destroy our spiritual reach back into nature.

We slew the ugly dragon that had kept us from our holy grail, our natural spirituality. Fools Crow, Black Elk, and Eagle Feather were our Red Cloud, Sitting Bull, and Crazy Horse. The spirit of Black Elk whispered in our ears during the Sun Dance. Nick Black Elk's son, Ben Black Elk, brought the old seer's pipe to the Sun Dance at Pine Ridge. He gave it to me to carry in the Sun Dance. Yes, Black Elk's pipe! Maybe that is another reason that I am so close to him. I'll tell you more about that in another book.

Everett called out Jamie's name, and I spoke out in my broken Lakota to tell Fools Crow that she was a *pejuta winan waste aloh, heh, Seneca oyate* (a well-meaning medicine woman of the Seneca people). Fools Crow seemed to sense this salutation, and after staring hard at Jamie he took her hand and held it. Jamie presented Fools Crow with 144 red tobacco ties, and he held them to his heart while she held his hand. She took a rattle and sang to him in Sioux words and in Seneca. I gathered that he liked her singing because he sat up attentively on the bed and gripped her free hand, and at one time even winked at her. I returned to my chair to visit with the Lone Hills and also to allow Jamie some privacy with the holy man, even though we were in the same room.

In a letter to me Jamie Sams states the following:

> Then I sang him over and he tapped out the beat with his hand. When I finished, I moved to the floor and held his hand while he took my Medicine Pouch in his hand, I took it off and opened it for him and gave him the Mountain Lion Claw. He held it up to the sky and back to his heart, then he grabbed my left hand with as much force as a twenty-year-old and slapped the claw into my palm holding my hand tight over it and winked at me. In so doing, he let me know that he knew me and why I had come and was happy. That is when the burning started in my hand and when we made ready to leave.
>
> He has been with me in twenty-eight doctoring lodges I have conducted since and is my constant friend and companion.

Jamie gave Fools Crow an expensive, woolen Pendleton blanket and also gave money to the Lone Hills because they had experienced considerable expense to care for the old man. I contributed to a needed part for Everett's car. I say this because I want to teach a point and hopefully some practical etiquette when it comes to making a worthwhile offering to Native Americans, especially holy men and holy women—medicine people whom you might go to visit or whose help you might seek out. Do not just take them a little wad of tobacco. They can't eat tobacco! Their travel is not covered by a nostalgic sack of Bull Durham. Somewhere, someone wrote that the way to approach a medicine person or a spiritual person is to offer him or her some tobacco. That statement is only partially true!

We had visited another holy man on the reservation and I believe his situation is worthy of comment to make my point. I had danced with this man in the Sun Dance years before. He is very poor and he is also proud; therefore, I will not give out his name. When we drove up to his cabin, his son was working on his car. The car's starter was in need of replacement. Jamie had brought several bags of groceries, including fresh meat and vegetables, and she made some soup for the holy man while I took the son into town to find a car part. This holy man had hardly a thing to eat in his outdoor icebox.

When you go to visit a holy person, it is proper Indian etiquette to stop first at a store and buy some fresh beef—a good quality cut too. Don't think of buying a ring of baloney and a box of crackers, not unless you wish to insult your host. Buy at least a twenty-five-pound sack of potatoes and a head of cabbage, along with some onions and carrots or celery. Usually you will find a tasty stew or soup waiting after your visit or after the ceremony if one has taken place. One of the nicest gifts you can take as an extra is raspberries, blackberries, or blueberries. If you can't find fresh berries, buy at least six to ten cans of them for a wonderful dessert we call *wojapi*. Do not buy "dab" style. Buy so that plenty of food will be left over for the holy person's family. If the Great Spirit has blessed you with plenty, then also offer your host a cash contribution. Be tasteful about the manner in which you do this. Have it in an envelope and give it in privacy. Better yet, offer your gift to the spouse and do it in a quiet manner.

Jamie should be commended for her generosity and her considerate way of giving. In this particular situation, we were going to see Fools Crow, a revered holy man. This man's ceremony had once revealed that my life would be protected in Vietnam and that I would return. There was such a contrast in the frail figure of less than a hundred pounds whom I saw reclining in the small cabin compared to the strong, powerful person who had conducted the *Yuwipi* Ceremony that dark night several decades before. Everett and his wife told us of the special care the old holy man needed. When I discovered that Everett's car was not working because of a starter problem, we offered money to get the needed part. Everett was too proud to ask for anything, but he did accept our offering for the part after Jamie used the excuse that his car should be in good working order in case Fools Crow became ill again.

Most Native Americans do not like to ask for help even if they are desperately in need. Non-Indian priests and ministers have a program for obtaining financial help to keep their churches operating and themselves as well. If you belong to a parish or a congregation, by all means support your house of worship. I do not have any problem with donating to a church that I attend occasionally, even though I am not a member and do not intend to become one. I go there because I learn a lot for my earth walk through what one particular minister has to say. He strikes a chord, a message I need to hear. When you visit a native spiritual person, then have the dignity and the foresight to support that person too.

When we left the Lone Hills the evening sky was like red dawn. We drove out onto the highway and headed south. The setting sun had painted the sky red, arcing to bright violet, almost refusing to go on to the deepening shades of night. Far to the west were three streaks in the sky like comets, but I told myself they were the contrails of military planes, no doubt refueling while they prowled aloft with weapons that could end a lot of life upon the planet if they were ever unleashed. We all hope they will never be used, and those awesome weapons were some of the main reasons people gathered for the Harmonic Convergence. A lot of the world scoffed at the time, especially the news media. But no one is scoffing at the tremendous world change that has resulted almost overnight since the people gathered on that day in August of 1987. A whirlwind of global change has come about since the Berlin Wall cracked.

Jamie told me to hold her hand, the hand Fools Crow had held. After feeling the heat in Jamie's hand I believed I was privileged to a meaningful sign issued by Fools Crow or whatever mystery was responsible. The inner portion of Jamie's hand was hot! The rest of her hand was as cool as mine. The next day when we drove into the yard to visit another spiritual person, her hand heated up again. To me, Fools Crow had acknowledged what Jamie is doing: standing up for native spirituality and listening deeply in order to preserve the past. I believe he was also acknowledging that holy women and medicine women from all tribes must come forth and have the courage to establish their rightful and needed role in spiritual leadership.

Some would say the old holy man was passing her some of his medicine. I don't believe "medicine" can be passed. Your life-style is the basis for your medicine. You can learn from those who exhibit mystical power and certainly you should attempt to follow their good example, but it is the way you conduct yourself, your own intense and selfless inspection of spiritual knowledge, that will allow medicine power to flow. Everyone gains a degree of medicine power when more truth comes into his or her life. Consequently, you can lose your flow with the universe when you allow yourself to be distracted away from your natural path through the various selfish roads of life. I just do not believe that medicine power can be passed on, or that you can pick it up by having a spiritual elder's pipe or objects. Yes, you can certainly learn from them, and the best way to do that is to assist them in ceremonies and consequently spend time with them. I would much prefer to have had the experiences I had with Bill Eagle Feather than to possess his green jade pipe. I would rather have read *Black Elk Speaks* the many times that I have read it and have known Ben, the son of Black Elk, than to be the owner of Black Elk's pipe, wherever it may be.

It is what you put into your mind that is important, not what you carry externally. Memory, yes memory, will be the only entity that you carry over into the spirit world. Take a look at a computer. It is an allowance by the Great Spirit. Its memory power is allowed. It carries over its memory even after it is shut off and, we could say, "dead." Bill Eagle Feather would say, "Now here is a teaching from what the Creator is allowing us two-leggeds to work with and observe." If you have the intellect to search for a teaching, then view this example. If you are a know-it-all jealous detractor, then do your scoffing. Maybe you will have an interesting visit sometime with Chief Eagle Feather, in the spirit world. I had a know-it-all brother who really knew very little because he would never listen, yet he was always detracting. He carried very little wisdom memory (spiritual growth knowledge) on into the spirit world. In the end, your conduct and your seeking, not the possession of items or a disparaging attitude, will establish your medicine power.

We watched the streaks of the line makers far, far out on the horizon. One line maker was a leader and was out in front. That way shower was Fools Crow in my thoughts. The other two followed. The leader was blotted out by a high thin cloud, disappearing, and only the two remained.

We drove along, silent. I had a strong feeling that Jamie's prediction about Fools Crow was going to be true. I was pretty sure it was the last time I would see Fools Crow.

"The bullets will bounce from your airplane. You will see the enemy over a hundred times and you will return to dance with a small boy at the Sun Dance grounds." The message of the spirit, Big Road, who spoke out in the *Yuwipi* at Fools Crow's cabin almost within sight of the Lone Hills's trailer house, called out to me. I remembered the sharp pain in my side when my dominant mother jabbed me hard with her elbow in the darkness of the ceremony. "Stand up and pray for your life," she commanded. "Give something back for what they will be giving to you."

When you have been given a window to your life through a powerful truth that a man such as Fools Crow lived, and through that truth an accurate foretelling ceremony can come forward, you reflect back on many things as you drive away from the last time you will see such a spiritual leader, at least through earth eyes. At the end of Bill Eagle Feather's time I had this same experience, this same feeling, and he even had his spirit straddle my pickup with two lightning bolts when he departed into the spirit world. The incident scared a non-Indian passenger who happened to be riding with me. To this day this person thinks I am a little different, because all I could do was hold my sides from laughing so hard at the way my passenger reacted. I still smile every time I remember the occasion. A hard laugh is a good memory, good medicine. Two lightning bolts straddling you is a sign and not something to be afraid of. Yes, there is definitely a culture gap among us, but with a sense of humor we can make light of the differences. After I finally quit laughing at my frightened passenger, I realized something big had happened, and that evening Wanita Lone Wolf called to tell me that Uncle Bill had left.

The sky darkened as I drove in silence with Jamie. Combat missions circled through my thoughts, and in memory I found myself lining up on the runway at Chu Lai air base. It seemed I flew a lot of missions on dark, starless nights. Once I flew five missions within a twenty-four-hour period. I was fresh from a lengthy rest and my squadron was scheduled for hot-pad duty. Two flight crews waited in the emergency hut, dressed in full battle gear. When the phone rang the pilots would run for their Phantom jets while the radar operators who rode the backseats would take the coordinates and situation of the emergency. At times, we would be called to protect a helicopter shot down and its crew about to be captured. Or Marines were under attack and the Phantoms with their heavy loads would streak out to them at the speed of sound. The time I flew the five missions, two helicopters had been shot down. It was my understanding that the crew and Marines from one of them were captured and never heard from again. We managed to save the other chopper and its cargo of Marines, but a couple of covering planes were lost to ground fire.

As I said, I was fresh, and I knew where the downed planes were, so I was sent back repeatedly. I never left my plane. I ate in it while it was being refueled and reloaded with weapons. I even went to the bathroom off the back end. The Phantoms are big. You can walk back on the tail above the idled engines and hold on to the ruddered shark fin and answer nature's call. That is allowed when men are being killed and captured and you have to get right back out. Formality and dogmas are soon dispensed with when shells fly and lives are on the line. Minorities get hired quickly! And the sons of the white chiefs vanish from the field of combat, only to show up later as our political leaders. In the old days, an Indian chief had his sons beside him in the front lines of battle. This code of honor prevented a lot of needless war.

Fools Crow and Bill Eagle Feather, I owe you for the absence of fear in combat. To this day I never fear the death that rode the skies in that whole fruitless war. I guess my undisturbed sleep and dreams are proof. I wish I could teach this to some of my comrades. Nor do I feel guilty for having fought in that war. I think of the "killing fields" and the millions who died needlessly after we left. Millions have fled what we were fighting against. Few ever go back to it. After the Berlin Wall cracked, countries across the world turned against the Communist repression we were fighting.

However, I do not condone the puppet dictators whom our country manipulates and supports as long as they do our leaders' bidding. The result of this selfish policy is that the people of those nations have no democracy. Even a madman like Hussein was helped by our country before his invasion of Kuwait. I do not condone any dictator who has installed himself in power and administers reprisals against those who seek democratic government. These men are even worse than the untruthful Blue Man of Black Elk's vision; they should be fought against and removed.

Mother Earth has spoken out strongly for the environment, and now it appears that not only the nation but the world is starting to listen. It is a good thing that we are beginning to listen. She could simply do a polar shift and correct many of our errant attitudes and behavior overnight. Action must follow the listening, however. I dream of bombs and battleships and sophisticated tanks being made into pipes—yes, simple circular pipes that will carry water.

After I returned to the Rainbow Tribe, a week passed by and Fools Crow quietly entered the spirit world. Hundreds of people attended the funeral and burial. A box wagon with orange wheels carried his remains five miles to the cemetery near Kyle on the Pine Ridge Sioux Reservation. A riderless horse with a brown, red, white, black, and yellow star blanket and an eagle feather warbonnet attached to it preceded the green wagon, which was drawn by a pair of horses.

In a *Rapid City Journal* article, Fools Crow was quoted as saying that his vision quests had directed him into a life of healing and tribal leadership. He also stated that he saw alcoholism and jealousy as the greatest curses for the Indian people. This is a very powerful statement for me because I have observed the almost total absence of alcohol and jealousy within the Rainbow Tribe, This absence, along with an absence of materialism, is a great strength for them. I believe that the factionalization, the turning of Indians against one another, done by the boarding schools and the missionaries has been a major source of these curses that Fools Crow spoke of.

All Indian children were separated from their parents at the age of six and placed in boarding schools. Abnormal rules were created to subvert the ones who displayed a free spirit, and the children were encouraged to spy on one another. Let this happen in any elite suburb of the nation and you will have a skyrocketing alcoholism rate. The Federal Bureau of Investigation hasn't helped matters by keeping records on practically every Indian who has spoken up against bureaucratic corruption. I wouldn't be a bit surprised to learn that the FBI has a record on most of our holy men, including Fools Crow. The agency has also paid informers to keep us agitated at one another. This is sickening and disgusting, especially when our Sioux veterans have had more volunteer military combat duty for our country than the entire FBI and federal Marshals Service combined. It is not hard to understand why our people become demoralized.

I often wonder about the people who lived in the old life-style. It seems that there was much more harmony in those times. The separation in the boarding schools, the destruction of our spirituality and spiritual leaders by the missionaries, and the situation of the reservations where little could be hunted or planted have all contributed to the disunity.

Alcohol has played its part as well in turning the people against one another. I have never known an alcoholic who was not jealous and demeaning in one way or another. Some tribes have returned to the Natural Way and have almost totally conquered alcoholism. The Rainbow Tribe has little use for alcohol, realizing that it is unnatural. The philosophy of traditionalism is, If it is not natural, it will not work fruitfully in the spiritual realm. If you want to load yourself up on paranoia and hate, drink alcohol. If you want to do the worst thing possible to come out of a relationship that is difficult to get over, drink alcohol. It will fill you with tortuous anxiety and help you make the worst possible decisions. Anxiety, depression, jealousy, hate, and despair—if you like to wallow in that kind of unspiritual doom, stay with alcohol. I have no experience with drugs, but I understand they are even worse. Even those who brought man-made alcohol here are starting to realize its dangers for society. One obvious reason why the pre-European, high-minded North American Indians could come up with such a precious gift as democracy was that they had never been exposed to the curse of mind and morals that alcohol brings.

I call on tribal peoples to understand the need for the rest of the world, the non-Indian world, to improve its philosophy and spirituality by observing the wisdom of the Natural Way. It is a big world but we all have to live together. We are much more dependent upon that world than we realize. We have proved in the past one hundred years of reservation life that we are a surviving people. The weak detractors among us fear that we will lose our culture by sharing. We will not lose anything. Rather, we will gain strength by sharing, for the ugly prejudice we have all suffered from will be severely reduced by our new and appreciative friends. We must not be naive. Brochures are still spread around by racists offering a reward for the killing or spearing of Indians, and we are referred to as squaws and bucks. Indian people need friends to combat these racists who still abound. Our new spiritual friends in the Rainbow Tribe will stand beside us to combat racism. In the end we will all be in the same spirit world, and the generations to come of all colors will appreciate that the new friends we generated also helped the environment.

I ask the white people who do not respect our Indian Way and somehow wish to "save" us—I ask you not to get so shook up because we are going in our own direction. The "saviors" destroyed enough of our culture with their boarding schools and narrow-minded book-thumping zeal. Start to realize that you are only two-leggeds and do not know any more than we do. We are all mere beings here, and there are many mysteries. One mystery you should recognize is the natural connection found in all things created—a creation over which you do not have dominion. Give us the religious freedom that has finally been allowed the Jewish people. Granted, Mother Earth is a powerful ally for us, as are the six powers, but there are only a few of us in relation to the rest of the world's population.

Eight pallbearers wearing feathered headdresses covered Fools Crow's casket with a tan, turquoise, red, brown, yellow, and green star quilt. A wool blanket was placed crosswise over the quilt. The pallbearers shoveled dirt into the grave while heated rocks were placed in a pit at the foot of the grave. Burning sage tinged the air with its scent when water was poured onto the rocks to generate steam that would carry Fools Crow's spirit and the prayers of his friends into the spirit world.

The newspaper article also stated that Fools Crow believed that respect, generosity, courage, knowledge, and wisdom were keys to the survival of Indian culture. "These values start from the home. They are taught there and expressed there and carried into the world. You must first better understand yourself before you can express yourself to others. The Lakota values help you to do this."

Fools Crow said he realized the world was changing and that life was not like it used to be, but modern problems must be dealt with through cooperation and without losing sight of the old ways. "We need peace and understanding and unity of all young men, young women and elders—both Indian and non-Indian alike. We must all stand together and work together for the reason of peace and tranquility of life for all."[1]

▼   ▼   ▼   ▼   ▼

Fools Crow did indeed have a mystical power that few in this day and age will match. His source of power resided in his truth. He walked the long, narrow pipe stem of life as an example of a man who grew more powerful through ceremony. He did not lack courage to share his knowledge either. It seems that this trait is indispensable for those who wish to travel deeply into the mysticism of the Natural Way. Fools Crow said:

> The power and ways are given to us to be passed on to others. To think or do anything else is pure selfishness. We only keep them and get more by giving them away, and if we do not give them away we lose them. . . .
>
> The survival of the world depends upon our sharing what we have and working together. If we don't, the whole world will die. First the planet, and next the people. The

ones who complain and talk the most about giving away medicine secrets are always those who know the least.[2]

Fools Crow, the Teton spiritual chief of the Sioux, had little time for people who attempted to keep blessings to themselves.

If you lack courage or vision to do ceremony, then at least have the courage to take a stand for Mother Earth. Do not regret an answer of doing nothing when the generations unborn eternally greet you in the spirit world.

I thank the Rainbows for coming into my life. They have given me a newfound confidence in two-leggeds. I thank Fools Crow and Bill Eagle Feather for beginning my path to them. I thank Black Elk for allowing the first Rainbow, John Neihardt, to come into the vision of the Sacred Hoop. I dislike predictions, but this time I sense that the Rainbow Tribe will endure and will bring good wisdom to fruition.

Mitakuye oyasin!

NOTES

▼ ▼ ▼

FOREWORD

1. Joseph Epes Brown, *The Sacred Pipe: Black Elk's Account of the Seven Sacred Rites of the Oglala Sioux* (Norman: University of Oklahoma Press, 1953), pp. x and xii.
2. Quoted in Thomas Mails, *Fools Crow* (Tulsa, OK: Council Oaks Books, 1991), p. 11.

CHAPTER ONE. Reconnecting with the Natural Way

1. Joseph Campbell, *The Power of Myth* (New York: Doubleday, 1988), p. 88.
2. Ibid.
3. Joseph Campbell, *Transformation of Myth Through Time* (New York: Harper & Row, 1990), p. 46.
4. According to Alikawahu, a Kansa Indian interviewed in 1880 by James Owen Dorsey, "On the other side [of the Mississippi River?] by the *tciyeta* [ocean] which is at Nyu Yak [New York], dwelt the people at the very first." Waqube-ki, a Kansa Indian who lived in the late 1800s, stated that the tribe's sacred objects, including the medicines, the pipes, and the clam shell, "were brought from the shore of the great water at the east." These shells trace back to the Atlantic coast. William Unrau, *The Kansa Indians: A History of the Wind People, 1673–1873* (Norman: University of Oklahoma Press, 1986), p. 16.
5. Brown, *The Sacred Pipe,* p. 46.
6. Ohiyesa (Wahpeton Sioux), *The Soul of the Indian* (Lincoln: University of Nebraska Press, 1980), p. 113.
7. Ibid., p. 109.
8. Eugene V. Debs in *Lifetime Speaker's Encyclopedia,* vol. 2, edited by Jacob M. Braude (Englewood Cliffs, NJ: Prentice-Hall, 1962), p. 862, Selection 6783.
9. See also John G. Neihardt Trust Letterhead, John G. Neihardt Center, Bancroft, NE, 1991.

CHAPTER TWO. Thunder Owl and the Rainbows

1. Vine DeLoria, Jr., *Custer Died for Your Sins* (New York: Avon Books, 1969), p.108.

CHAPTER THREE. Rainbow and Celtic Relationship

1. Jeffrey Goodman, *American Genesis: The American Indian and the Origins of Modern Man* (New York: Berkley Books, 1982), p. 199.
2. *San Bernardino Sun,* October 27, 1980, cited in ibid.
3. Charles Gallenkamp, *Maya: The Riddle and Rediscovery of a Lost Civilization,* 3d rev. ed. (New York: Penguin, 1987), p. 107; Jose Arquelles, *The Mayan Factor* (Santa Fe, NM: Bear & Co., 1987), p. 204.
4. Gallenkamp, *Maya*, p. 105.
5. Robert Silverberg, *The Mound Builders* (Athens: Ohio University Press, 1970), pp. 10 and 11.
6. Jack Weatherford, *Native Roots* (New York: Crown, 1991), p. 9.
7. Silverberg, *Mound Builders,* p. 11.
8. Mike McCormack, "Echoes of Irish History," *Heritage Line Newsletter,* May/June 1991, p. 8.
9. Barry Fell, *America B.C.* (New York: Simon & Schuster, Pocket Books, 1976), p. 218.
10. Mary Lou Skinner Ross, "Celtic Wisdom and Other," *Spiritual Frontiers Fellowship National Newsletter* (Independence, Mo.), July 1989.

CHAPTER FOUR. The Path of the Rainbow

1. Raymond DeMallie, *The Sixth Grandfather* (Lincoln: University of Nebraska Press, 1985), p. 12.
2. "Lost Tribes, Lost Knowledge," *Time,* Sept. 23, 1991, pp. 46, 48.
3. Jack Weatherford, *Indian Givers* (New York: Fawcett Columbine, 1990), p. 138.

CHAPTER FIVE. Rainbows in Sweat Lodge

1. Ed McGaa, Eagle Man, *Mother Earth Spirituality* (San Francisco: Harper & Row, 1990), chapter 16, "Building a Sweat Lodge."
2. Skipp Porteous, "Are We Reuniting Church and State in the Schools?" *Utne Reader,* January/February 1991, p. 86. Originally published in *The Freedom Writer,* June/July 1990.
3. Brown, *The Sacred Pipe,* p. 59.

CHAPTER SIX. Rainbows in Vision Quest

1. Elisabet Sahtouris, *Gaia: The Human Journey from Chaos to Cosmos* (New York: Simon & Schuster, 1989), p. 74.
2. Ibid., p. 70.
3. Philip Carr-Gomm, *The Druid Tradition* (Shaftesbury, Dorset, and Rockport, MA: Element, 1991), p. 87.

CHAPTER SEVEN.
Rainbows Finding Their Natural Names
and *Wotai* Stones

1. William K. Powers, *Yuwipi* (Lincoln: University of Nebraska Press, 1982), pp. 11–12.
2. Ibid., p. 91.
3. Ibid.
4. Ibid.

CHAPTER EIGHT. Rainbows Discovering Spirit Guides

1. William Stoltzman, S.J., *The Pipe and Christ* (Chamberlain, S.D.: Tipi Press, 1986), p. 103.
2. William K. Powers, *Sacred Language: The Nature of Supernatural Discourse in Lakota* (Norman: University of Oklahoma Press, 1986), pp. 134–135.
3. Pat Robertson, *Answers to 200 of Life's Most Probing Questions* (Nashville, Thomas Nelson, 1984), "Angels and Demons" chapter, p. 118.
4. In respect for Little Crow's Dakota heritage, I have retained spellings consistent with Dakota pronunciation in this section.

CHAPTER NINE. Spirit-calling Ceremony

1. William Stoltzman, S.J., *How to Take Part in Lakota Ceremonies* (Pine Ridge, S.D.: Red Cloud Indian School, 1986), p. 61.
2. Ibid., p. 62.
3. Ibid., pp. 62, 63.
4. Stephen E. Feraca, *Wakinyan: Contemporary Teton Dakota Religion* (Browning, MT: Museum of the Plains Indian, 1963), p. 36, quoted in Powers, *Yuwipi,* p. 94.

CHAPTER TEN. Healing with Ceremony and Medicine

1. Jamie Sams, *Medicine Cards* (Santa Fe, NM: Bear & Co., 1988), p. 105.

CHAPTER ELEVEN. Gatherings

1. Barbara Cole, "A Gathering" notification, February 1991, Maineville, OH.

CHAPTER TWELVE. The Call to Lead

1. Frank Fools Crow, quoted in *Rapid City Journal,* Dec. 5, 1989, p. B3.
2. Ibid., quoted in Mails, *Fools Crow,* pp. 11 and 18.

Suggested Readings

▼ ▼ ▼

Adams, Barbara Means. *Prayers of Smoke*. Berkeley, CA: Celestial Arts, 1990.

Arquelles, Jose. *The Mayan Factor*. Santa Fe, NM: Bear & Company, 1987.

Bend, Cynthia, and Tayja Wiger. *Birth of a Modern Shaman*. St. Paul, MN: Llewellyn, 1988.

Brown, Joseph Epes. *The Sacred Pipe: Black Elk's Account of the Seven Sacred Rites of the Oglala Sioux*. Norman: University of Oklahoma Press, 1953.

Brown, Tom. *The Vision*. New York: Berkley, 1991.

Brown, Vinson, and William Willoya. *Warriors of the Rainbow*. Happy Camp, CA: Naturegraph, 1962.

Bryde, John F. *Modern Indian Psychology*. Vermillion, SD: Department of Indian Studies, University of South Dakota, 1971.

Campbell, Joseph. *The Power of Myth*. New York: Doubleday, 1988.

Campbell, Joseph. *Transformation of Myth Through Time*. New York: Harper & Row, 1990.

Carr-Gomm, Philip. *The Druid Tradition*. Shaftesbury, Dorset, and Rockport, MA: Element, 1991.

DeLoria, Vine, Jr. *Custer Died for Your Sins*. New York: Avon Books, 1969.

Eastman, Charles A. (Ohiyesa). *From the Deep Woods to Civilization*. Lincoln: University of Nebraska Press, 1916.

Eastman, Charles A. (Ohiyesa). *The Soul of the Indian*. Lincoln: University of Nebraska Press, 1980.

Ehrlich, Paul R., and Anne H. Ehrlich. *Healing the Planet*. Reading, MA: Addison-Wesley, 1991.

Fell, Barry. *America B.C.* New York: Simon & Schuster, Pocket Books, 1976.

Fire, John (Lame Deer), and Richard Erdoes. *Lame Deer: Seeker of Visions*. New York: Simon & Schuster, 1972.

Fortunate Eagle, Adam. *Alcatraz! Alcatraz!* Berkeley, CA: Heyday Books, 1992.

Gallenkamp, Charles. *Maya: The Riddle and Rediscovery of a Lost Civilization*. 3d rev. ed. New York: Penguin, 1987.

Goodman, Jeffrey. *American Genesis: The American Indian and the Origins of Modern Man*. New York: Berkeley Books, 1982.

McGaa, Ed, Eagle Man. *Mother Earth Spirituality*. San Francisco: Harper & Row, 1990.

Mails, Thomas. *Fools Crow*. Tulsa, OK: Council Oaks Books, 1991.

Medicine Eagle, Brooke. *Buffalo Woman Comes Singing*. New York: Ballantine, 1991.

Miller, David Humphreys. *Custer's Fall: The Indian Side of the Story*. Lincoln: University of Nebraska Press, 1957.

Neihardt, John G. *Black Elk Speaks.* New York: William Morrow, 1932. Reprint. Lincoln: University of Nebraska Press, 1957.

Powers, William K. *Oglala Religion.* Lincoln: University of Nebraska Press, 1977.

Powers, William K. *Sacred Language: The Nature of Supernatural Discourse in Lakota.* Norman: University of Oklahoma Press, 1986.

Powers, William K. *Yuwipi.* Lincoln: University of Nebraska Press, 1982.

Ross, Allen Charles. *Mitakuye Oyasin.* Fort Yates, ND: BEAR, 1989.

Sahtouris, Elisabet. *Gaia: The Human Journey from Chaos to Cosmos.* New York: Simon & Schuster, 1989.

Sams, Jamie. *Medicine Cards.* Santa Fe, NM: Bear & Co., 1988.

Sams, Jamie. *Other Council Fires Were Here Before Ours.* San Francisco: Harper Collins, 1991.

Sams, Jamie. *Sacred Path Cards.* San Francisco: Harper Collins, 1990.

Sandoz, Mari. *Crazy Horse: The Strange Man of the Oglalas.* Lincoln: University of Nebraska Press, 1961.

Silverberg, Robert. *The Mound Builders.* Athens: Ohio University Press, 1970.

Standing Bear, Luther. *My Indian Boyhood.* Lincoln: University of Nebraska Press, 1988.

Stoltzman, William, S.J. *How to Take Part in Lakota Ceremonies.* Pine Ridge, SD: Red Cloud Indian School, 1986.

Sun Bear. *Sun Bear: The Path of Power.* Spokane, WA: Bear Tribe Publishing, 1983.

Unrau, William. *The Kansa Indians: A History of the Wind People, 1673–1873.* Norman: University of Oklahoma Press, 1986.

Vanderwerth, W. C. *Indian Oratory: Famous Speeches by Noted Chieftains.* Norman: University of Oklahoma Press, 1971.

Vestal, Stanley. *Warpath: The True Story of the Fighting Sioux Told in a Biography of Chief White Bull.* Boston: Houghton Mifflin, 1934. Reprint. Lincoln: University of Nebraska Press, 1984.

Weatherford, Jack. *Indian Givers.* New York: Fawcett Columbine, 1990.

Weatherford, Jack. *Native Roots.* New York: Crown, 1991.